Bible Crosswords 101

Vol. 1

ISBN 978-1-60260-877-1

Crosswords were created using licensed Crossword Weaver software (www.crosswordweaver.com).

Puzzles were prepared by Kathryn Hake, Mary A. Hake, Vicki J. Kuyper, and Sarah Simmons in association with Snapdragon Group℠, Tulsa, Oklahoma, USA.

All scripture quotations, unless otherwise noted, are taken from the King James Version of the Bible.

Published by Barbour Publishing, Inc., P.O. Box 719, Uhrichsville, Ohio 44683, www.barbourbooks.com

Our mission is to publish and distribute inspirational products offering exceptional value and biblical encouragement to the masses.

ecpa Member of the Evangelical Christian Publishers Association

Printed in the United States of America.

Bible Crosswords 101

Vol. 1

BARBOUR PUBLISHING

1

Genesis

by Mary A. Hake

ACROSS

1 First man God created
5 Likeness, as of God (Gen. 1:27)
9 God put one on Cain (Gen. 4:15)
13 When God created (Gen. 1:1)
15 Venture
16 Beginning of Hebrew day (Gen. 1:5)
17 Created with 19 Across
18 Attorney General (abbr.)
19 First created thing (Gen. 1:1)
21 CA city (abbr.)
22 Opposite of cold
25 Falls, border China, Vietnam
29 "Eyes of them ___ were opened" (Gen. 3:7)
31 Alcoholics Anonymous (abbr.)
32 Layered vegetable (Num. 11:5)
33 God's beautiful garden
35 Arithmetic
37 Creator
38 First gender God created
39 Adam to his sons
42 The Appalachian Trail (abbr.)
43 Builder of ark
46 Land of Abram's birth (Gen. 11:31)
47 Wrath
49 First word of each Creation command
51 Ever-living (1 Tim. 1:17)
53 Iowa (abbr.)
54 Sacrifice animal (Gen. 22:13)
56 First word of Bible
57 It lasted for 40 days and 40 nights (Gen. 7:4) (pl.)
58 Highest authority (1 Pet. 2:13)
59 Son of Noah (Gen. 5:32)
60 Pasta sauce
61 Designated
65 Phone co.
66 God called the light this (Gen. 1:5)
69 Hebrew name for God
70 Eve's first son
72 Biblical "your" (Gen. 3:10)
73 The land Pison flows through (Gen. 2:11)
74 Close to

DOWN

1 Honest president's nickname
2 Satan, aka the serpent (Gen. 3:1)
3 God said Abram would live to old ___ (Gen. 15:15)
4 Ancient coin
5 Lodging place (Gen. 43:21)
6 Jacob called Reuben his ___ (Gen. 49:3)
7 Article before a vowel
8 Abbreviation for text messager's concluding remark
9 When the angels hastened Lot (Gen. 19:15)
10 The Lord called, "Where ___ thou?" (Gen. 3:9)
11 A cheer
12 Kentucky (abbr.)
14 What God called darkness
15 Italian city
17 First woman
20 Lamech's first wife (Gen. 4:19)
22 Cain killed him
24 Electrical unit
26 Garlic mayonnaise
27 Land east of Eden (Gen. 4:16)
28 Opposite of 38 Across
30 Number of ribs God took (Gen. 2:21)
31 Near
34 Palm fruit
36 Grandson of 59 Across (Gen. 10:13)

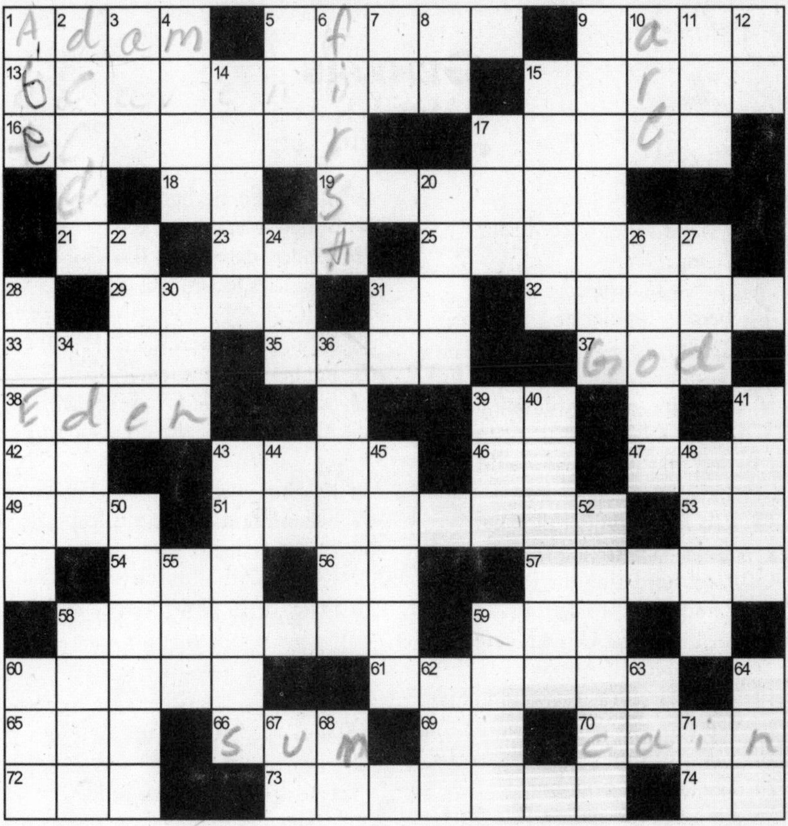

39 "And I will ___enmity between thee and the woman" (Gen. 3:15)
40 Ark's landing place (Gen. 8:4)
41 What God called waters (Gen. 1:10)
43 Mighty hunter (Gen. 10:9)
44 Russian river
45 Sharpens
48 Pharaoh took one from his hand (Gen. 41:42)
50 God removes the speech of them (Job 12:20)
52 Descendant of Cain (Gen. 4:18)
55 Able, as in war (2 Kings 24:16)
58 Third son of first parents (Gen. 4:25)
59 Corridor
60 Gentle tap
62 Hawaiian necklace
63 District Attorney (abbr.)
64 Some
67 Exclamation (Isa. 1:4)
68 Teen category (abbr.)
71 Type of explosive (abbr.)

2

Genesis

by Mary A. Hake

ACROSS

1 It was a tower of confusion (Gen. 11:9)
5 Lot's wife turned back and became a pillar of ___ (Gen. 19:26)
9 Estimated time en route (abbr.)
10 "Joseph __ a fruitful bough" (Gen. 49:22)
13 God told Abram he would __ a blessing (Gen. 12:2)
14 Rebekah's family called her "___ sister" (Gen. 24:60)
15 River bordering the Promised Land (Gen. 15:18)
18 Region of the United States (abbr.)
19 What Jacob's wives were to his sons
20 Valley of slimepits (Gen. 14:10)
24 The ark was a big one
26 Biblical exclamation (Isa. 55:1)
27 Personal retirement savings (abbr.)
28 Plain where the tower was built (Gen. 11:2)
32 Alphanumeric (abbr.)
33 Nothing
34 Danish King from Beowulf
36 "We shall all stand before the judgment ____ of Christ" (Rom. 14:10)
38 Telegram company (abbr.)
39 Pouch
40 Defeated by Chedorlaomer (Gen. 14:5 NIV)
44 Abraham's great-nephew (Gen. 22:21)
46 Sarah told the king, "__ is my brother" (Gen. 20:5)
47 Work Adam may have done in Eden
48 Era of Genesis
49 Special Forces fighting terrorists
52 Where Haran died (Gen. 11:28)
53 Biblical expression (Ps. 70:3)
56 Ishmael's fourth son (Gen. 25:13)
58 Noah's grandson (Gen. 11:10)
61 Rachel's sister (Gen. 29:16)
63 Space available for use (abbr.)
64 Abraham gave the Lord food to ___ (Gen. 18:8)
66 KJV for "before" (Ex. 1:19)
67 Second note of the musical scale
68 Business degree (abbr.)
69 King of Zeboiim (Gen. 14:2)
70 Sister of 23 Down (Gen. 11:29)

DOWN

1 Hagar's well was between Kadesh and ____ (Gen. 16:14)
2 Next to
3 Father of Esau's wife Judith (Gen. 26:34)
4 Job did not sin with his ___ (Job 2:10)
5 Father of 58 Across (Gen. 11:10)
6 Unit of weight (abbr.)
7 Ninth son of Ishmael (Gen. 25:13–15)
8 Son of Abraham and Keturah (Gen. 25:2)
11 Beersheba's former name (Gen. 26:33)
12 Abram's servant Eliezer's home (Gen. 15:2)
16 Common Hungarian surname
17 Hitler's elite corps
21 Charged particle
22 Rachel's son through Bilhah (Gen. 30:6)
23 Nahor's wife (Gen. 11:29)
25 Son of Bethuel and Reumah (Gen. 22:24 NIV)

If you enjoyed
Bible Crosswords 101
Volume 1

Check out these other titles for hours of fun!

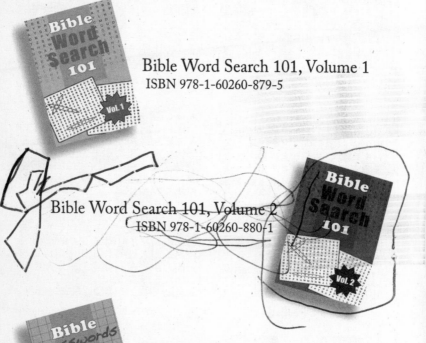

Bible Word Search 101, Volume 1
ISBN 978-1-60260-879-5

Bible Word Search 101, Volume 2
ISBN 978-1-60260-880-1

Bible Crosswords 101, Volume 2
ISBN 978-1-60260-878-8

5.1875" x 8", paperback, 224 pages, $4.99 each

Available wherever Christian books are sold!

S	P	A	C	E		H	A	N	G		B	A	B	E
N	I	C	H	E		O	D	O	R		I	D	O	L
A	N	N	U	L		P	A	R	E		G	I	R	D
P	E	E	R		C	O	M	M	A	S		O	N	E
			C	Y	A	N			T	E	A	S	E	R
R	O	D	H	A	M			S	E	E	M			
O	B	I		M	E	A	G	E	R		O	R	B	S
L	O	V	E			R	O	E			S	I	L	O
L	E	A	D		K	I	D	N	E	Y		P	E	N
			G	O	O	D			V	E	R	S	U	S
A	P	P	E	A	R			D	I	N	E			
O	L	E		K	E	G	F	U	L		C	A	P	E
R	E	A	D		A	L	A	N		C	O	V	E	Y
T	A	C	O		N	E	C	K		W	R	I	T	E
A	D	E	N		S	E	E	S		A	D	D	E	D

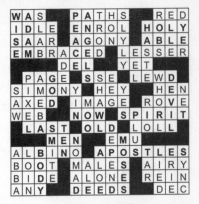

Puzzle 97: 3 John

W	A	S			P	A	T	H	S			R	E	D
I	D	L	E		E	N	R	O	L		H	O	L	Y
S	A	A	R		A	G	O	N	Y		A	B	L	E
E	M	B	R	A	C	E	D		L	E	S	S	E	R
				D	E	L			Y	E	T			
	P	A	G	E		S	S	E		L	E	W	D	
S	I	M	O	N	Y		H	E	Y			H	E	N
A	X	E	D		I	M	A	G	E		R	O	V	E
W	E	B			N	O	W		S	P	I	R	I	T
	L	A	S	T		O	L	D		L	O	L	L	
			M	E	N			E	M	U				
A	L	B	I	N	O		A	P	O	S	T	L	E	S
B	O	O	T		M	A	L	E	S		A	I	R	Y
B	I	D	E		A	L	O	N	E		R	E	I	N
A	N	Y			D	E	E	D	S			D	E	C

Puzzle 98: Jude

D	E	L	A	Y		A	B	L	E		E	D	G	E
O	Z	O	N	E		S	L	A	P		H	E	R	A
F	R	O	G	S		C	O	S	H		F	L	O	G
F	A	K	E		E	I	T	H	E	R		H	A	L
			L	E	V	I			S	A	B	I	N	E
A	G	A	S	S	I			F	U	M	E			
N	O	N		P	L	I	E	R	S		A	B	B	A
T	U	T	U			R	Y	E			R	E	A	P
E	P	I	C		G	O	E	T	H	E		A	L	I
			L	I	O	N			U	G	A	N	D	A
I	S	L	A	N	D			U	R	G	E			
T	W	O		C	H	R	I	S	T		G	O	L	D
E	A	T	S		E	A	S	E		F	E	V	E	R
M	I	T	E		A	C	L	U		F	A	E	N	A
S	N	O	W		D	E	E	P		A	N	N	O	Y

Puzzle 99: Revelation

A	G	O			S	A	G	A	S			D	N	A
C	U	P	S		C	L	A	S	P		O	R	A	L
A	R	E	A		A	L	P	H	A		M	A	M	A
D	U	N	G	A	R	E	E		S	I	E	G	E	S
				M	S	G			M	C	G			
	T	R	E	E		E	A	R		Y	A	W	L	
P	R	A	W	N	S		L	O	W			H	A	S
S	I	D	E		U	N	I	T	S		P	I	T	A
T	A	I			N	O	V		W	O	R	T	H	Y
	L	I	F	E		W	E	B		D	O	E	S	
			A	R	T			E	G	O				
P	I	L	L	A	R		C	H	U	R	C	H	E	S
I	R	I	S		A	F	O	O	T		D	A	R	N
L	O	V	E		C	E	L	L	S		T	R	I	O
E	N	E			T	E	D	D	Y			P	E	W

Puzzle 100: Revelation

D	N	A			E	R	A	S	E			P	U	P
R	O	S	E		M	E	M	O	S		J	U	S	T
I	T	E	M		A	G	E	N	T		U	R	S	A
P	E	R	U	V	I	A	N		E	L	D	E	R	S
				I	L	L			S	E	A			
	E	B	O	N		E	G	G		T	H	O	U	
B	A	R	L	E	Y		R	O	W			L	P	N
A	V	I	D		I	M	A	G	E		R	I	P	E
R	E	D			P	I	T		T	R	I	V	E	T
	S	E	G	O		L	A	B		A	G	E	D	
			A	R	T			A	S	K				
B	I	T	T	E	R		A	L	L	E	L	U	I	A
O	B	I	E		A	S	S	A	Y		S	T	O	W
D	I	M	S		P	H	I	A	L		D	A	T	A
E	S	E			S	E	A	M	Y			H	A	Y

Puzzle 101: Revelation

A	R	B		B	A	S	S	O		A	G	A	P	E
B	O	A		U	N	P	I	N		P	Y	R	E	X
B	O	B		M	O	U	N	T		O	P	E	R	A
A	M	E	N		I	N	G	O	T	S		S	U	M
			R	A	N				E	T	A			
	H	E	A	R	T	S		S	A	L	U	T	E	
S	E	A		T	E	M	P	O		E	N	O	C	H
C	A	R	T		D	I	A	N	A		T	I	L	E
A	L	T	A	R		T	R	I	B	E		L	A	Y
	S	H	R	I	N	E		C	H	R	I	S	T	
			E	B	B				O	R	B			
S	A	P		B	E	T	T	E	R		M	E	A	T
P	L	U	T	O		Y	O	U	R	S		V	I	I
A	A	R	O	N		P	U	R	E	E		I	R	K
T	R	E	E	S		E	R	O	D	E		L	Y	E

Puzzle 91: Hebrews

G	O	O	D			A	T	S	E	A		C	A	L
N	A	K	E	D		T	H	U	M	B		A	L	I
A	T	A	L	E		L	E	M	U	R		R	E	V
W	H	Y		P	R	A	Y			A	B	O	V	E
			S	A	Y	S		A	S	H	A	M	E	D
E	N	T	I	R	E		S	W	E	A	R			
R	E	A	C	T			P	A	L	M		P	E	P
M	A	R	K		B	E	R	Y	L		B	O	N	A
A	T	E		F	I	R	E			B	I	R	D	S
			M	E	T	R	E		D	U	R	E	S	S
S	T	R	A	U	S	S		F	O	O	D			
H	O	U	N	D			O	O	Z	Y		A	D	D
I	N	N		I	T	E	M	S		E	R	R	O	R
P	A	T		S	A	G	A	S		D	A	I	L	Y
S	L	Y		T	B	O	N	E			M	A	T	S

Puzzle 92: James

G	R	A	D		U	M	B	O			L	U	R	E
R	U	D	E		L	O	O	K		S	O	N	A	R
E	M	M	A		S	T	A	R		C	R	O	W	N
A	B	I	D	E	T	H		A	S	I	A			
T	A	T		Y	E	S			H	O	N	E	S	T
			H	E	R		S	K	I	N		M	A	R
B	L	O	O	D		V	E	I	N	S		A	L	I
A	E	R	Y		D	A	I	S	Y		L	I	V	E
B	A	D		L	O	I	N	S		H	A	L	E	D
E	V	E		A	N	N	E		C	O	D			
S	E	R	E	N	E			S	O	N		S	A	G
			I	C	E	D		C	R	E	A	T	O	R
A	D	A	G	E		A	M	E	N		L	O	R	E
L	I	G	H	T		L	O	N	E		A	N	T	E
B	E	E	T			E	W	E	R		N	E	A	T

Puzzle 93: 1 Peter

E	V	A	D	E		R	U	B			L	A	P	S
L	I	B	E	L		A	S	L		B	O	U	L	E
D	R	O	L	L		P	E	A		O	T	T	E	R
E	T	U	I		D	I	S	C	U	S		O	A	F
R	U	N		C	A	D		K	N	O	B			
	E	D	G	A	R			G	I	R	A	F	F	E
			A	S	K		L	E	T		R	O	A	R
F	E	A	S	T		G	E	M		E	R	R	O	R
C	O	S	H		S	A	D		A	V	E			
A	S	S	E	R	T	S			M	I	N	E	R	
			D	U	A	L		G	E	L		L	E	E
D	O	G		P	R	I	S	O	N		H	E	W	S
O	V	A	T	E		G	O	D		N	O	V	A	S
F	A	L	S	E		H	A	L		O	P	E	R	A
F	L	A	P			T	R	Y		W	I	N	D	Y

Puzzle 94: 2 Peter

E	G	G			D	R	E	F	T			L	A	W
T	O	A	D		E	A	G	E	R		A	I	D	E
N	O	V	A		A	B	I	D	E		T	E	A	R
A	D	E	N	I	T	I	S		A	S	S	U	R	E
				S	H	E			T	O	E			
	P	A	U	L		S	S	E		N	A	M	E	
L	A	P	S	E	S		P	T	A			O	N	E
I	D	E	A		I	D	E	A	L		O	R	E	S
E	R	R			N	E	W		A	F	L	A	M	E
	E	Y	E	S		C	S	T		I	D	L	Y	
			A	S	H			I	O	N				
S	P	A	R	T	A		A	D	V	O	C	A	T	E
P	A	N	T		R	A	M	I	E		P	R	A	Y
A	C	T	H		S	H	E	E	R		S	A	M	E
S	E	E			H	A	N	D	S			B	E	D

Puzzle 95: 1 John

S	T	U	B			A	P	N	E	A		G	A	B
T	A	P	I	R		B	L	U	R	B		R	U	E
E	R	O	D	E		H	E	N	R	I		E	R	A
P	E	N		W	H	O	A			D	R	E	A	D
			F	A	I	R		G	R	E	A	T	L	Y
U	N	H	U	R	T		U	N	I	T	Y			
C	O	U	L	D			S	U	C	H		N	I	L
L	O	L	L		F	L	E	S	H		L	O	S	E
A	K	A		B	E	A	R			F	O	O	L	S
			D	E	E	D	S		C	O	R	N	E	T
A	M	N	E	S	T	Y		W	E	L	D			
P	E	A	C	E			L	O	O	K		M	O	O
I	N	K		E	A	T	E	R		S	P	E	A	K
S	S	E		C	R	E	E	L		Y	E	N	T	A
H	A	D		H	E	A	R	D			A	S	H	Y

Puzzle 96: 2 John

Puzzle 85: 2 Thessalonians

Puzzle 86: 1 Timothy

Puzzle 87: 2 Timothy

Puzzle 88: Titus

Puzzle 89: Philemon

Puzzle 90: Hebrews

C	L	E	A	R		A	B	B	A		A	C	A	D
R	U	M	B	A		W	O	R	D		P	A	R	E
O	R	I	O	N		A	L	O	E		R	U	D	E
P	E	R	U		D	R	O	W	N	S		S	O	D
			N	E	E	D			O	I	L	E	R	S
S	L	E	D	G	E			S	I	N	E			
N	O	V		O	P	E	N	E	D		T	R	A	M
A	V	I	S			Y	E	A			S	A	R	I
G	E	L	T		P	E	W	T	E	R		T	E	N
			E	E	L	S			A	E	G	E	A	N
T	E	M	P	L	E			E	S	P	N			
A	X	E		L	A	R	V	A	E		A	R	E	S
K	I	N	G		S	E	A	S		A	W	A	R	E
E	L	S	E		E	L	L	E		B	E	G	I	N
N	E	A	T		D	Y	E	D		C	R	U	E	T

Puzzle 79: 2 Corinthians

S	T	I	C	K			S	E	E	M		F	F	A
S	E	V	E	N	S		A	X	L	E		E	O	N
T	A	Y	L	O	R		W	H	O	M		T	U	G
			T	W	I	G		A	P	O	S	T	L	E
	V	A	I	N		R	U	L	E		P	E	E	L
D	I	S	C		G	A	T	E		H	E	R	D	S
I	T	S		F	A	C	E		S	E	A			
S	A	N	J	O	S	E		W	O	R	K	E	T	H
			U	G	H		G	O	O	D		L	O	O
S	C	U	D	S		E	A	R	N		P	A	S	T
T	O	N	E		W	I	L	L		S	O	N	S	
P	A	R	A	P	E	T		D	E	P	T			
A	R	E		O	A	H	U		W	E	A	S	E	L
U	S	A		O	R	E	S		E	N	G	I	N	E
L	E	D		L	Y	R	E			T	E	N	E	T

Puzzle 80: Galatians

H	A	T	S			M	A	M	B	A		A	W	L
A	G	R	E	E		A	L	O	O	F		C	I	O
T	R	A	W	L		S	P	O	O	F		R	L	V
H	E	M		A	G	E	S			A	S	I	D	E
			L	I	A	R		B	U	I	L	D	E	D
S	T	R	O	N	G		B	E	R	R	Y			
C	A	U	S	E			L	E	S	S		K	I	N
A	I	N	T		G	R	A	N	T		D	I	D	O
B	L	T		B	R	I	M			S	Y	N	O	D
			A	R	I	S	E		N	E	E	D	L	E
A	T	H	L	E	T	E		A	F	A	R			
S	H	E	B	A			M	U	L	L		A	F	C
T	E	A		D	R	A	I	N		E	N	S	U	E
E	R	R		T	A	I	N	T		D	E	I	G	N
R	E	D		H	Y	M	N				W	A	S	T

Puzzle 81: Ephesians

S	A	F	E		T	O	A	D			C	O	D	A
T	R	I	P		O	N	C	E		O	R	I	O	N
R	A	R	E		U	S	E	S		B	E	L	L	Y
A	B	S	E	N	C	E		K	E	E	P			
P	S	T		O	A	T			M	Y	T	H	I	C
			C	A	N		T	H	E	E		I	L	L
F	L	E	S	H		F	O	U	N	D		K	I	A
L	A	S	T		B	L	A	N	D		H	E	A	D
O	U	T		A	L	A	S	T		B	I	R	D	
A	G	E		B	A	T	T		S	O	S			
T	H	R	A	S	H			C	A	L		P	E	A
S			B	E	S	T		R	I	D	D	I	N	G
	R	A	I	N		E	L	O	N		O	V	E	R
L	I	N	D	T		L	E	S	T		C	O	M	E
T	O	T	E			L	O	S	S		S	T	Y	E

Puzzle 82: Philippians

S	M	A	R	T		R	P	M			A	I	L	S
T	A	B	O	O		E	R	A		U	N	D	U	E
A	R	S	O	N		P	A	N		N	Y	L	O	N
I	C	E	D		L	A	Y	O	F	F		E	S	T
N	U	N		K	E	Y		F	L	E	W			
	S	T	U	N	S			G	O	D	H	E	A	D
			S	E	T		V	O	W		O	G	L	E
M	A	C	A	W		R	E	D		H	O	G	A	N
C	L	O	G		L	E	T		S	O	S			
G	E	N	E	T	I	C			A	P	H	I	D	
			S	A	K	E		D	I	E		D	I	P
A	G	E		S	E	I	Z	E	D		S	E	E	R
G	O	G	E	T		V	I	M		P	H	A	S	E
A	B	O	V	E		E	T	A		H	O	T	E	L
R	I	S	E			D	I	S		D	W	E	L	L

Puzzle 83: Colossians

T	W	O		T	U	R	B	A	N	S		H	E	M
O	A	H	U		N	U	R	S	E		C	U	T	E
T	R	I	P		C	L	O	K	E		A	G	U	A
A	P	O	S	T	L	E	S		D	E	C	E	I	T
				H	E	R			Y	E	A			
	S	A	G	A		S	A	W		L	O	R	D	
M	O	S	A	I	C		B	A	D			E	R	E
I	B	I	S		A	L	O	N	E		F	L	O	E
L	E	D			D	A	D		W	I	R	I	N	G
	R	E	A	D		Y	E	S		N	I	C	E	
			B	E	G			O	A	F				
H	I	G	H	L	Y		A	D	M	O	N	I	S	H
O	S	L	O		R	O	N	D	O		B	O	T	A
A	L	A	R		O	F	T	E	N		E	W	E	R
R	E	D			S	T	I	N	G	S		A	W	E

Puzzle 84: 1 Thessalonians

C	P	A		F	O	B		S	E	C		D	K	R
L	O	G		O	B	A	D	I	A	H		E	N	E
A	U	G		R	I	S	O	T	T	O		G	E	E
S	C	R	A	M		E	W	E		S	H	A	L	L
S	H	O	W	E	D				H	E	I	S	T	S
			A	D	A	B		O	I	N	K			
H	O	L	Y		Y	E	L	L	S		E	A	S	T
I	R	E				G	O	D				C	A	W
P	E	E	P		R	A	T	E	R		S	E	G	O
			A	G	O	N		N	A	V	Y			
S	T	A	R	E	D				W	I	N	D	U	P
M	U	L	T	I		P	A	W		S	C	O	N	E
A	L	L		S	W	A	H	I	L	I		V	I	A
S	S	E		H	O	R	A	T	I	O		E	T	C
H	A	Y		A	W	E		H	E	N		R	Y	E

Puzzle 73: Acts

A	B	S		C	A	M	E	L		A	P	H	I	D
S	U	E		A	B	E	L	E		C	R	E	D	O
I	L	L		B	O	A	S	T		C	O	A	L	S
A	B	L	E		U	N	E	S	C	O		P	E	T
			S	O	N	S			O	U	R			
	F	R	A	U	D			H	O	N	O	U	R	
C	E	O		T	E	N	S	E		T	O	N	A	L
W	A	Y	S		D	O	R	I	C		T	I	M	E
O	R	A	L	B		W	A	S	H	Y		F	I	G
	S	L	E	E	P			T	I	E	D	Y	E	
			W	A	S				L	A	Y			
A	W	L		R	I	B	A	L	D		E	Y	E	D
C	H	I	M	E		A	F	I	R	E		A	R	E
T	I	R	E	S		G	R	E	E	N		R	I	B
G	R	A	N	T		S	O	U	N	D		N	E	T

Puzzle 74: Romans

S	L	A	Y		D	I	S	H		L	A	G	O	S
L	I	V	E		I	N	T	O		A	B	O	D	E
I	B	O	A		S	W	A	B		C	O	V	E	T
D	R	I	N	K		A	B	B	R	E	V			
E	A	D		P	E	R	S	I	A		E	A	T	
			S	H	O	D		T	W	O		C	O	W
A	B	B	A		S	L	Y			F	L	U	T	E
W	E	E	K	S		Y	E	N		F	E	R	A	L
A	F	T	E	R			T	I	P		F	A	L	L
R	I	O		I	N	N		C	A	S	T			
E	T	N	A		B	E	C	O	M	E		A	A	N
			C	R	A	V	A	T		E	D	I	F	Y
S	W	A	M	I		A	R	I	D		I	D	O	L
S	A	K	E	S		D	O	N	E		N	E	R	O
E	R	A	S	E		A	M	E	N		E	D	E	N

Puzzle 75: Romans

T	U	E		C	A	S	E	S		C	A	S	T	E
I	N	N		A	B	I	D	E		O	P	E	R	A
L	T	D		P	U	R	G	E		V	E	X	E	S
L	O	S	S		N	E	E	D	L	E		Y	E	T
			O	D	D				E	R	R			
	M	A	N	I	A	C		S	T	E	E	L		
G	A	L		G	N	A	S	H		D	A	I	L	Y
A	G	E	D		T	U	B	A	S		P	L	E	A
P	I	P	E	D		S	E	L	L	S		A	D	M
	C	H	E	E	S	E		L	I	P	I	C		
			P	S	U				G	Y	P			
T	A	P		P	R	E	A	C	H		R	A	C	E
A	L	I	B	I		B	R	O	T	H		W	A	Y
L	O	C	U	S		B	E	L	L	E		A	R	E
C	E	A	S	E		S	A	T	Y	R		Y	E	S

Puzzle 76: 1 Corinthians

A	D	A	M	S		B	O	O			A	L	U	M
B	E	B	E	K		E	R	R		E	V	E	R	Y
E	S	S	A	Y		F	E	D		L	E	A	S	T
L	I	E	N		D	O	S	A	G	E		D	A	H
E	R	N		E	E	G		I	N	C	A			
	E	T	U	D	E			N	A	T	U	R	A	L
			M	A	D		B	E	T		T	O	R	E
R	E	A	L	M		D	I	D		R	H	E	T	T
A	S	I	A		W	E	D		T	O	O			
P	E	R	U	S	A	L			H	A	R	R	Y	
			T	A	R	E		S	I	N		H	A	Y
S	A	P		I	N	G	O	T	S		K	I	N	E
A	W	A	I	T		A	T	E		C	O	N	K	A
T	O	U	C	H		T	I	E		A	L	O	E	S
E	L	L	E			E	S	P		B	E	S	E	T

Puzzle 77: 1 Corinthians

L	A	M	B			S	B	W			H	O	M	E
A	L	O	E		S	P	E	E	D		I	B	I	S
W	I	L	L		T	I	T	L	E		M	O	N	T
	F	L	O	W	E	R		L	E	S	S	E	N	
			V	A	P	I	D		D	U	E			
A	L	I	E	N		T	E	N		B	L	A	M	E
R	E	N	D	E	R		B	U	T		F	L	E	A
R	A	D		D	E	M	O	N	I	C		I	R	S
A	S	I	A		P	A	R		C	H	A	N	C	E
S	T	A	N	D		D	A	B		O	B	E	Y	
			O	U	R		H	E	N	R	I			
	A	C	T	I	O	N		H	I	D	D	E	N	
N	O	A	H		C	A	R	O	B		E	P	I	C
O	S	S	E		I	D	O	L	S		T	E	N	D
B	E	E	R			O	D	D			H	E	A	T

Puzzle 78: 2 Corinthians

Puzzle 67: Mark

Puzzle 68: Luke

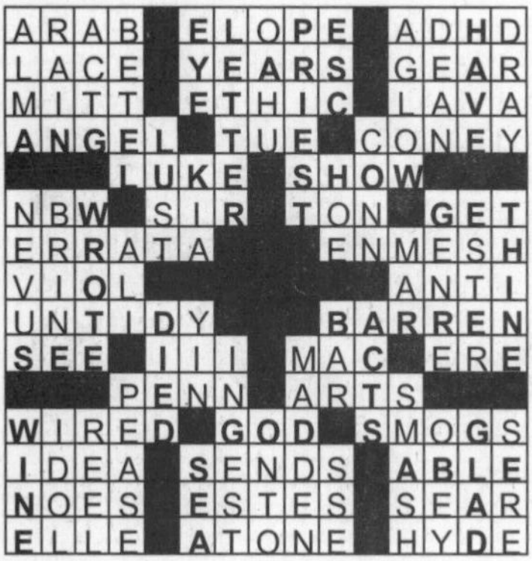

Puzzle 69: Luke

Puzzle 70: John

Puzzle 71: John

Puzzle 72: Acts

D	E	M	E		M	A	J	O	R		E	D	G	E
O	R	A	L		O	L	I	V	E		T	I	E	R
Z	E	R	U	B	B	A	B	E	L		U	S	E	R
			D	R	Y			R	A	D	I	O		
K	O	R	E	A		M	A	L	T	A		B	E	N
I	I	I			S	A	W	Y	E	R		E	L	F
A	L	B	A	C	O	R	E			I	D	Y	L	L
			C	O	W	S		M	A	U	I			
H	U	R	T	S			D	I	P	S	T	I	C	K
U	S	E		T	H	R	O	N	E			R	U	E
B	A	G		L	I	E	G	E		A	P	E	R	Y
		E	G	Y	P	T			N	B	E			
L	O	N	E		P	O	E	T	I	C	A	L	L	Y
A	N	T	E		O	R	G	A	N		C	O	P	E
D	E	S	K		S	T	O	N	E		E	T	N	A

Puzzle 61: Haggai

B	A	S	E			C	A	L	I	F		M	A	C
A	L	U	L	A		E	D	E	M	A		O	U	R
S	M	E	L	L		A	D	O	P	T		O	N	E
H	A	D		P	A	S	S			H	O	S	T	S
			E	A	S	E		E	V	E	R	E	S	T
B	R	A	N	C	H		A	D	O	R	E			
L	A	R	V	A			N	E	W	S		M	U	D
O	K	A	Y		S	I	G	N	S		S	O	R	E
W	E	B		M	A	D	E			H	I	N	G	E
			H	O	V	E	L		P	O	T	T	E	R
P	A	N	A	C	E	A		F	I	R	E			
S	T	A	L	K			N	E	T	S		I	R	E
A	S	K		I	N	D	I	A		E	N	D	O	W
L	E	E		N	O	U	N	S		S	I	D	L	E
M	A	D		G	R	E	A	T			P	O	O	R

Puzzle 62: Zechariah

M	A	N	N	A		G	R	E	A	T		O	C	T
A	R	E	A	S		R	A	L	P	H		A	L	I
N	E	A	T	H		A	S	K	E	W		S	O	N
S	A	R	I		A	C	P			A	B	I	D	E
			O	N	C	E		H	A	R	A	S	S	
C	A	N	N	O	T		P	O	R	T	S			
L	E	A	S	T		N	E	S	T		K	E	E	P
A	R	M			B	O	A	T	S			E	P	A
N	O	E	L		A	B	C	S		D	A	L	E	S
			O	V	U	L	E		L	E	N	S	E	S
	A	B	R	A	D	E		M	A	N	Y			
W	O	R	D	S			W	O	W		M	A	D	E
E	R	E		T	R	E	A	D		L	O	V	E	D
P	T	A		L	I	N	D	A		P	R	O	U	D
T	A	D		Y	O	D	E	L		N	E	W	S	Y

Puzzle 63: Malachi

S	T	E	A	D		B	R	A	G		T	A	S	K
P	E	P	S	I		L	U	R	E		A	G	U	E
A	L	I	A	S		A	T	T	Y		H	O	L	Y
T	L	C		C	A	S	H		S	T	I	N	K	S
			L	I	V	E			E	A	T			
E	S	C	A	P	E		M	A	R	X	I	S	M	
S	C	O	W	L		T	A	R	S			T	A	N
P	R	U	N	E		W	I	T		A	F	O	R	E
Y	A	P			P	I	N	S		W	O	O	D	S
	M	E	S	S	A	G	E		S	A	U	D	I	S
			P	A	R			T	O	I	L			
M	A	L	A	Y	A		F	O	N	T		S	E	A
U	S	E	D		B	R	A	D		I	S	A	A	C
G	I	V	E		L	I	R	A		N	O	T	R	E
S	A	I	D		E	M	M	Y		G	L	E	N	S

Puzzle 64: Matthew

B	E	D				B	A	D				F	D	A
O	W	I	N	G		O	W	E		T	H	R	O	B
D	E	V	I	L		A	L	L		H	E	E	L	S
	R	E	P	A	S	T		I	S	R	A	E	L	
			S	S	E				E	A	T			
E	P	A		S	C	R	I	B	E	S		S	P	A
P	A	L	S	Y		E	N	E		H	U	M	A	N
I	D	E	A			N	A	G			T	I	L	E
C	R	U	D	E		D	N	A		H	E	L	E	N
S	E	T		A	B	S	E	N	C	E		E	S	T
			P	S	I				R	A	N			
	A	W	A	I	T	S		B	Y	L	A	W	S	
O	C	H	R	E		I	W	O		E	M	A	I	L
C	H	E	E	R		N	O	R		D	E	L	T	A
T	E	N				S	O	N				K	E	G

Puzzle 65: Matthew

S	C	A	M			A	R	G	A	L		U	S	S
C	O	B	A	L		S	E	R	V	O		M	P	H
U	M	B	R	A		I	V	I	E	S		L	I	E
M	A	R	I	M	B	A		P	R	E	P	A	R	E
			N	B	E		A	P	T		S	U	I	T
P	I	C	A		F	A	C	E		W	A	T	T	S
S	O	N		D	O	V	E		G	E	L			
I	N	S	P	I	R	E		C	A	L	M	I	N	G
			L	E	E		V	E	I	L		C	O	O
G	L	E	A	M		A	E	O	N		S	E	N	D
O	I	L	S		J	U	T		E	T	A			
S	T	O	M	P	E	D		C	R	A	N	I	A	L
P	E	P		A	S	I	D	E		L	E	D	G	E
E	R	E		P	U	T	I	N		C	L	E	A	N
L	S	D		A	S	S	E	T			Y	A	R	D

Puzzle 66: Mark

A	L	P	S	■	S	T	A	T	S	■	G	A	T	E
J	O	H	N	■	A	R	G	U	E	■	O	X	E	N
A	S	I	A	■	V	I	O	L	A	■	G	I	R	D
R	E	L	I	G	I	O	N	S	■	S	H	A	M	E
■	■	■	L	O	O	■	■	A	R	T	■	L	S	D
N	A	Y	■	D	R	A	W	■	A	U	G	■	■	■
E	G	O	S	■	S	C	O	U	N	D	R	E	L	S
S	A	G	A	■	■	N	U	N	■	■	I	D	O	L
T	R	A	N	S	C	E	N	D	S	■	D	O	N	E
■	■	■	G	N	U	■	D	O	E	S	■	M	E	W
A	C	V	■	A	T	E	■	■	N	O	D	■	■	■
W	H	E	L	P	■	A	P	R	I	L	R	A	I	N
F	A	R	O	■	I	G	L	O	O	■	A	L	O	E
U	S	S	R	■	C	L	E	A	R	■	F	E	T	A
L	E	A	D	■	Y	E	A	R	S	■	T	S	A	R

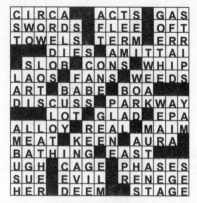

Puzzle 55: Obadiah

C	I	R	C	A	■	■	A	C	T	S	■	G	A	S
S	W	O	R	D	S	■	F	L	E	E	■	O	F	T
T	O	W	E	L	S	■	T	E	R	M	■	E	R	R
■	■	■	D	I	E	S	■	A	M	I	T	T	A	I
■	S	L	O	B	■	C	O	N	S	■	W	H	I	P
L	A	O	S	■	F	A	N	S	■	W	E	E	D	S
A	R	T	■	B	A	B	E	■	B	O	A	■	■	■
D	I	S	C	U	S	S	■	P	A	R	K	W	A	Y
■	■	■	L	O	T	■	G	L	A	D	■	E	P	A
A	L	L	O	Y	■	R	E	A	L	■	M	A	I	M
■	M	E	A	T	■	K	E	E	N	■	A	U	R	A
■	■	■	B	A	T	H	I	N	G	■	E	A	S	T
U	G	H	■	C	A	G	E	■	P	H	A	S	E	S
S	U	E	■	E	V	I	L	■	R	E	N	E	G	E
H	E	R	■	D	E	E	M	■	■	S	T	A	G	E

Puzzle 56: Jonah

C	U	B	A	■	H	U	L	A	■	I	M	A	G	E
E	V	I	L	■	A	N	O	N	■	R	I	S	E	R
D	U	S	T	■	S	P	A	T	■	O	C	H	E	R
A	L	O	O	F	■	A	T	H	E	N	A	■	■	■
R	A	N	■	C	A	C	H	E	T	■	H	A	T	S
■	■	■	W	A	L	K	■	M	A	L	■	A	R	E
A	F	R	O	■	T	E	E	■	■	A	G	R	E	E
B	E	E	R	S	■	D	A	D	■	W	O	O	E	R
E	L	A	T	E	■	■	T	O	M	■	E	N	D	S
A	L	L	■	A	L	B	■	W	A	Y	S	■	■	■
M	A	M	A	■	S	I	E	N	N	A	■	C	A	P
■	■	■	M	A	D	C	A	P	■	M	E	R	C	Y
H	E	A	P	S	■	E	G	O	S	■	M	A	U	L
E	V	I	L	S	■	P	L	U	S	■	U	N	T	O
Y	E	M	E	N	■	S	E	R	E	■	S	E	E	N

Puzzle 57: Micah

E	Y	E	S	■	■	L	A	B	E	L	■	H	I	M
D	O	V	E	S	■	A	M	I	N	O	■	O	N	E
A	K	E	E	M	■	Z	E	B	E	C	■	M	A	N
M	E	N	■	E	D	E	N	■	■	U	P	E	N	D
■	■	■	A	L	A	S	■	E	N	S	U	R	E	S
S	L	O	W	L	Y	■	S	C	O	T	T	■	■	■
L	O	B	E	S	■	■	T	O	N	S	■	G	O	D
A	C	I	D	■	P	L	A	N	E	■	K	I	N	E
W	O	E	■	C	O	I	N	■	■	C	I	R	C	A
■	■	■	W	O	U	N	D	■	G	A	N	D	E	R
A	N	D	A	N	T	E	■	K	O	N	G	■	■	■
L	O	I	N	S	■	■	E	N	V	Y	■	O	C	T
T	O	N	■	U	N	C	L	E	■	O	M	A	H	A
E	S	E	■	L	O	U	S	E	■	N	A	H	U	M
R	E	D	■	T	R	E	E	S	■	■	T	U	B	E

Puzzle 58: Nahum

F	D	A	■	■	A	T	R	I	P	■	■	E	V	E
L	E	V	I	■	V	E	I	L	S	■	B	R	A	Y
E	V	E	R	■	A	M	P	L	Y	■	E	A	S	E
A	I	R	S	H	I	P	S	■	C	O	A	S	T	S
■	■	■	■	A	L	L	■	■	H	U	N	■	■	■
■	A	B	E	L	■	E	W	E	■	T	O	I	L	■
I	G	L	O	O	S	■	A	G	O	■	■	D	I	E
M	O	O	N	■	L	Y	S	O	L	■	L	A	V	A
P	R	O	■	■	Y	E	T	■	E	I	T	H	E	R
■	A	D	A	M	■	S	E	A	■	O	D	O	R	■
■	■	■	W	S	W	■	■	L	A	W	■	■	■	■
B	R	E	A	T	H	■	H	A	B	A	K	K	U	K
R	E	E	K	■	O	P	E	R	A	■	P	E	N	N
I	D	L	E	■	R	E	A	M	S	■	H	Y	D	E
E	O	S	■	■	L	A	P	S	E	■	■	S	O	W

Puzzle 59: Habakkuk

R	A	S	H	■	■	A	T	S	E	A	■	A	S	H
O	C	H	E	R	■	C	H	A	R	M	■	W	O	E
S	H	A	M	E	■	T	E	T	R	A	■	A	L	A
E	G	G	■	S	H	O	E	■	■	R	A	K	E	R
■	■	■	H	E	A	R	■	F	A	I	R	E	S	T
S	P	R	I	N	T	■	G	E	T	A	T	■	■	■
W	R	E	S	T	■	■	O	A	T	H	■	D	O	N
B	O	S	S	■	H	E	N	R	Y	■	H	E	R	O
S	S	T	■	B	O	R	G	■	■	P	A	E	A	N
■	■	■	L	E	W	I	S	■	B	R	I	D	L	E
W	H	E	E	D	L	E	■	P	O	O	R	■	■	■
H	A	S	T	E	■	■	M	O	A	B	■	O	D	D
I	T	S	■	W	O	M	E	N	■	E	D	G	E	R
S	E	A	■	E	R	R	E	D	■	D	O	L	L	Y
T	R	Y	■	D	E	S	K	S	■	■	E	E	L	S

Puzzle 60: Zephaniah

MICA UCLA FEAST
ADHD POUR AMBER
LOIS TACT TESTY
ELL HOLY PAN
SINEWS CALDRON
OWN PALL ERA
MAVEN ARMY MAN
IDOL SAILS KILN
NOD SKIN GETBY
IRK AIDS BEE
MEASURE TEMPLE
OCT BIAS AXE
ABODE FRAU DUTY
COLOR FORT OGRE
POEMS AWAY CHAD

Puzzle 49: Ezekiel

SHINA FACE SWAB
CAROB ALAN HERE
ALONE IOWA ASEA
TEN DONE MORTAR
KNIT END
DANIEL CELESTA
ORANG DAYS UMP
LINGO ORE ALTAR
ESC GUTS BOOZE
EYESORE INURES
GOD TOED
SPURNS THUG BED
POLE EVER AFORE
ALAS NILE TULIP
SKIS DALE ERECT

Puzzle 50: Daniel

DATE SCRAM TSP
YIELD ELITE APR
EDEMA ROBES BOO
DEN NAVY HELIX
FIRE BRAVELY
DECREE PIECE
AURAL UTAH SBA
DRAY TIMED CULL
SON DURA BASEL
TUNAS DARIUS
HALOGEN WALL
AMINO WHYS SEW
DIM ULTRA AGAPE
ESE TOWEL MOREL
SHY STONE DIED

Puzzle 51: Daniel

NAB TEPEE FLU
ABET ILIAD CLOG
SLAW BEERI HEAL
AEROBICS TWEEDY
EAT SOW
ABED SET OSLO
GDANSK LIE OPT
MIKE PRIMP OVEN
TEE HOT ARDENT
URGE BEG ADDS
OLD RAN
LOAMMI FAITHFUL
ELLE STEPS ELSE
SEER CUREL NESS
SOS SENSE ART

Puzzle 52: Hosea

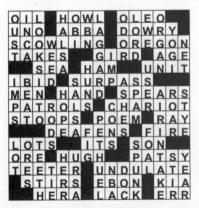

OIL HOWL OLEO
UNO ABBA DOWRY
SCOWLING OREGON
TAKES GIRD AGE
SEA HAM UNIT
IBID SURPASS
MEN HAND SPEARS
PATROLS CHARIOT
STOOPS POEM RAY
DEAFENS FIRE
LOTS ITS SON
ORE HUGH PATSY
TEETER UNDULATE
STIRS EBON KIA
HERA LACK ERR

Puzzle 53: Joel

GEE SCRUB SLEDS
RUN HOUSE HOOKS
ACT OCTET AISLE
SHRIEK HYMN
PRES THEE SAVE
SEER VIALS LAX
ATOMS TOAST
CREOLE COARSE
WHELP FRUIT
AID KARAT EGIS
SNOW IRON GENE
OKRA NUANCE
SWORN BODES DIM
SAUDI IRATE ESE
WRIST ABYSS RED

Puzzle 54: Amos

RAPS ALOE AIDE
ERIE BIND ASIAN
CALL AGED SHINE
ABOLISH YULE
PST NET SESAME
LSD CLUE BOA
ADMIT CHEAP NOR
GOAD WHEAL LENT
INK CROWD MARSH
NNE ROWS BUD
GARDEN PET OFF
RAGS EATABLE
BERET ACLU BEAR
ARISE MITT ESPN
REPS EASY LESS

Puzzle 43: Isaiah

ECHO CHEEP ALL
BRIDE HALSA LOO
BIRDS ISLES GOV
SBE CANT THOSE
GODS SPOILED
ADDERS STORM
CARAT HERS MST
TIER SLEPT DEAR
SSW FLOE MANSE
CRISP CAYUSE
CASSATT FIGS
RUTTY WRAP NBE
ERA IDAHO IDEAL
DAN NYLON EARLS
OLD GETAT TOME

Puzzle 44: Jeremiah

ACCT CHILD ABS
CHASM EERIE GEE
HIPPO CREEL ARE
ENE HAIR ICIER
CALL SAVANTS
AMELIA WAFER
RIGOR OVER BOW
TRIP THREW CANE
YES DIET BOATS
JUDAH HARLOT
AFEARED WALK
BERRA WOMB OFT
ALE BRIER OCHER
TLC LACES ADIEU
EAT EGYPT SOLE

Puzzle 45: Jeremiah

GATES HIS ABBA
AROMAS ESC LORD
BEAUTY ALI AREA
LASS RAREST EAR
EST AINT SHARD
AWAY JOEL
ABODE JEREMIAH
BLUR LAW ONCE
STRICTER INNER
FIRE LARD
MATTE SINS WSW
HOE YELPED SOMA
AURA GEL ETYMON
STIR USA SENATE
THEM MST ACNED

Puzzle 46: Lamentations

CALF EDICT ASSN
AJAR MACHO BLUE
NAME IDEAS BUNS
EXPORT DISTRESS
NETS NEW
CNS BEAR SORROW
LIE EDGES YEAR
ANGEL ANT TENSE
STAY SEEDY DIS
PHLEGM WAYS SST
OAT KNOB
SWINDLES ANOMIE
AIDE ITEMS NOSY
ASEA GREAT ELLE
REAR NANNY SEES

Puzzle 47: Lamentations

SOB HAS STOOGE
ABR FADE PEPPER
USE LION RATTLE
DEADER SWAMI
ISSUE ROOT MITT
STM FIRE FUROR
BRASS FAMINE
SST UTE BIC SSE
ATHENS DUNES
FEEZE ERRS OBI
EPEE RAIN FLASH
KLUTZ PIERRE
MEDIAN ZEUS OAF
ORIENT LEFT NET
BARLEY ELF SLY

Puzzle 48: Ezekiel

ESC SHIPS MOM
TALC HANOI TEAR
AGAR EMCEE EATS
AMEBA GOETH
TIFF PENT
AFTER ABR CHAFF
LEE REJOICE DUE
GIN SIGNS ASL
AGO DETECTS GEL
ENNUI AYE NEEDY
SPAS SOON
TRUST TWANG
POOR STOAT COON
ATOP ELUDE TEEN
REF ACTOR SSE

Puzzle 37: Proverbs

CAB STOMP THROW
RUE LABOR HEALS
ETC AMINO AANDW
CHASTE FAIR
HOLE BLIP TAKE
ERMA SUITE KIN
RHONE SWINE
DOCENT HIRING
GUSHY DAVID
ALL AMITY OWNS
BLOW BOTH WHAT
OUCH POSEUR
PAIRS AFTER ESE
ABODE WROTE LEE
TRUSS KITES SAT

Puzzle 38: Ecclesiastes

ISAAC HEAPS SBE
MICRO AGGRO ERA
PREEN SIREN PAT
ACS SEA GAVE
GOD ARM ECHELON
OVERVIEW HIM
RAMIE ARIES REV
GLIB KNORR NAME
EST MOTTO AFTER
DAH ENABLING
WOMANLY SLY ODE
HUED ROE LSD
ITS BADLY SALTS
CDS OBESE ADIEU
HOY WILES LADEN

Puzzle 39: Ecclesiastes

COTE MAMMA ACES
OPEN SNOOP SOLO
MEET GETUP KOLN
ENTRY WETLY KEG
SHEEP HEEDS
ANENT AIMED
SPIT PAW BREEZE
WON ASPIRIN ARE
INCUBI NOR STAR
MYRRH SEDAN
ENOCH SPOKE
SPA RIOTS TWERP
KISS GUILD IDOL
EPEE ASKER NADA
WEST REEDY GREY

Puzzle 40: Song of Solomon

MALTA RAIN CAPS
AFOUL AXLE ARIA
NAVEL VILE SENT
ERE EYES DOTAGE
AGIN FIR
FLAGON EMULOUS
LABOR HAIL SOD
EBONY ATE PLANE
WED GLEN LOGAN
LEBANON WATERS
ALA OATH
BANNER AFRO ASH
ELAN LEFT NICHE
DOVE EPEE ICIER
SEED DAWN CEDAR

Puzzle 41: Song of Solomon

FACT DIGS WARNS
ILLS ETNA AWAIT
CLAP LEAK DAILY
HEM DIMWIT KNEE
UNPLUG AWE
ASH FIRE WSW
SPITTOON DEATH
FOUR RUT XRAY
CURSE ENORMITY
ALL GOOD EOS
FOR JOTHAM
BASE BALEEN ERE
ALERT ROTC SAGS
SMEAR TOUT PROS
SADLY SKIS ATTY

Puzzle 42: Isaiah

Puzzle 31: Job

Puzzle 32: Psalms

Puzzle 33: Psalms

Puzzle 34: Psalms

Puzzle 35: Proverbs

Puzzle 36: Proverbs

F	O	R	E	■	■	W	R	A	P	■	C	R	A	B
E	V	E	N	■	W	H	I	R	R	■	H	I	V	E
T	E	N	T	■	R	A	C	K	O	■	A	P	E	D
A	R	T	I	F	I	C	E	■	P	A	P	E	R	S
■	■	■	C	A	S	K	■	P	H	I	L	■	■	■
P	R	I	E	S	T	■	D	U	E	L	I	S	T	■
L	O	R	D	■	S	T	A	R	T	■	N	O	O	K
A	L	I	■	■	■	A	V	E	■	■	■	F	A	N
N	E	S	T	■	P	L	I	E	D	■	R	I	S	E
■	S	H	E	L	L	E	D	■	I	D	E	A	T	E
■	■	■	S	E	A	S	■	S	N	I	P	■	■	■
C	H	A	T	T	Y	■	J	U	G	G	L	I	N	G
Y	O	G	I	■	A	S	A	P	H	■	I	D	E	A
S	A	U	L	■	C	O	V	E	Y	■	C	O	R	P
T	R	A	Y	■	T	S	A	R	■	■	A	L	O	E

Puzzle 25: 1 Chronicles

A	L	P	O	■	■	D	E	G	A	S	■	C	R	Y
C	A	R	L	O	■	A	M	I	N	O	■	H	U	E
T	W	E	E	T	■	V	I	N	Y	L	■	A	L	A
G	N	P	■	H	E	I	R	■	■	O	F	F	E	R
■	■	■	M	E	L	D	■	H	A	M	M	E	R	S
D	I	S	A	R	M	■	B	E	F	O	G	■	■	■
A	B	Y	S	S	■	■	I	R	A	N	■	S	A	T
R	I	N	K	■	C	E	D	A	R	■	H	U	G	H
E	S	C	■	L	O	R	D	■	■	B	O	G	I	E
■	■	■	S	E	A	M	Y	■	I	R	V	I	N	E
C	A	N	T	A	T	A	■	T	R	E	E	■	■	■
O	B	E	Y	S	■	■	U	R	S	A	■	C	P	A
M	A	R	■	H	O	U	S	E	■	S	C	O	R	N
A	C	V	■	E	A	S	E	S	■	T	A	L	O	N
S	K	Y	■	S	T	A	R	S	■	■	N	A	M	E

Puzzle 26: 2 Chronicles

A	S	P	■	■	■	P	R	E	■	■	■	A	T	E
S	H	E	B	A	■	O	U	R	■	M	A	N	O	R
H	O	A	R	D	■	O	B	S	■	A	L	T	A	R
■	E	L	I	J	A	H	■	T	U	R	B	I	D	■
■	■	■	M	U	G	■	■	■	S	I	A	■	■	■
T	E	N	■	S	O	L	O	M	O	N	■	L	O	W
H	E	A	R	T	■	A	L	I	■	A	C	U	T	E
A	R	T	Y	■	■	D	I	M	■	■	A	C	H	E
N	I	T	E	R	■	E	V	E	■	P	L	I	E	D
K	E	Y	■	I	G	N	E	O	U	S	■	D	R	S
■	■	■	N	B	A	■	■	■	N	E	B	■	■	■
■	G	R	A	B	B	Y	■	D	O	U	A	L	A	■
A	L	A	M	O	■	E	S	E	■	D	R	E	S	S
S	E	V	E	N	■	A	P	E	■	O	F	F	E	R
L	E	E	■	■	■	R	A	M	■	■	■	T	A	I

Puzzle 27: 2 Chronicles

S	E	B	S	■	■	S	C	A	L	**P**	■	**H**	I	T
T	U	L	I	**P**	■	A	L	D	E	**R**	■	**O**	N	E
A	R	I	S	**E**	■	K	A	Z	O	**O**	■	**U**	S	A
B	O	P	■	**O**	B	E	Y	■	■	**P**	O	**S**	E	S
■	■	■	O	**P**	U	S	■	A	T	**H**	L	**E**	T	E
S	**E**	P	A	**L**	S	■	**A**	C	H	**E**	D	■	■	■
A	**Z**	U	R	**E**	■	■	**M**	E	A	**T**	■	D	**K**	G
A	**R**	T	S	■	G	H	**O**	S	T	■	T	O	**I**	L
R	**A**	T	■	B	R	A	**N**	■	■	**P**	R	O	**N**	E
■	■	■	F	L	I	N	**G**	■	**G**	**E**	O	R	**G**	E
S	M	I	L	I	N	**G**	■	**L**	**O**	**R**	**D**	■	■	■
C	**Y**	**R**	**U**	**S**	■	■	**G**	**O**	**D**	**S**	■	A	C	S
A	L	A	■	T	A	B	**O**	O	■	**I**	G	L	O	O
M	A	T	■	E	X	A	**L**	T	■	**A**	I	M	E	D
P	R	E	■	R	E	N	**D**	S	■	■	N	A	D	A

Puzzle 28: Ezra

A	C	T	■	**W**	**A**	T	T	■	S	T	A	T	U	S
W	O	E	■	**A**	**R**	I	A	■	W	H	O	O	S	H
A	V	E	■	**L**	**O**	**R**	**D**	■	A	I	R	W	A	Y
R	E	P	U	L	**S**	E	■	■	T	N	T	■	■	■
E	**Y**	**E**	**S**	■	E	D	**G**	E	■	**G**	**A**	**T**	**E**	**S**
■	**S**	**E**	**A**	**S**	■	■	**O**	R	B	■	■	R	A	P
■	■	■	G	**A**	G	■	**D**	I	E	■	C	A	S	E
M	I	M	E	**T**	I	C	■	**E**	**S**	**C**	**A**	**P**	**E**	**D**
E	R	A	S	■	**S**	**O**	**N**	■	T	A	R	■	■	■
E	**A**	**R**	■	■	T	W	**O**	■	■	**D**	**O**	**W**	**N**	■
K	N	E	A	D	■	S	**T**	E	**M**	■	L	**A**	O	S
■	■	■	C	O	P	■	■	P	**E**	N	S	**I**	V	E
T	E	N	U	R	E	■	**L**	O	**R**	E	■	**T**	E	E
S	**P**	**I**	**R**	**I**	**T**	■	**A**	C	**C**	T	■	**E**	**N**	**D**
P	**A**	**L**	**A**	**C**	**E**	■	**W**	H	**Y**	S	■	**D**	**A**	**Y**

Puzzle 29: Nehemiah

U	M	**P**	■	T	I	L	D	**E**	■	E	D	U	C	E
P	E	**A**	■	A	R	E	A	**S**	■	S	E	R	E	R
P	A	**L**	■	**F**	**I**	**G**	**H**	**T**	■	P	I	N	O	N
E	N	**A**	C	T	S	■	■	**H**	**A**	**N**	**G**	■	■	■
R	I	**C**	A	■	■	S	H	**E**	D	■	**N**	**A**	**D**	**A**
S	**E**	**E**	**K**	■	**S**	W	A	**R**	M	■	■	N	**I**	P
■	■	■	**I**	**D**	**E**	**A**	**S**	■	■	E	S	T	**E**	E
■	B	A	N	Y	**A**	N	■	**F**	**A**	**S**	**T**	**E**	**D**	■
R	O	U	G	E	■	■	**N**	**A**	**S**	**T**	**Y**	■	■	■
E	**A**	**T**	■	■	A	**P**	I	**S**	H	■	L	A	I	**D**
D	R	O	**P**	■	F	**E**	L	**T**	■	■	E	M	M	**A**
■	■	■	**U**	**N**	**T**	**O**	■	■	B	**O**	S	O	M	**S**
G	E	N	**R**	E	■	**P**	R	E	E	**N**	■	R	U	**T**
O	R	B	**I**	T	■	**L**	E	V	E	**L**	■	**A**	**R**	**E**
D	E	E	**M**	S	■	**E**	**V**	**E**	**R**	**Y**	■	L	E	**D**

Puzzle 30: Esther

M	A	D	E		S	T	O	W			E	V	I	L
A	L	A	R		T	R	U	E		D	A	I	R	Y
D	I	V	A		R	A	I	N		A	R	I	S	E
A	B	I	S	H	A	I		T	E	N	T			
M	I	D		Y	I	N			S	C	H	E	M	A
			G	M	T		B	A	T	E		S	O	L
O	F	T	E	N		T	R	I	E	D		T	W	O
M	O	O	T		B	E	A	N	S		B	E	E	N
A	R	T		F	E	A	S	T		H	O	R	D	E
H	U	E		I	L	L	S		S	A	W			
A	M	M	I	E	L			A	L	I		S	S	E
			C	L	E	G		C	O	R	N	E	T	S
R	A	P	I	D		A	V	O	W		O	A	R	S
O	P	E	N	S		T	I	R	E		P	L	E	A
D	R	A	G			H	A	N	D		E	S	P	Y

Puzzle 19: 2 Samuel

L	E	V	I		S	C	E	N	T			B	U	L
S	L	I	D		T	O	R	A	H		P	A	P	A
D	I	E	D		U	N	I	T	E		U	S	E	S
			O	L	D		C	O	N	F	R	O	N	T
P	R	E		O	I	L				L	E	N	D	S
L	A	Y	A	B	O	U	T		B	A	R	S		
O	V	E	R			C	R	E	A	K				
D	E	S	K		N	A	I	A	D		I	O	T	A
				R	I	S	E	R			O	A	R	S
		K	E	E	P		S	T	A	T	U	T	E	S
S	T	A	I	N				H	U	R		H	E	N
H	A	R	D	T	A	C	K		G	Y	M			
E	P	E	E		G	U	I	S	E		E	A	R	N
B	E	E	R		A	B	N	E	R		A	R	E	A
A	D	M			R	A	G	E	S		L	E	V	Y

Puzzle 20: 1 Kings

S	C	A	R		M	A	T	T		W	A	S	P	S
H	U	L	A		O	M	R	I		S	H	O	R	E
I	R	O	N		N	O	E	L		W	I	D	O	W
P	I	T		I	T	S	E	L	F		A	S	S	N
S	A	H	A	R	A				A	S	H			
			M	A	N		P	A	S	O		A	C	E
	A	B	I	N	A	D	A	B		W	A	L	L	S
W	H	Y	S			E	N	D			L	E	A	P
B	A	T	H	S		J	E	A	L	O	U	S	Y	
N	B	E		B	A	A	L		A	W	L			
			O	W	L				B	E	A	S	T	S
H	E	E	L		A	W	A	K	E	D		H	I	T
A	P	R	I	L		A	B	E	L		G	O	B	I
S	E	R	V	E		F	L	E	E		E	V	I	L
H	E	S	E	D		T	E	N	D		M	E	A	L

Puzzle 21: 1 Kings

S	T	A	F	F		S	A	C			G	A	T	E
T	H	R	E	E		P	L	Y		M	E	S	H	A
A	R	M	E	D		L	E	T		E	T	H	E	R
G	O	O	D		C	A	S	H	E	D		Y	E	S
G	N	U		H	I	T		E	P	I	C			
	G	R	E	E	T			R	E	C	A	N	T	S
			L	A	Y		S	E	E		M	E	A	L
D	A	V	I	D		C	I	A		B	E	T	T	Y
A	X	I	S		E	R	R		M	A	L			
B	E	E	H	I	V	E			O	A	S	I	S	
			A	M	I	D		S	O	L		G	A	L
G	M	T		P	L	I	G	H	T		E	L	L	E
L	E	A	V	E		T	O	E		G	R	O	U	P
A	N	G	E	L		O	R	E		E	M	O	T	E
D	U	S	T			R	E	P		M	A	S	E	R

Puzzle 22: 2 Kings

A	R	C		S	H	O	D		E	A	C	H		
B	O	A		C	O	D	A		T	H	A	I	S	
B	O	R	R	O	W	E	D		C	O	R	N	E	R
A	D	V	I	L			A	C	H	Y		D	R	Y
		E	N	D		M	I	D			L	I	F	E
W	H	I	G		T	O	S	T	A	D	A			
E	O	N		H	O	O	T		B	E	C	A	M	E
P	U	T	D	O	W	N		B	A	B	Y	L	O	N
T	R	O	U	P	E		A	U	N	T		L	A	D
			D	I	L	E	M	M	A		R	O	B	S
A	B	L	E			N	A	P		B	O	W		
S	R	I		A	B	E	L			A	B	A	S	E
H	O	S	H	E	A		G	A	R	M	E	N	T	S
	S	T	O	O	L		A	H	A	B		C	A	P
		S	E	N	D		M	A	G	I		E	R	N

Puzzle 23: 2 Kings

A	R	O	M	A		A	F	A	R		O	P	U	S
B	O	N	U	S		B	A	D	E		D	E	L	L
B	E	L	L	S		S	C	A	B		D	A	T	A
A	S	Y	L	U	M		E	M	U	S		C	R	Y
			A	M	A	S	S		K	O	R	E	A	
J	A	P	H	E	T	H			E	Y	E			
U	S	E			H	E	L	P	S		N	E	E	D
S	H	E	M			T	O	E			T	U	B	E
T	Y	P	E		W	H	O	L	E			R	E	M
			E	R	A			E	Y	E	S	O	R	E
	G	E	T	A	T		A	G	E	N	T			
S	E	X		W	E	I	R		S	C	O	P	E	S
O	N	C	E		R	O	M	P		A	N	O	D	E
N	O	E	S		E	W	E	R		S	E	R	G	E
S	A	L	T		D	A	D	O		E	S	T	E	R

Puzzle 24: 1 Chronicles

L	O	T		A	G	A	P	E		A	B	L	E	N
O	N	E		B	E	T	E	L		C	R	O	W	D
S	E	A		B	R	E	A	D		T	O	W	E	R
S	I	S	E	R	A			E	A	S	T			
E	D	E	N			M	A	R	X		H	O	H	O
S	A	L	T		R	I	N	S	E			D	E	W
			I	T	A	L	Y			A	D	O	R	E
	S	H	R	I	N	K		C	E	D	A	R	S	
S	H	E	E	P			S	I	H	O	N			
T	O	B			S	H	E	A	F		C	A	V	E
M	E	E	T		A	U	T	O			E	V	I	L
			A	D	D	S			G	I	D	E	O	N
G	R	E	B	E		T	R	I	A	D		N	L	A
A	A	R	O	N		L	E	N	T	O		G	E	T
S	T	A	R	S		E	X	C	E	L		E	T	H

Puzzle 13: Judges

A	N	T	I			A	D	L	I	B		A	F	T
B	E	R	R	A		M	A	Y	O	R		L	I	E
B	R	A	S	S		A	R	E	N	A		T	O	N
A	D	M		K	N	I	T			M	E	A	N	T
			L	I	O	N		D	E	B	O	R	A	H
E	R	R	A	N	D		B	U	L	L	S			
S	U	I	N	G			R	O	S	E		B	O	V
P	L	O	D		H	O	U	S	E		L	E	V	I
Y	E	T		C	O	R	N			C	O	N	A	N
			M	A	N	E	T		B	O	T	T	L	E
E	S	C	A	P	E	S		P	U	A	H			
S	H	U	N	T			A	R	M	S		O	B	I
T	A	R		A	M	B	L	E		T	A	K	E	N
E	V	E		I	O	T	A	S		S	O	R	E	S
R	E	D		N	O	U	N	S			F	A	S	T

Puzzle 14: Judges

A	G	O		S	A	K	E	S		S	E	V	E	N
L	A	D		B	L	E	A	T		C	R	I	M	E
T	W	O		E	M	P	T	Y		O	A	S	I	S
O	K	R	A		I	T	S	E	L	F		A	R	T
			B	I	G				A	F	C			
	M	A	R	T	H	A		D	W	E	L	L	S	
P	E	Z		S	T	R	A	W		D	E	A	L	T
O	N	T	O		Y	O	K	E	S		F	U	E	L
I	D	E	A	L		S	A	L	T	S		D	E	C
	S	C	H	E	M	E		T	R	U	E	S	T	
			U	S	A				A	P	T			
T	O	P		O	R	P	H	A	N		C	A	M	E
A	L	L	O	T		T	O	N	G	S		B	O	N
L	E	A	C	H		S	H	E	E	P		B	A	D
L	O	T	T	O		D	O	W	R	Y		A	B	S

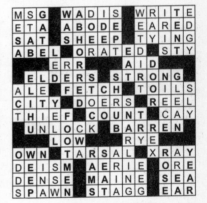

Puzzle 15: Ruth

M	S	G		W	A	D	I	S		W	R	I	T	E
E	T	A		A	B	O	D	E		E	A	R	E	D
S	A	T		S	H	E	E	P		T	Y	I	N	G
A	B	E	L		O	R	A	T	E	D		S	T	Y
			E	R	R				A	I	D			
	E	L	D	E	R	S		S	T	R	O	N	G	
A	L	E		F	E	T	C	H		T	O	I	L	S
C	I	T	Y		D	O	E	R	S		R	E	E	L
T	H	I	E	F		C	O	U	N	T		C	A	Y
	U	N	L	O	C	K		B	A	R	R	E	N	
			L	O	W				R	Y	E			
O	W	N		T	A	R	S	A	L		X	R	A	Y
D	E	I	S	M		A	E	R	I	E		O	R	E
D	E	N	S	E		M	A	I	N	E		S	E	A
S	P	A	W	N		S	T	A	G	G		E	A	R

Puzzle 16: 1 Samuel

Y	A	C	H	T			G	A	F	F		F	E	B
A	P	I	A	R	Y		O	B	O	E		A	V	E
M	E	A	N	I	E		T	O	R	E		V	I	A
			N	A	S	A		A	C	T	I	O	N	S
	H	E	A	D		F	I	R	E		D	U	C	T
G	A	T	H		B	I	N	D		S	I	R	E	S
Y	I	N		B	O	R	N		T	W	O			
P	L	A	C	A	T	E		R	A	I	M	E	N	T
			A	S	H		F	I	L	M		P	A	S
A	L	I	V	E		B	O	O	K		W	I	M	P
C	O	N	E		S	O	R	T		F	A	C	E	
C	A	S	S	A	T	T		S	A	U	L			
E	V	E		L	O	T	H		D	E	N	T	I	N
S	E	C		M	O	L	E		S	L	U	I	C	E
S	S	T		A	D	E	N			S	T	E	E	R

Puzzle 17: 1 Samuel

C	O	D	A			A	R	E	N	A		P	A	L
O	P	E	R	A		C	A	R	O	B		O	B	I
D	E	A	T	H		H	I	N	D	I		S	O	N
E	N	D		I	R	O	N			G	U	I	D	E
			O	L	E	O		C	H	A	S	T	E	N
A	L	A	R	U	M		T	H	A	I	S			
W	A	X	E	D			H	I	L	L		J	I	M
A	C	E	S		E	G	Y	P	T		T	O	N	E
Y	E	S		A	D	A	M			G	O	A	T	S
			S	M	O	T	E		G	I	L	B	O	A
P	R	E	S	U	M	E		G	O	L	D			
H	O	S	T	S			F	I	V	E		A	L	B
A	P	T		I	N	T	E	R		A	E	R	I	E
S	E	E		N	E	W	E	L		D	W	E	L	T
E	S	E		G	R	O	S	S			E	A	T	S

Puzzle 18: 2 Samuel

S	M	O	G	■	A	B	L	E	■	■	S	T	U	B
W	A	V	E	■	G	L	O	B	■	G	H	A	N	A
E	C	O	N	■	L	U	T	E	■	R	I	G	O	R
A	H	I	E	Z	E	R	■	R	Y	A	N	■	■	■
R	I	D	■	E	A	T	■	■	O	P	E	N	E	D
■	■	■	I	B	M	■	C	A	K	E	■	A	V	E
P	A	L	L	U	■	L	O	V	E	S	■	H	I	N
A	B	E	L	■	Z	E	R	O	S	■	A	B	C	S
R	U	E	■	A	A	N	D	W	■	W	R	I	T	E
A	S	K	■	B	R	O	S	■	B	I	D	■	■	■
N	E	S	S	I	E	■	■	H	O	N	■	T	E	D
■	■	■	E	D	D	Y	■	E	R	E	M	I	T	E
A	H	I	R	A	■	A	R	A	D	■	I	G	A	L
S	I	R	E	N	■	W	O	V	E	■	C	E	L	L
S	P	E	D	■	■	L	E	E	R	■	A	R	E	S

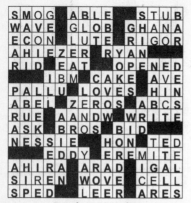

Puzzle 7: Numbers

R	A	G	S	■	O	N	C	E	■	R	A	S	T	A
E	T	U	I	■	V	O	L	T	■	T	A	P	I	R
H	A	I	R	■	E	V	E	N	■	A	R	E	L	I
O	L	D	■	B	R	O	G	A	N	■	O	W	E	D
B	E	E	V	E	S	■	■	■	U	R	N	■	■	■
■	■	■	A	T	E	■	R	E	N	O	■	F	D	A
■	G	A	T	H	E	R	E	D	■	D	A	R	E	D
S	U	S	I	■	■	A	G	O	■	■	D	E	A	D
E	L	E	C	T	■	G	A	M	A	L	I	E	L	■
A	P	T	■	L	A	E	L	■	L	I	T	■	■	■
■	■	■	A	C	S	■	■	■	M	O	S	A	I	C
S	C	A	B	■	H	E	B	R	O	N	■	U	T	E
A	R	N	O	N	■	D	E	A	N	■	F	R	E	D
P	O	N	D	O	■	A	M	I	D	■	L	A	M	A
S	W	E	E	T	■	M	A	N	S	■	U	S	S	R

Puzzle 8: Numbers

G	A	L	■	■	A	D	M	A	H	■	■	I	C	E
O	R	E	O	■	B	R	A	K	E	■	P	R	E	Y
D	E	V	I	■	H	E	N	C	E	■	R	O	D	E
S	A	I	L	B	O	A	T	■	D	R	O	N	E	S
■	■	■	■	A	R	M	■	■	S	I	X	■	■	■
■	S	C	A	D	■	S	A	D	■	E	Y	R	A	R
S	C	A	R	E	D	■	V	I	I	■	■	E	L	I
R	O	C	K	■	I	C	I	E	R	■	E	V	I	L
A	U	T	■	■	D	I	M	■	S	L	E	E	V	E
S	T	I	F	F	■	A	S	K	■	E	L	L	E	■
■	■	■	E	O	S	■	■	A	H	A	■	■	■	■
D	E	P	A	R	T	■	A	D	U	L	T	E	R	Y
E	D	A	S	■	R	A	V	E	N	■	O	L	E	O
E	D	I	T	■	A	R	E	S	T	■	E	S	A	U
R	A	N	■	■	W	I	S	H	■	■	■	E	R	R

Puzzle 9: Deuteronomy

T	E	N	S	■	■	P	A	N	■	■	D	O	S	E
W	A	R	P	■	A	L	L	O	W	■	I	D	E	A
I	T	■	O	■	S	A	L	M	I	■	Z	O	A	R
N	S	■	K	E	P	T	■	A	L	T	A	R	S	■
■	■	■	E	A	S	E	L	■	D	A	H	■	■	■
S	H	R	U	G	■	S	E	C	■	D	A	C	C	A
H	O	O	P	L	A	■	A	P	T	■	B	E	O	R
A	N	Y	■	E	P	H	R	A	I	M	■	A	L	I
F	E	A	R	■	R	A	N	■	C	O	A	S	T	S
T	Y	L	E	R	■	D	E	W	■	O	B	E	S	E
■	■	■	J	E	W	■	D	R	I	E	R	■	■	■
■	S	T	O	L	O	N	■	A	F	R	A	I	D	■
V	I	I	I	■	M	O	T	I	F	■	H	O	O	F
O	P	E	C	■	B	O	O	T	Y	■	A	W	O	L
W	A	D	E	■	■	K	P	H	■	■	M	A	R	Y

Puzzle 10: Deuteronomy

B	O	A	R	■	A	D	A	R	■	L	A	S	S	O
A	B	B	A	■	K	I	N	E	■	E	A	S	E	L
N	E	B	N	■	A	S	I	A	■	T	R	E	A	D
K	Y	O	T	O	■	M	O	R	E	S	O	■	■	■
S	S	T	■	P	L	A	N	E	T	■	N	E	A	T
■	■	■	S	T	A	Y	■	D	A	N	■	A	G	E
S	T	E	P	■	W	E	D	■	■	F	O	R	G	E
P	A	V	E	D	■	D	A	B	■	L	A	T	I	N
A	B	I	D	E	■	■	Y	A	K	■	T	H	E	Y
S	O	T	■	L	O	T	■	S	I	N	S	■	■	■
M	O	A	B	■	F	I	J	I	A	N	■	C	S	T
■	■	■	A	S	T	R	A	L	■	E	L	A	T	E
H	E	L	L	O	■	A	C	I	D	■	A	L	O	N
U	R	B	A	N	■	D	O	C	K	■	C	E	N	T
B	A	C	K	S	■	E	B	A	L	■	E	B	E	S

Puzzle 11: Joshua

F	A	S	T	■	S	O	C	K	■	■	C	R	O	P
E	C	H	O	■	I	R	O	N	■	A	R	E	N	A
T	H	O	U	■	E	D	G	E	■	S	E	V	E	N
C	O	U	R	A	G	E	■	E	A	S	T	■	■	■
H	O	T	■	H	E	R	■	■	S	I	E	S	T	A
■	■	■	E	O	S	■	S	A	S	S	■	W	A	C
S	P	L	A	Y	■	C	A	R	E	T	■	A	S	H
T	E	A	R	■	D	O	U	B	T	■	A	N	T	I
R	A	N	■	M	A	N	N	A	■	L	I	K	E	N
A	R	K	■	U	R	S	A	■	G	A	D	■	■	■
P	L	A	T	T	E	■	■	B	I	N	■	C	P	A
■	■	■	R	E	S	T	■	R	A	D	I	O	E	D
S	T	E	A	L	■	A	L	A	N	■	N	A	D	A
H	A	P	P	Y	■	L	O	S	T	■	S	T	A	G
E	R	A	S	■	■	L	O	S	S	■	T	I	L	E

Puzzle 12: Joshua

Puzzle 1: Genesis

Puzzle 2: Genesis

Puzzle 3: Exodus

Puzzle 4: Exodus

Puzzle 5: Leviticus

Puzzle 6: Leviticus

27 Satan, the ___ serpent (Rev. 12:9)
29 Non ___ (not welcome)
30 ___ and Magog (Rev. 20:8)
32 Type of trees near two candlesticks (Rev. 11:4)
33 Elevated
34 Rod (Num. 4:12)
35 Shrill bark
37 "They are ___ with the showers" (Job 24:8)
39 Fisherman's tool (Luke 5:5)
42 Unit of length (abbr.)
43 Cheat
47 Collect leaves
49 Entryways of pearls (Rev. 21:21)
50 Aggregate of minerals
52 Mesopotamian diviner (Rev. 2:14)
55 Snares (Josh. 23:13)
57 Cunningly
58 Portend
59 Wading bird
60 "For the ___ is at hand" (Rev. 22:10)
61 Continent with seven churches (Rev. 1:4)
62 American Bar Association division
63 Beehive State
64 Ninth letter in Greek alphabet
65 "Wipe ___ all tears" (Rev. 7:17)
68 "Was granted that ___ should be arrayed in fine linen" (Rev. 19:8)

101

Revelation

by Kathy Hake

• • • • •

ACROSS

1 Cell stuff
4 Wipe out
9 Young dog
12 "Smoke ___ up for ever and ever" (Rev. 19:3)
14 Business mail
15 "___ and true are thy ways" (Rev. 15:3)
16 Detail
17 Representative
18 ___ Minor (Little Dipper)
19 Peru related
21 They fell down and worshipped God (Rev. 19:4)
23 "Love worketh no ___ to his neighbour" (Rom. 13:10)
24 This "gave up the dead which were in it" (Rev. 20:13)
25 Black (poet.)
28 "If he shall ask an ___" (Luke 11:12)
31 "What ___ seest, write in a book" (Rev. 1:11)
34 Grain sold for three measures for a penny (Rev. 6:6)
36 Line of cedar beams (1 Kings 6:36)
38 Licensed practical nurse
40 Eager
41 "To give life unto the ___ of the beast" (Rev. 13:15)
43 "The harvest of the earth is ___" (Rev. 14:15)
44 Color of dragon (Rev. 12:3)
45 Angel had key to bottomless ___ (Rev. 20:1)
46 Hot pot holder
48 Edible lily bulb
51 Scientist's office
53 "That the ___ men be sober" (Titus 2:2)
54 "Remember. . .whence thou ___ fallen" (Rev. 2:5)
56 "___ in faith" (James 1:6)
58 Bad tasting, like waters (Rev. 8:11)
61 "___: for the Lord. . .reigneth" (Rev. 19:6)
66 Off-Broadway award
67 "If we ___ to commune with thee" (Job 4:2)
69 Store
70 Fades, as Eli's eyesight (1 Sam. 3:2)
71 Vial
72 Input
73 Compass point
74 Sordid
75 "___ is withered away" (Isa. 15:6)

DOWN

1 Leaky faucet noise
2 Make a record (2 Thess. 3:14)
3 Israelite tribe (Rev. 7:6)
4 Modern message system
5 Delight
6 "Be unto our God for ever and ever. ___" (Rev. 7:12)
7 Jesus (Rev. 14:14)
8 Author Eleanor
9 Angels were "clothed in ___ and white linen" (Rev. 15:6)
10 Russia
11 Parent-teacher groups
13 Large bird
15 "Lion of the tribe of ___" (Rev. 5:5)
20 Angel "gathered the ___ of the earth" (Rev. 14:19)
22 "___ us be glad" (Rev. 19:7)
25 Roof overhang
26 Jerusalem was "prepared as a ___" (Rev. 21:2)

29 "Behold, I am ___" (Rev. 1:18)
30 "The name of the wicked shall ___" (Prov. 10:7)
32 Color of stone overcomers will receive (Rev. 2:17)
33 Building materials
34 Santa Barbara time
35 One day this will no longer shine (Rev. 7:16)
37 Istanbul to Patmos dir.
39 "Hast tried them which ___ they are apostles" (Rev. 2:2)
42 "___ is come salvation" (Rev. 12:10)
43 Not against
47 Incense gives off a pleasant one
49 Cohort of the beast is a ___ prophet (Rev. 19:20)
50 The Tribulation, e.g.
52 "___, he cometh with clouds" (Rev. 1:7)
55 Parcel of land
57 God's prophets were this
58 "I will even make the ___ for fire great" (Ezek. 24:9)
59 Overcomers will rule with a rod made of this (Rev. 2:27)
60 The beast is wounded, but would do this (Rev. 13:14)
61 "Thou art neither ___ nor hot" (Rev. 3:15)
62 Kansas time zone during summer
63 Traditional angel instrument
64 Canal
65 "As white as ___" (Rev. 1:14)
68 Charge

100

Revelation

by Vicki J. Kuyper

ACROSS

1 "I knew a man in Christ above fourteen years ___" (2 Cor. 12:2)
4 Epics
9 Genetic code
12 "The washing of pots and ___" (Mark 7:8)
14 Hug
15 Voiced
16 Samaria, e.g.
17 First letter of Greek alphabet and part of one of Jesus' monikers
18 What Cain may have called Eve
19 Denim work trouser
21 Attacks
23 Chinese flavoring
24 Tiny measurement (abbr.)
25 Those who overcome will eat from the "___ of life" (Rev. 2:7)
28 "He that hath an ___, let him hear" (Rev. 2:7)
31 Small boat
34 Shrimps
36 "I was brought ___, and he helped me" (Ps. 116:6)
38 KJV "hath"
40 "On either ___ of the river, was there the tree of life" (Rev. 22:2)
41 Dimensions
43 Mediterranean bread
44 ___ chi
45 Second to last mo.
46 Those who walk in white are this (Rev. 3:4)
48 "The book of ___" (Rev. 3:5)
51 The trust of those who forget God is like a spider's ___ (Job 8:14)
53 KJV "doeth"
54 "From whence thou ___ fallen" (Rev. 2:5)
56 Pride
58 "I make a ___" (Rev. 3:12)
61 John originally recorded this book for seven ___ (Rev. 1:4)
66 Colored part of eye
67 "Many knew him, and ran ___ thither" (Mark 6:33)
69 Mend with stitches
70 The church of Ephesus had left its first ___ (Rev. 2:4)
71 Paul spent time in prison ___
72 Peter, John, and James, e.g.
73 Crete to Patmos dir.
74 ___ bear
75 Church bench

DOWN

1 University (abbr.)
2 Teacher
3 "Who is worthy to ___ the book" (Rev. 5:2)
4 Former wounds
5 Maintain
6 What Paul must have done in light of all he saw
7 Faithful sidekick of sackcloth
8 Hiccup
9 "Burn incense unto their ___" (Hab. 1:16)
10 Overcomers will receive a new one (Rev. 2:17)
11 "___, ___ that great city Babylon" (Rev. 18:10) (same wd.)
13 Droop
15 Jesus is Alpha and ___ (Rev. 1:8)
20 "These things saith the ___" (Rev. 3:14)
22 Chilly
25 "The fiery ___" (1 Pet. 4:12)
26 Plural spherical measures
27 "Save one little ___ lamb" (2 Sam. 12:3)

35 "Every ___ shall see him" (Rev. 1:7)
37 Green, lima, or fava
38 Lacking hair (Lev. 13:41)
39 Capital of Western Samoa
41 Ca. University
45 "In him dwelleth all the fulness of the ___ bodily" (Col. 2:9)
46 "They should not ___ the grass of the earth" (Rev. 9:4)
47 "Is there any taste in the white of an ___?" (Job 6:6)
50 Business abbr.
52 Sea between Turkey and Greece
53 Objects
54 Beau
55 Game of chance
56 Sap (2 wds.)
59 "They which run in a ___ run all" (1 Cor. 9:24)
60 Patmos is one (Rev. 1:9)
62 "Thou shalt make them as a fiery ___" (Ps. 21:9)
63 Comedian Jay
64 Cart for hauling heavy things
66 "A time to rend, and a time to ___" (Eccl. 3:7)
68 Agricultural education organization

99

Revelation

by Kathy Hake

ACROSS

1 "Thou shalt not ___ to offer the first of thy ripe fruits" (Ex. 22:29)
6 "No man. . .was ___ to open the book" (Rev. 5:3)
10 Curtain border (Ex. 36:11)
14 Atmosphere layer
15 Hit
16 Mythical wife of Zeus
17 "I saw three unclean spirits like ___" (Rev. 16:13)
18 Weighted weapon (Brit.)
19 Whip, as Romans did Jesus
20 False
21 "On ___ side of the river, was there the tree of life" (Rev. 22:2)
23 Nickname for Harold or Henry
24 Israelite tribe (Rev. 7:7)
26 Ancient central Italy people
28 Tennis player Andre
31 Be angry
32 Ephraim's son (1 Chron. 7:27)
33 Hand tool
36 Father God (Mark 14:36)
40 Skirt
42 Cereal grass
43 "Thrust in thy sickle, and ___" (Rev. 14:15)
44 Style of poetry
45 Famous German author
48 NASA's Earth-observing instrument
49 First beast (Rev. 4:7)
51 African nation
53 Small land mass (Rev. 6:14)
56 "Pharisees began to ___ him vehemently" (Luke 11:53)
57 Number of witnesses (Rev. 11:3)
58 "They lived and reigned with ___ a thousand years" (Rev. 20:4)
61 Precious metal (Rev. 21:18)
65 Corrodes
67 "Take thine ___, eat, drink, and be merry" (Luke 12:19)
68 High temperature (Acts 28:8)
69 Small amount (Luke 12:59)
70 Organization concerned with civil liberties
71 Passes at the bull
72 "As white as ___" (Rev. 1:14)
73 "Yea, the ___ things of God" (1 Cor. 2:10)
74 Pester

DOWN

1 To put aside
2 Jewish scribe (Ezra 7:6)
3 "He that sat was to ___ upon like a jasper" (Rev. 4:3)
4 "Seven stars are the ___ of the seven churches" (Rev. 1:20)
5 Affirmative reply (Mark 7:28)
6 Computer code
7 "I will not ___ out his name out of the book of life" (Rev. 3:5)
8 Beat, like Jews did to Paul
9 One of seven churches (Rev. 1:11)
10 30 to 300 gigahertz
11 Headquarters of British India
12 Moan (2 Cor. 5:4)
13 "Fourth beast was like a flying ___" (Rev. 4:7)
21 Wicked (Rev. 2:2)
22 Sacrificial animal (Ex. 29:16)
25 Extrasensory perception
27 Beast's "feet were as the feet of a ___" (Rev. 13:2)
28 Stake
29 Ascend (2 wds.)
30 Counteractive
31 Guitar finger marker
34 Jesus "shall rule them with a rod of ___" (Rev. 19:15)

20 Former British colony
22 Snake-like fish
25 Computer screen dot
26 Very tiny life-form (var.)
27 "Keep yourselves in the love of ___" (Jude 1:21)
29 Shoulder covering
30 Graphical record of electrical activity of brain
32 Coil
33 Being Michael the archangel contended with (Jude 1:9)
34 "___ no corruption" (Acts 13:37)
35 Goes with yang
37 Positive confirmation (Rom. 3:29)
39 Simon Peter's fishing tool (John 21:11)
42 Type of animal utterance
43 Former capital of Brazil
47 Adding term
49 "___ the shepherd" (Mark 14:27)
50 "___ thousands of his saints" (Jude 1:14)
52 Require
55 Rover
57 Israelites' leader (Jude 1:9)
58 NT term for father (Gal. 4:6)
59 Cut of beef
60 Michael and the devil were disputing over this (Jude 1:9)
61 Succulent plant (John 19:39) (sing.)
62 Dark, viscous material
63 Told a falsehood (Ps. 78:36)
64 Canal
65 In ___ (together)
68 Fermented drink

98

Jude

by Kathy Hake

• • • • •

ACROSS

1 "It ___ needful for me to write unto you" (Jude 1:3)
4 "Make his ___ straight" (Mark 1:3)
9 Color of fair evening sky (Matt. 16:2)
12 Doing nothing (Matt. 20:6)
14 Register (var.)
15 "On your most ___ faith" (Jude 1:20)
16 French and German river
17 Suffering, as Jesus experienced in garden (Luke 22:44)
18 "Now unto him that is ___ to keep you" (Jude 1:24)
19 Hugged, as Paul did disciples (Acts 20:1)
21 Moon is this type of light (Gen. 1:16)
23 New Jersey's neighbor (abbr.)
24 "___ ye have not, because ye ask not" (James 4:2)
25 Summon
28 South southeast
31 Salacious (Acts 17:5)
34 Selling of a church office
36 Express surprise
38 She "doth gather her brood under her wings" (Luke 13:34)
40 Chopped
41 "Renewed in knowledge after the ___ of him that created him" (Col. 3:10)
43 Wander, as Israelites did in wilderness
44 Spider's home (Job 8:14)
45 "___ unto him that is able to keep you from falling" (Jude 1:24)
46 Part of Trinity (Jude 1:19)
48 End time (Jude 1:18)
51 Past times, of ___ (Jude 1:4)
53 Lounge
54 Males (Jude 1:4)
56 Large Australian bird
58 Colorless person
61 Followers of Jesus Christ (Jude 1:17)
66 Shoe
67 Group to appear before God three times a year (Ex. 23:17)
69 Incorporeal
70 Stay
71 "Man shall not live by bread ___" (Luke 4:4)
72 Tack
73 "Said he at ___ time, Sit on my right hand" (Heb. 1:13)
74 Actions (Jude 1:15)
75 Twelfth month (abbr.)

DOWN

1 "To the only ___ God our Saviour" (Jude 1:25)
2 Enoch was seventh from ___ (Jude 1:14)
3 Block
4 "Mercy unto you, and ___" (Jude 1:2)
5 Heavenly beings (Jude 1:6)
6 Walked, as Israelites did across land (Josh. 14:9)
7 Term of affection
8 Craftily
9 Steals, as men of Shechem did at mountaintop (Judg. 9:25)
10 English Language and Literacy
11 Tinter, as Lydia "seller of purple" (Acts 16:14)
13 "Their lies caused them to ___" (Amos 2:4)
15 "Came with ___, and found Mary, and Joseph, and the babe" (Luke 2:16)

37 Tears
38 Type of dressing
39 Male offspring (Gen. 5:4)
41 Sword blade (Josh. 11:11)
45 Residents of Asian peninsula
46 "He that doeth ___ hath not seen God" (3 John 1:11)
47 Japanese money
50 Deciduous tree (Judg. 6:11)
52 Account (3 John 1:12)
53 Large trunk artery
54 Appeal earnestly (Mic. 6:2)
55 Serenity (3 John 1:14)
56 Submerges in liquid
59 Rejoicing
60 Person's countenance (3 John 1:14)
62 Zealous
63 Nickname for Andrew's brother (Matt. 10:2)
64 Kept watch
66 Put on
68 Clean Water Act

97

3 John

by Kathy Hake

• • • • •

ACROSS

1 Time span (James 5:17)

6 "Lift up the hands which ___ down" (Heb. 12:12)

10 Young one (Luke 2:12)

14 Corner

15 Aroma

16 False god (1 Cor. 8:7)

17 Invalidate

18 Trim off (Deut. 21:12)

19 Encircle with belt or band (Acts 12:8)

20 Look at

21 Punctuation marks

23 Alone in character (Matt. 23:8)

24 Greenish-blue color

26 Tormentor

28 Mrs. Clinton's middle name

31 "Members of the body, which ___ to be more feeble" (1 Cor. 12:22)

32 Sash with wide flat bow

33 Frugal

36 Globes

40 "Whom I ___ in the truth" (3 John 1:1)

42 Deer (2 Sam. 2:18)

43 Farm building

44 Guide (Gen. 33:14)

45 Organ (Lev. 7:4)

48 Ink's mate (3 John 1:13)

49 "He that doeth ___ is of God" (3 John 1:11)

51 Against

53 "When he shall ___, we may have confidence" (1 John 2:28)

56 Eat dinner (John 21:12)

57 Bullfight cheer

58 Container full

61 Mantle

65 Study (Matt. 21:42)

67 Assembly on Literature for Adolescents

68 Small flock

69 Mexican sandwich

70 Nape (Gen. 27:16)

71 "With ink and pen ___ unto thee" (3 John 1:13)

72 Gulf in Arabian Sea

73 Observes with eye

74 Joined (Acts 11:24)

DOWN

1 Take a picture

2 Yearn (Lev. 26:39)

3 Inflammatory disease

4 "Casteth them out of the ___" (3 John 1:10)

5 Teleost fish of order Apodes

6 Mount (2 wds.)

7 First man

8 Rule

9 "I have no ___ joy" (3 John 1:4)

10 Grand

11 Bye-bye

12 "Which have ___ witness of thy charity" (3 John 1:6)

13 Greater in age (3 John 1:1)

21 "When the brethren ___ and testified" (3 John 1:3)

22 View (3 John 1:14)

25 Edible tuber

27 Mattathias's father (Luke 3:25)

28 Move by revolving (Gen. 29:8)

29 Slender woodwind

30 Leading lady

31 "He that doeth evil hath not ___ God" (3 John 1:11)

34 Waterless, like dry and thirsty land

35 "He that doeth good is of ___" (3 John 1:11)

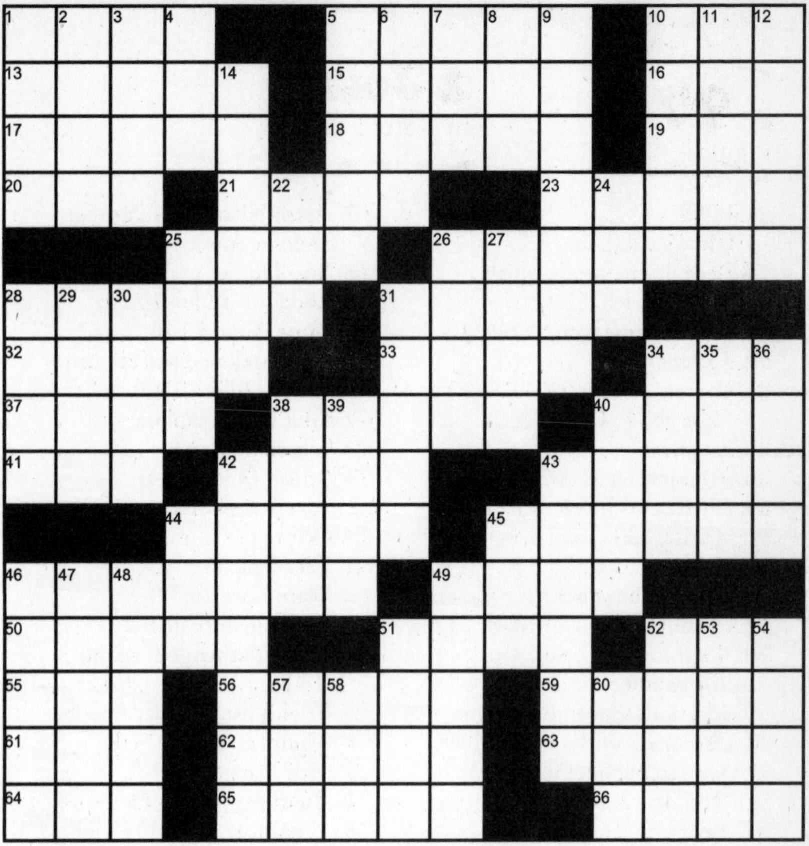

31 Consumers
34 Midday (Ps. 55:17)
35 Land surrounded by water (Isa. 23:2)
36 For fear that (2 Pet. 3:17)
38 "Make straight paths for your ___" (Heb. 12:13)
39 Woman (2 John 1:5)
40 Christ (2 John 1:3)
42 Request earnestly (2 John 1:5)
43 Informal
44 Gregorian calendar's last month (abbr.)
45 Business executive
46 Imitative
47 Elite intellectuals' society
48 Without clothes (Rev. 3:17)
49 Earth's inhabitants (1 John 5:19)
51 Stare lewdly
52 "Te work of ___ hands" (Deut. 4:28)
53 Solemn promise (Heb. 6:17)
54 Affirmative
57 "Many deceivers ___ entered into the world" (2 John 1:7)
58 Oolong
60 Annual climbing leguminous plant

96

2 John

by Kathy Hake

• • • • •

ACROSS
1 Hurt one's toe
5 Sleep disorder
10 Talk
13 Tropical American mammal
15 Endorsement
16 Aromatic Mediterranean plant (Luke 11:42)
17 Eat away
18 ___ Matisse, painter
19 Distinctive period of time
20 Writing tool (Judg. 5:14)
21 Horse command
23 "Let him be your ___" (Isa. 8:13)
25 Comely
26 "I rejoiced ___ that I found of thy children walking in truth" (2 John 1:4)
28 Uninjured
31 Accord (Eph. 4:13)
32 "The children of Israel ___ not stedfastly behold the face of Moses" (2 Cor. 3:7)
33 "We therefore ought to receive ___" (3 John 1:8)
34 Nix
37 Relax
38 "Who confess not that Jesus Christ is come in the ___" (2 John 1:7)
40 Fail to keep (2 John 1:8)
41 Alias
42 Bring forth (James 3:12)
43 Unwise ones (Rom. 1:22)
44 "Biddeth him God speed is partaker of his evil ___" (2 John 1:11)
45 Trumpet's cousin
46 Pardon
49 Join metal
50 "Grace be with you, mercy, and ___" (2 John 1:3)
51 Heed (2 John 1:8)
52 Cow speak
55 "I would not write with paper and ___" (2 John 1:12)
56 Diner (Isa. 55:10)
59 "___ face to face, that our joy may be full" (2 John 1:12)
61 Solar system exploration
62 Fish basket
63 Gossip
64 Possessed (2 John 1:5)
65 Listened to (2 John 1:6)
66 Pale

DOWN
1 Short distance (1 Sam. 20:3)
2 Weed in wheat field (Matt. 13:40)
3 "Truly my soul waiteth ___ God" (Ps. 62:1)
4 "Neither ___ him God speed" (2 John 1:10)
5 "___ that which is evil" (Rom. 12:9)
6 Appeal (Deut. 17:8)
7 Joshua's father (Num. 11:28)
8 Sin (Isa. 9:16)
9 "He that ___ in the doctrine of Christ" (2 John 1:9)
10 Salute (2 John 1:13)
11 Relating to ear
12 Bright
14 Recompense for worthy behavior (2 John 1:8)
22 Slug
24 Light beam
25 Complete (2 John 1:8)
26 African antelope
27 Poor's opposite (Luke 16:19)
28 Public research university in LA
29 Cranny
30 ___ hoop (child's toy)

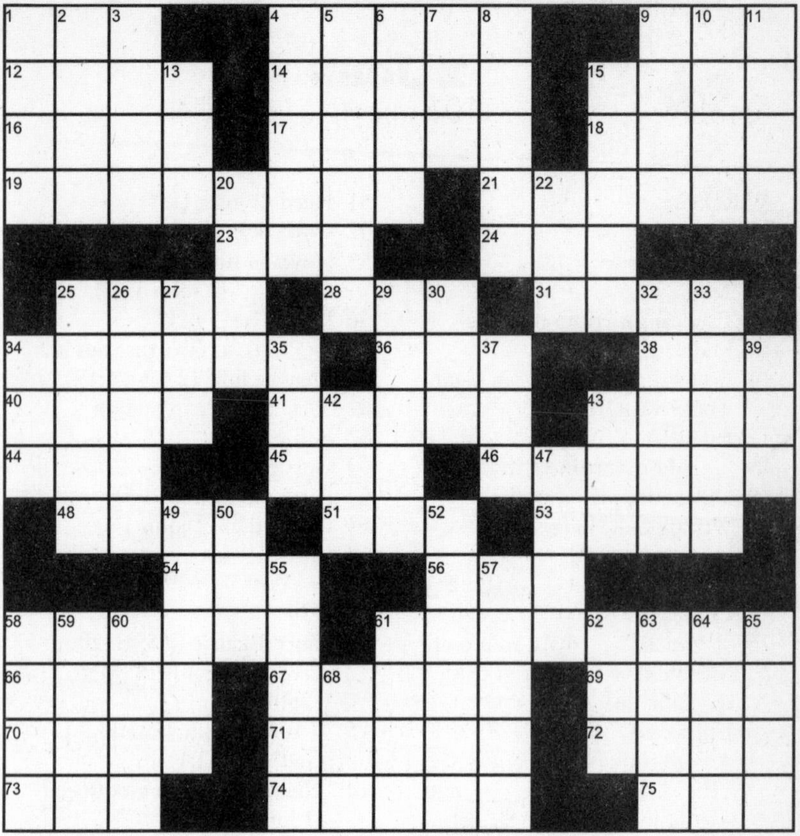

37 Wing-like structure
39 East southeast
42 Christmas month (abbr.)
43 New's opposite (1 John 2:7)
47 Pale sherry
49 Planet (1 John 5:8)
50 Stainless steel
52 Made neater
55 Rasping
57 Pull-___ (sweaters)
58 Baths
59 Step (2 Sam. 6:13) (sing.)
60 Wager
61 So be it (1 John 5:21)
62 Cycles per second
63 City in Judah's inheritance (Josh. 15:52)
64 Subdue (Mark 5:4)
65 Looked at (1 Sam. 18:9)
68 Expression of triumph (Isa. 44:16)

95

1 JOHN

by Kathy Hake

ACROSS

1 Chick holder (Jer. 17:11)
4 Laundry detergent brand
9 Collection of rules (1 John 3:4)
12 Amphibian
14 Avid
15 Assistant, like Joshua was for Moses
16 Variable star
17 Endure (1 John 2:24)
18 Rend (Hos. 13:8)
19 Inflammation of the glands
21 Affirm (1 John 3:19)
23 That girl
24 Foot's forepart (Lev. 8:23)
25 Saul (Acts 13:9)
28 Midway between south and southeast
31 "Believe on the ___ of his Son Jesus" (1 John 3:23)
34 Slips
36 School group
38 "Beloved, let us love ___ another" (1 John 4:7)
40 Whim
41 Utopian
43 Metal-bearing minerals
44 Violate moral standard (Ps. 95:10)
45 "A ___ commandment I write" (1 John 2:8)
46 "His eyes were as ___ ___ of fire" (Rev. 19:12) (2 wds.)
48 Sight organs (1 John 1:1)
51 Clock time
53 Lazily
54 Deciduous ornamental or timber tree (Isa. 44:14)
56 Cation
58 Ancient Greek city
61 "We have an ___ with the Father" (1 John 2:1)
66 Yearn (Amos 2:7)
67 Synthetic fabric
69 Commune with God (1 John 5:16)
70 Pituitary hormone
71 Light
72 "Whosoever denieth the Son, the ___ hath not the Father" (1 John 2:23)
73 Behold (1 John 5:16)
74 "Our ___ have handled" (1 John 1:1)
75 Sleeping place (Luke 8:16)

DOWN

1 Gas burner
2 "It is ___ for me to draw near to God" (Ps. 73:28)
3 Shared (1 John 5:10)
4 Termination of life (1 John 5:16)
5 Hydrophobia
6 Breastplate (var.)
7 Federal government (abbr.)
8 Handle
9 In ___ of (instead of)
10 Twelfth Jewish month (Est. 9:1)
11 "They ___ not of us" (1 John 2:19)
13 Rachel's son (Gen. 30:6)
15 Afloat (2 wds.)
20 Island (Rev. 1:9)
22 Jesus Christ is God's (1 John 3:23)
25 Religious military man
26 Mimicry
27 North American country
29 Spits out (Rev. 3:16) (var.)
30 Seventh letter of Greek alphabet
32 Righteous
33 Foe (Rom. 12:20)
34 Tell falsehood (1 John 1:6)
35 Transgression (1 John 1:7)

31 Food and Agriculture Organization
32 Deviate from direct course (Ps. 119:118)
34 Directed (2 Pet. 3:18)
36 Farm Credit Administration
37 Winged goddess of dawn
38 Balaam's animal (2 Pet. 2:16)
39 Empty tank signifier
40 Morally wrong (2 Pet. 2:12)
42 Shining light (2 Pet. 1:19)
43 "Glory both now and for ever. ___" (2 Pet. 3:18)
45 Indian monetary unit
47 Matthias was numbered with ___ apostles (Acts 1:26)
48 Recompense (2 Pet. 2:13)
50 "Lord knoweth how to deliver the ___" (2 Pet. 2:9)
52 Written material
53 Take off your hat
54 Ovoid
55 Festive
57 Fly as an eagle (Prov. 23:5)
58 Shoshonean
60 Measuring tool (abbr.)
62 Currently (2 Pet. 3:7)

94

2 Peter

by Kathy Hake

• • • • •

ACROSS

1 Get away
6 Scrape together, as Jesus' disciples did ears of corn (Luke 6:1)
9 Israelites made seven ___ around Jericho's walls on seventh day
13 Smear
14 American Sign Language
15 Ancient Greek government
16 Absurd
17 Legume
18 Semi-aquatic mammal
19 Decorative needle case
20 Disk thrown in field event
22 Lout
23 Be inclined (1 Pet. 4:4)
24 Blackguard
25 Handle
27 Author Poe
29 Long-necked mammal
33 "If any of you lack wisdom, let him ___ of God" (James 1:5)
34 "___ him not be ashamed" (1 Pet. 4:16)
35 Sea's mighty noise (Ps. 96:11)
36 Dine (2 Pet. 2:13)
39 Jasper is one type (Ex. 28:20)
40 "Those that were clean escaped from them who live in ___" (2 Pet. 2:18)
41 Bludgeon (Brit.)
42 Unhappy and grieved (Mark 10:22)
43 Lane (abbr.)
44 Attests
46 Ore digger
49 Plural
50 Harden
51 Shelter (Zeph. 1:12) (sing.)
53 Mammal that returned to own vomit (2 Pet. 2:22)
56 Place of seeming confinement (1 Pet. 3:19)
58 Cuts, as Noah does gopher wood to build ark
59 Elliptical
61 "Hasting unto the coming of the day of ___" (2 Pet. 3:12)
62 Kinds of stars
63 "___ prophets also among the people" (2 Pet. 2:1)
64 Movie *2001*'s talking computer
65 Drama set to music
66 Wave
67 Prove (1 Pet. 4:12)
68 Stormy (Ps. 55:8)

DOWN

1 "Submit yourselves unto the ___" (1 Pet. 5:5)
2 "Add to your faith ___" (2 Pet. 1:5)
3 Be plentiful (2 Pet. 1:8)
4 Restaurant
5 Building addition
6 Sudden
7 Purposes (Titus 3:14)
8 Onyx (Ex. 39:13) (2 wds.)
9 Abraham's nephew (2 Pet. 2:7)
10 Vehicle
11 Controversial defense (Deut. 17:8)
12 Subject
15 Balaam's father (2 Pet. 2:15)
20 Absence of light (2 Pet. 1:19)
21 Part
24 Threw (2 Pet. 2:4)
26 Unfruitful (2 Pet. 1:8)
28 Slashed, as David's sword did in battle
30 "Looking ___ and hasting unto the coming of the day of God" (2 Pet. 3:12)

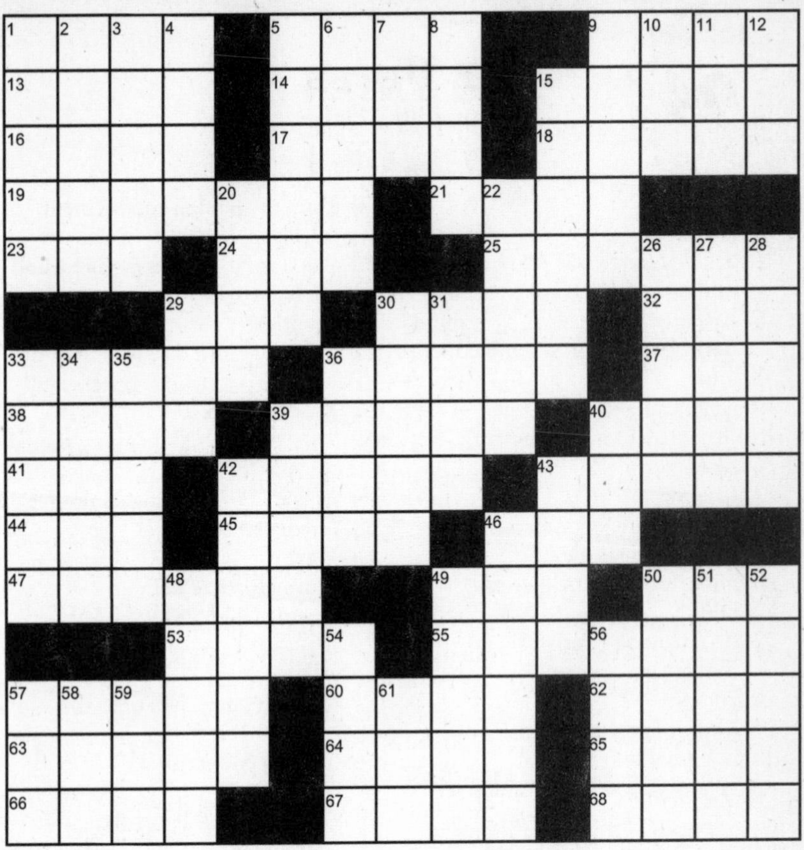

28 Tested (1 Pet. 1:7)
29 Used to attract attention
30 River
31 "Greet ye one another with a ___ of charity" (1 Pet. 5:14)
33 "As newborn ___, desire the sincere milk" (1 Pet. 2:2)
34 "I will never ___ thee" (Heb. 13:5)
35 "Joying and beholding your ___" (Col. 2:5)
36 Conceited (1 Pet. 1:18)
39 Beneficiary
40 Male child (Judg. 16:26)
42 Pointed weapon (1 Kings 18:28)
43 Polish
46 "The same is made the head of the ___" (1 Pet. 2:7)
48 Number of souls saved by ark (1 Pet. 3:20)
49 View
50 Rock (1 Pet. 2:8)
51 Main artery
52 Express respect for (1 Pet. 5:14)
54 Valley (2 Sam. 18:18)
56 Mr. Greenspan
57 Vestment
58 "It is appointed unto men once to ___" (Heb. 9:27)
59 "Cast me not off in the time of old ___" (Ps. 71:9)
61 Cut grass

93

1 PETER

by Kathy Hake

ACROSS

1 High school finisher
5 Convex shape
9 Entice
13 Lacking in refinement or grace (2 Cor. 11:6)
14 Peer at (1 Pet. 1:12)
15 Water radar
16 Austen novel
17 "When they saw the ___" (Matt. 2:10)
18 "Ye shall receive a ___ of glory" (1 Pet. 5:4)
19 Liveth, as God's Word (1 Pet. 1:23)
21 Country where Peter ministered (1 Pet. 1:1)
23 Intertwine
24 Favorable answer (Matt. 17:25)
25 "Your conversation ___ among the Gentiles" (1 Pet. 2:12)
29 "___ price is far above rubies" (Prov. 31:10)
30 John the Baptist was clothed with camel's hair and ___ (Mark 1:6)
32 "They ___ my path" (Job 30:13)
33 "With the precious ___ of Christ" (1 Pet. 1:19)
36 Geological formations of minerals (Job 28:1)
37 Alarm interface
38 Visionary (poet.)
39 Spring flower
40 "Being dead to sins, should ___ unto righteousness" (1 Pet. 2:24)
41 Having undesirable qualities (2 Cor. 5:10)
42 "Gird up the ___ of your mind" (1 Pet. 1:13)
43 Delivered, as to judge (Luke 12:58)
44 Abel's mother
45 Green Gables dweller
46 Common fish
47 Tranquil
49 Marcus was Peter's (1 Pet. 5:13)
50 Swag
53 Type of tea
55 Almighty Architect (1 Pet. 4:19)
57 Proverb
60 "Glory and dominion for ever and ever. ___" (1 Pet. 5:11)
62 Belief
63 God calls out of darkness into His marvelous ___ (1 Pet. 2:9)
64 Only
65 Parlay
66 Red root vegetable
67 Water pitcher
68 Well kept

DOWN

1 A meek and quiet spirit is "of ___ price" (1 Pet. 3:4)
2 Ballroom dancing
3 Acknowledge
4 Departed (1 Pet. 4:5)
5 Long loose overcoat
6 Lepidopterous insects (Job 13:28)
7 Reptile in Boidae family
8 *Hibiscus esculentus*, used in making gumbo
9 Navigation system
10 Spanish "one"
11 Sore and diseased, as leprous flesh (Lev. 13:15)
12 *Haliaetus albicilla* (var.)
15 Isaac and Jacob were Abraham's
20 "Leah was tender ___" (Gen. 29:17)
22 Agleam
26 Electronic message
27 Soothe

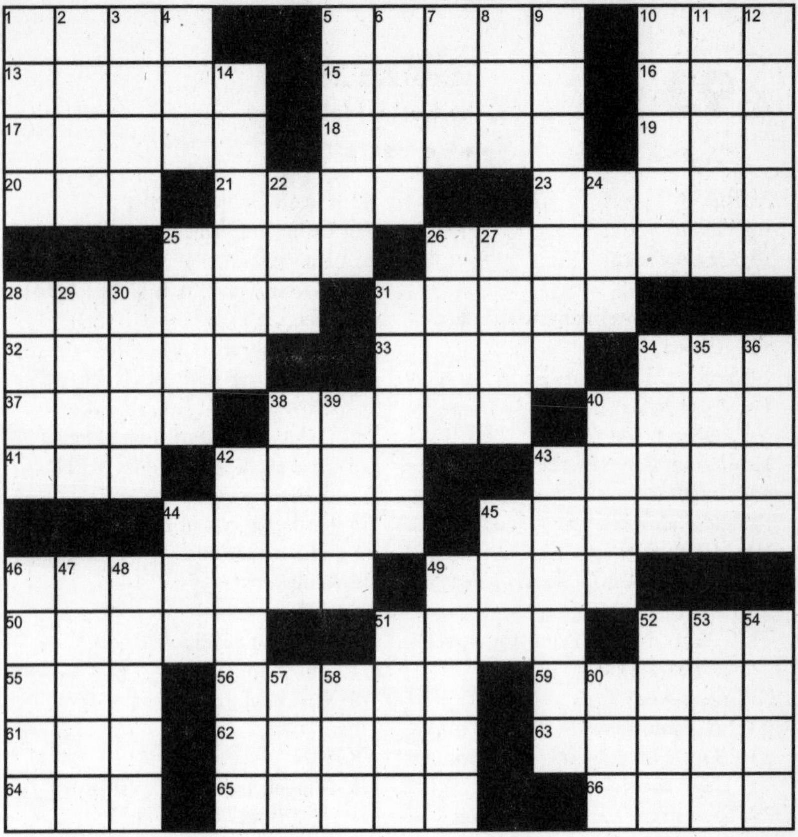

26 Life is a vapor that quickly vanishes ___ (James 4:14)
27 Buy, ___, get gain (James 4:13)
28 River in southeastern Serbia
29 Dandy
30 Ripped , as king did garments (2 Sam. 13:31)
31 Lark
34 Read attentively
35 "Thy praise unto the ___ of the earth" (Ps. 48:10)
36 "As the flower of the grass he shall ___ away" (James 1:10)
38 Pieces of metal used to control horses (James 3:3)
39 Stumbles, as proud (Ps. 119:21)
40 Its home is a nest (Prov. 27:8)
42 Participant in feud
43 Kept afloat
44 "Prayer of a righteous ___ availeth much" (James 5:16)
45 Group of twelve (abbr.)
46 They are "turned about with a very small helm" (James 3:4)
47 Keyed
48 Little
49 Moat
51 Asian nation
52 Operatic solo
53 Dunce
54 Bones in Ezekiel's vision (pl.)
57 Check
58 Self
60 Male sheep (Ex. 29:18)

92

JAMES

by Kathy Hake

ACROSS

1 "Every ___ gift. . .is from above" (James 1:17)

5 His disciples were ___ when Jesus walked on water (2 wds.)

10 Western state (abbr.)

13 Unclothed (James 2:15)

15 Priest put oil on this part of right hand (Lev. 14:28)

16 Originally known as Cassius Clay

17 Dickens's ___ *of Two Cities* (2 wds.)

18 Monkey's cousin

19 Minister (abbr.)

20 "___ art thou cast down?" (Ps. 43:5)

21 What to do when afflicted (James 5:13)

23 "Wisdom that is from ___ is first pure" (James 3:17)

25 Tells

26 Guilty (2 Tim. 2:15)

28 "That ye may be perfect and ___" (James 1:4)

31 Make solemn declaration or oath (James 5:12)

32 Respond

33 Type of branches waved for Jesus (John 12:13)

34 Spiritedness

37 John's surname (Acts 15:37)

38 Transparent gem (Ex. 28:20)

40 ___ fide

41 Consume, as John did little book (Rev. 10:10)

42 "The tongue is a ___" (James 3:6)

43 Type of tamed animal (James 3:7)

44 Metric linear unit (Brit.)

45 Coercion

46 Classical composer

49 Eaten for sustenance (James 2:15)

50 Hunting dog

51 Slimy

52 "Which of you. . .can ___ to his stature?" (Luke 12:25)

55 Where Good Samaritan took injured man (Luke 10:34)

56 Wise men brought three ___ to Jesus

59 Wrongdoing (James 5:20)

61 Caress

62 Epic stories

63 Cyclic (James 2:15)

64 Skilled in deception

65 Cut of beef

66 Welcome rugs

DOWN

1 Chew on bones (Zeph. 3:3)

2 Swear not by any ___ (James 5:12)

3 Yes

4 One of first original Thirteen Colonies (abbr.)

5 Book of maps

6 "We put bits in the horses' mouths, that ___ may obey us" (James 3:3)

7 "How great is the ___ of them!" (Ps. 139:17)

8 Flightless bird

9 He "believed God, and it was imputed unto him for righteousness" (James 2:23)

10 Rebound

11 Tylenol's competitor

12 "Ye have ___ in pleasure on the earth" (James 5:5)

14 "___ in peace, be ye warmed and filled" (James 2:16)

22 Grain

24 Secure, as a door (Neh. 7:3)

25 "Prayer of faith shall save the ___" (James 5:15)

26 "Nor faint when thou ___ rebuked" (Heb. 12:5)
28 Father's sister
29 Cures, as Jesus did sick and lame (Luke 6:7)
30 "Laid the foundation of the ___" (Heb. 1:10)
31 "Whosoever shall ___ thee on thy right cheek" (Matt. 5:39)
32 Audible
33 Labors, unlike lilies (Matt. 6:28)
34 Acclaim
35 Severe heart problem
37 Golfer's goal
39 __ you! (attention getter)
41 Hurt, as devil did child (Luke 9:42)
43 Loathed (Job 19:19)
46 Hair ornaments
48 "They do alway ___ in their heart" (Heb. 3:10)
51 Compass direction
53 Computer makers
56 Jesus ___ on ground and made clay to heal blind man's eyes (John 9:6)
57 Axillary
58 "Having. . .our bodies washed with ___ water" (Heb. 10:22)
60 Font
61 Visit places
62 European monetary unit
64 Corrupt (Heb. 3:12)
65 Weightless
66 Small fry (var.)
68 Priest sprinkled blood on this part of foot (Ex. 29:20)
70 "But we ___ Jesus" (Heb. 2:9)

91

HEBREWS

by Kathy Hake

• • • • •

ACROSS

1 Stock or currency schemer
4 Lowest adult male singing voice
9 Divine, unconditional love
14 Constrictor
15 Unfasten
16 Glass kitchenware
17 Move up and down
18 "But ye are come unto ___ Sion" (Heb. 12:22)
19 Pageant
20 Prayer ending (Heb. 13:21)
22 Blocks of metal
24 "Things which we have spoken this is the ___" (Heb. 8:1)
25 Move quickly, as Peter did to sepulchre (Luke 24:12)
27 Seventh letter of Greek alphabet
29 "Hear his voice, harden not your ___" (Heb. 3:15)
32 "___ all them that have the rule" (Heb. 13:24)
35 "The sand which is by the ___ shore" (Heb. 11:12)
36 Musical time
38 "By faith ___ was translated" (Heb. 11:5)
40 Used to carry ark of the Lord (1 Sam. 6:11)
42 False goddess (Acts 19:35)
44 Thin, flat slab of fired clay Ezek. 4:1)
45 Site of sacrifice (Heb. 13:10)
47 Israelite group (Heb. 7:14)
49 "Let us ___ aside every weight" (Heb. 12:1)
50 Place of worship (Acts 19:24)
52 "So ___ was once offered" (Heb. 9:28)
54 Recede
55 Globe
56 "Trees of the Lord are full of ___" (Ps. 104:16)
59 "Ye have in heaven a ___ and an enduring substance" (Heb. 10:34)
63 Esau sold birthright for morsel of ___ (Heb. 12:16)
67 "Former" planet
69 "Blessed be ye poor: for ___ is the kingdom of God" (Luke 6:20)
71 "The walls of Jericho fell down, after they were compassed about ___ days" (Heb. 11:30) (Rom. num.)
72 His rod budded (Heb. 9:4)
73 Mush up
74 Make angry
75 Adam and Eve hid among them in garden (Gen. 3:8)
76 Wear away
77 Strong solution of sodium hydroxide

DOWN

1 Father
2 Upper area where disciples met (Acts 1:13)
3 Infant (Heb. 5:13)
4 Tramp
5 "God, hath ___ thee" (Heb. 1:9)
6 Twisted, as threads (Ex. 35:25)
7 "I ___ praise unto thee" (Heb. 2:12)
8 On top of
9 "Consider the ___ and High Priest" (Heb. 3:1)
10 Con
11 Greek god of war
12 South American country
13 Test
21 U.S. Parks Service designation
23 Beverage

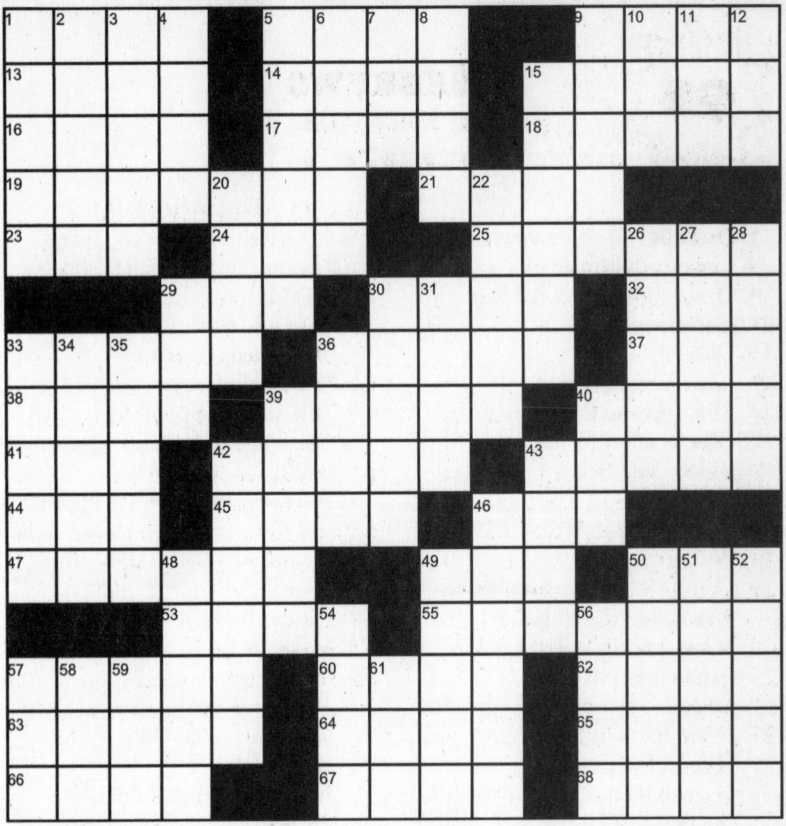

27 Practice
28 "Make straight ___ for your feet" (Heb. 12:13)
29 "Consider ___ another to provoke unto love" (Heb. 10:24)
30 "A priest for ever after the ___ of Melchisedec" (Heb. 5:6)
31 Tabernacle curtain (Heb. 9:3)
33 Type of coin disciples were not to carry (Matt. 10:9)
34 "Mother of the Internet" ___ Perlman
35 Smooth, thin-walled nut
36 Hindu goddess
39 Short notes
40 "I will be to them a ___" (Heb. 8:10)
42 "___, the days come, saith the Lord" (Heb. 8:8)
43 Built, as tabernacle (Heb. 9:2)
46 Dutch town in northern province
48 Disorder
49 Isaac and Jacob, for example (Heb. 11:9)
50 Mount where God gave Moses Ten Commandments (Ex. 19:18)
51 Body parts placed under yokes (Jer. 27:12)
52 Blood and ___ were sprinkled on the unclean (Heb. 9:13)
54 Isaac's son (Heb. 11:20)
56 Baby's drink (Heb. 5:13)
57 Compass point
58 ___ Baba and the forty thieves
59 "Hath trodden under foot the ___ of God" (Heb. 10:29)
61 American Cancer Society

90

Hebrews

by Kathy Hake

• • • • •

ACROSS

1 Deposits
5 Passed with flying colors
9 Opaque gem
13 Inspiration
14 Type of cheese
15 Spanish "friend"
16 "The LORD will ___ from Zion" (Amos 1:2)
17 Viscous liquids used to anoint the sick (Mark 6:13)
18 Regenerate (Heb. 6:6)
19 OT patriarch (Heb. 7:4)
21 Moses "forsook Egypt, not fearing the wrath of the ___" (Heb. 11:27)
23 Distress call
24 Sphere
25 Absorb (2 wds.)
29 "They all shall wax ___" (Heb. 1:11)
30 Egg-shaped
32 God bless the ___
33 Ember (Zech. 3:2)
36 Fear (Isa. 8:13)
37 Digital audio tape
38 "Let us run with patience the ___" (Heb. 12:1)
39 Herbaceous plant
40 Artist Van ___
41 Flurry
42 Knife edge
43 He led his people from Egypt (Heb. 3:16)
44 Term of address for a man (John 4:19)
45 Asian ruler
46 Crazy (1 Cor. 14:23)
47 Portuguese king
49 "After he ___ patiently endured, he obtained the promise" (Heb. 6:15)
50 IBM computer networking protocol
53 Conduit
55 Foes who became His footstool (Heb. 10:13)
57 Whining speech
60 "Moses ___, I exceedingly fear and quake" (Heb. 12:21)
62 Part of a foot
63 Liquid used in sacrifice (Heb. 13:11)
64 Land unit (1 Sam. 14:14)
65 Gennesaret, for example (Luke 5:1)
66 Beats
67 Soviet Union
68 Signal used to betray Jesus (Mark 14:44)

DOWN

1 Italian "dollars" (var.)
2 Philippine dish with marinated chicken or pork
3 Forty ___, time Israelites spent in wilderness (Heb. 3:17)
4 Abraham's wife (Heb. 11:11)
5 On the ship
6 "___ the wall like men of war" (Joel 2:7)
7 Moray
8 Evening
9 "I am Alpha and ___" (Rev. 1:8)
10 Fastener used to secure Samson's hair (Judg. 16:14)
11 "Strong meat belongeth to them that are of full ___" (Heb. 5:14)
12 Opposite of exalted (James 1:9)
15 Mr. Schwarzenegger
20 "___ fast the profession of our faith" (Heb. 10:23)
22 Abraham's son (Heb. 11:9)
26 Reward

31 Goads
34 Alated
35 "Let me ___ joy of thee in the Lord" (Philem. 1:20)
36 Elderly, like Paul (Philem. 1:9)
38 Seabird
39 "The grace of our ___ Jesus Christ" (Philem. 1:25)
40 Natural fiber (Matt. 12:20)
42 Upright, as king saw Ahimaaz (2 Sam. 18:27) (2 wds.)
43 Period of time (Philem. 1:15)
44 Type of comptroller
45 "I thank my ___, making mention of thee" (Philem. 1:4)
46 Female lead singers
47 Chosen (Mark 13:27)
48 Number of sacrificial rams (Num. 7:88)
49 Boss, like man who chose laborers (Matt. 20:1)
51 "Great joy and consolation in thy ___" (Philem. 1:7)
52 "His heart is as ___ as a stone" (Job 41:24)
53 Explosive igniter
54 Last word of Philemon
57 Type of belt
58 Toddler
60 Couple

89

PHILEMON

by Kathy Hake

• • • • •

ACROSS

1 "Not reckoned of grace, but of ___" (Rom. 4:4)
5 Japanese city
10 Variant (abbr.)
13 Elliptical
15 Antique
16 It is impossible for God to ___ (Heb. 6:18)
17 Trouble
18 Mont ___
19 "That which groweth of ___ own accord" (Lev. 25:5)
20 Conclusion (Heb. 3:6)
21 Skullcap
23 "If he hath wronged thee, or oweth thee ___" (Philem. 1:18)
25 Salamander
26 Relish type
28 Request (Philem. 1:8)
31 Unbounded two-dimensional shape (Isa. 44:13)
32 Consider (Philem. 1:17)
33 Jabber
34 Enemy's word (Ezek. 36:2)
37 Whetstone
38 Architect Frank ___ Wright
40 Type of bulbous plant (Job 8:11)
41 Particular person (Philem. 1:9)
42 Morally admirable (Philem. 1:6)
43 Non-hired worker, like Onesimus
44 Colorado Rockies' home field
45 Ready to go, with "up"
46 Lose courage
49 Dupery, like David and Michal played on Saul (1 Sam. 19:13)
50 Book by Homer
51 Caps
52 Farming club
55 Torture, as King Herod did to church (Acts 12:1)
56 Engine
59 Disgrace
61 "The LORD shall. . .and bring to pass his ___" (Isa. 28:21)
62 Higher up (Philem. 1:16)
63 "Even as a ___ cherisheth her children" (1 Thess. 2:7)
64 Hovel
65 Gunpowder need
66 Portent

DOWN

1 Curved roof
2 "Owest unto me ___ thine own" (Philem. 1:19)
3 "Though I might be much ___ in Christ" (Philem. 1:8)
4 Attach, as commandments around neck (Prov. 6:21)
5 Circle, as in planets
6 Your person (Philem. 1:19)
7 Type of limb
8 "Without honour. . .among his own ___" (Mark 6:4)
9 "Put that on mine ___" (Philem. 1:18)
10 Adjust
11 Flexible
12 Ill-natured
14 "Spoil you through philosophy and vain ___" (Col. 2:8)
22 Belonging to (Philem. 1:19)
24 North American Indian
25 "See that ___ render evil for evil unto any man" (1 Thess. 5:15)
26 What potter has power over (Rom. 9:21)
27 "I Paul have written it with mine own ___" (Philem. 1:19)
28 Sound reflection
29 Time of day Saul reached Damascus (Acts 22:6)
30 Sixth month

23 Their bellies were (Titus 1:12)
25 Where priests sacrificed (pl.)
27 French Canadian colony
29 God told Jesus, "Thou ___ my Son"
30 New Zealand bird
31 Shocked exclamation
33 Nocturnal flying mammal (Lev. 11:19)
35 Sinking ship's signal
36 Airline
37 Pastor's title (abbr.)
38 Heaters (Neh. 12:38)
39 "Thy servant was ___ here and there" (1 Kings 20:40)
41 Prod
42 Mantle
44 Academy award
46 Musical theaters
47 Messiah
49 Phase
51 Distribute
52 Created polio vaccine
53 Cast metal (Dan. 2:34)
54 De __ ("from the beginning") (Latin)
56 "All the merryhearted do ___" (Isa. 24:7)
57 Humped ox
59 Cat sound
61 Friend

88

Titus

by Mary A. Hake

ACROSS

1 Feel for (Phil. 2:20)
5 Beverage brewed from malt and hops
8 Section
12 Unleavened bread (Ex. 29:23)
13 "I will also ____ the hearts of many" (Ezek. 32:9)
14 Macedonian
15 Deduce
16 "Be obedient unto their ___ masters" (Titus 2:9)
17 Holy ___ (Spirit)
18 Dirt (Ezek. 17:8)
19 "Thou art my ____ place" (Ps. 32:7)
21 A ball's stand
22 That female
23 What Jacob did with pottage (Gen. 25:29)
24 Zeus's wife
26 "A very ____ thing that I should be judged" (1 Cor. 4:3)
28 Quarantine
32 Bashful
33 Deli order
34 Paul said the witness was (Titus 1:13)
35 One day the lion shall eat this like the ox (Isa. 11:7)
38 U.N. food organization
39 Fabric dyeing art
40 Debt is what is ____
41 "___ them in mind" (Titus 3:1)
42 Mongrel dog
43 Redeemer (Titus 2:13)
45 Partner (abbr.)
48 Organization (abbr.)
49 "To ___ out our liberty which we have" (Gal. 2:4)
50 Advanced degree
52 "He cannot ___, because he is born of God" (1 John 3:9)
55 Young women should be (Titus 2:5)
57 Zilch
58 Pleasant smell
60 U.S. espionage bureau
61 Danger (Rom. 8:35)
62 A bishop should be "a ___ of hospitality" (Titus 1:8)
63 Chicken's offering (Job 6:6)
64 "Behold every one that is proud, and ____ him" (Job 40:11)
65 "Profess that they ___ God" (Titus 1:16)
66 "Wife see that ___ reverence her husband" (Eph. 5:33)
67 "Not fulfil the ___ of the flesh" (Gal. 5:16)

DOWN

1 Indian boats
2 Assert
3 "The earth shall ___ to and fro" (Isa. 24:20)
4 "Brethren, if any of you do ___" (James 5:19)
5 "___ foolish questions" (Titus 3:9)
6 "Certain ___ fellows of the baser sort" (Acts 17:5)
7 Out of nothing (Latin) (2 wds.)
8 The tree planted (Isa. 44:14)
9 "Not accused of ___ or unruly" (Titus 1:6)
10 Relief (Deut. 28:65)
11 Pay, often used with "up"
12 "We ___, even your perfection" (2 Cor. 13:9)
14 Violent (slang)
19 God asks us to be ___ (Titus 1:8)
20 An eagle stirs hers up (Deut. 32:11)

41 "Lead ___ silly women" (2 Tim. 3:6)
42 Onesiphorus ___ Paul in Rome (2 Tim. 1:16–17)
43 Orator (Acts 14:12)
45 Women's Army Corps
47 Western time zone
49 "The dead in Christ shall ____ first" (1 Thess. 4:16) (pl.)
50 "We cry, '___, Father' " (Rom. 8:15)
51 Fright (2 Tim. 1:7)
52 "Hold ___ the form of sound words" (2 Tim. 1:13)
53 Stack (Ezek. 24:9)
54 "They which creep ___ houses" (2 Tim. 3:6)
55 Loan (Luke 11:5)
56 Galilee and Aegean
59 Visible light

87

2 TIMOTHY

by Mary A. Hake

• • • • • •

ACROSS
1 Plateau
5 .16 of an inch
9 Air Battle Damage Report
13 Iridescent gem
14 National Association of Registered Agents and Brokers
15 Escape (2 Tim. 2:22)
16 Bluish green
17 Defense
18 "Make ___ proof of thy ministry" (2 Tim. 4:5)
19 False teachings
21 "To Timothy, my ___ beloved son" (2 Tim. 1:2)
23 Some vessels are made of this (2 Tim. 2:20)
24 Half (prefix)
25 Obstruct
28 Some are lacking this kind of affection (2 Tim. 3:3)
31 Said before (Gal. 5:21)
32 Christ abolished this (2 Tim. 1:10)
34 Trim
36 Main computer part
37 Street (abbr.)
38 African antelope
39 Cannabis
41 Salad plant
43 Mumble
44 Shoreline fortification
46 "Instructing those that ___ themselves" (2 Tim. 2:25)
48 Strikes
49 Trick
50 Influence (Gal. 4:17)
53 Hairdo (pl.)
57 Legume
58 Dublin citizens
60 Every ___ will bow to Jesus
61 Plant fiber used in ropes
62 Manservant
63 Lava maker
64 "Them also which used curious ___" (Acts 19:19)
65 God's ___ see all
66 Paul was beaten with these

DOWN
1 "Where ___ and rust doth corrupt" (Matt. 6:19)
2 Type of sword
3 European river
4 Supposed
5 Lost color
6 Spring flower
7 "Part of a ___ of dove's dung" (2 Kings 6:25)
8 "He ___ faithful" (2 Tim. 2:13)
9 "Entangleth himself with the ___" (2 Tim. 2:4)
10 Smudge
11 Wooded hollow
12 Depend on (2 Chron. 16:8)
14 Jesus was ___ to the cross
20 "Holy offerings ___ they in pots" (2 Chron. 35:13)
22 Flightless bird
24 "Fear of the LORD is to ___ evil" (Prov. 8:13) (pl.)
25 Unsatisfied ears do this (2 Tim. 4:3) (pres. tense)
26 Pouts
27 Fancy feather
28 Belly button (Prov. 3:8)
29 English-speaking person
30 He sent greetings (2 Tim. 4:21)
33 Dukes
35 Our hearts should be this (2 Tim. 2:22)
40 Mother and Father (2 Tim. 3:2)

27 "Let no man despise thy ___" (1 Tim. 4:12)
28 __ of the covenant
29 Kingly
30 Minerals
32 "___ your hands, all ye people" (Ps. 47:1)
33 Nest on a cliff
34 Nations brought Solomon tribute at an annual ___ (1 Kings 10:25)
35 Shredded
38 "Lie down in ____ pastures" (Ps. 23:2)
39 "When they have begun to ___ wanton" (1 Tim. 5:11)
41 Seem (Matt 23:38)
42 "Take ____ unto thyself" (1 Tim. 4:16)
45 "To sharpen every man his ___" (1 Sam. 13:20)
46 Publicist (2 wds.)
47 Struck (Ps. 78:20)
48 Conscious of (Luke 12:46)
49 Paul said younger women should do this (1 Tim. 5:14)
50 This brings destruction (1 Tim. 3:6)
51 All run in one (Heb. 12:1)
53 Servants under this should honor their masters (1 Tim. 6:1)
55 Without end (Rev. 1:6)
57 Sea that parted for Moses
58 Poem
60 Separate (abbr.)

86 1 TIMOTHY

by Mary A. Hake

• • • • • •

ACROSS

1 "I ___ seven golden candlesticks" (Rev. 1:12)
4 "One glory of the ____" (1 Cor. 15:41)
7 Engrave
11 Secret plan
13 Only God truly is (1 Tim. 1:17)
14 Curtain
15 Italian currency
16 Periods of time (Eph. 2:7)
17 Don't wear "costly ___" (1 Tim. 2:9)
18 Voluntarily refrain (1 Tim. 4:3)
20 One's good (1 Tim. 5:23)
22 "___ them about thy neck" (Prov. 6:21)
23 Neuter possessive pronoun
24 This "exercise profiteth little" (1 Tim. 4:8)
28 Moabite city (Deut. 2:9)
29 "Love of money is the ___ of all evil" (1 Tim. 6:10)
31 Soft bird sound
32 "We can ___ nothing out" (1 Tim. 6:7)
35 Earth (Latin)
36 Note of debt
37 What a problem faucet does
38 God told Moses, "___, ___ thee down" (Ex. 32:7) (2 wds.)
39 What Jesus did at Lazarus's tomb
40 "Whereunto thou ___ also called" (1 Tim. 6:12)
41 City of northern France
42 Stern
43 Filled pastry shell
44 Babylon did this to every shoulder (Ezek. 29:18) (pres. tense)
45 Male or female
46 Baboon
47 The girl (Luke 8:52)
48 Makes music louder (abbr.)
52 "If we ___ him, he also will ___ us" (2 Tim. 2:12) (same wd.)
54 "Joshua ___ ___ a long time" (Josh. 11:18) (2 wds.)
56 Fragrance
59 Scent
61 Ring-tailed lemur
62 Wood used for the temple
63 Unclean bird (Lev. 11:14)
64 Emergency and Remedial Response Division
65 God's beautiful garden
66 "Adam was first formed, then ___" (1 Tim. 2:13)
67 Doctor who studied fatal syndrome connected to children taking aspirin

DOWN

1 Smacking noise
2 Excuse
3 "Is ___ than an infidel" (1 Tim. 5:8)
4 "___ and wonders" (Heb. 2:4)
5 "The law is good, if a man ___ it lawfully" (1 Tim. 1:8)
6 River and lake in Scotland
7 "Have ___ concerning the faith" (1 Tim. 6:21)
8 Dark, oily substance
9 Accountant
10 Call to attention
12 Form lace
13 "___ for his Son from heaven" (1 Thess. 1:10)
14 One of 2 northern states
19 Light and open
21 Terminate
25 More frozen
26 Each curtain had 50 for hanging (Ex. 26:5)

28 "Brethren, be not ____ in well doing" (2 Thess. 3:13)
29 Bible book about Paul's journeys
30 "Count him not as an ___" (2 Thess. 3:15)
31 Impressive sword
32 Samson took the gate of the city, ___ and all (Judg. 16:3)
33 Stinky
34 Civil wrong
36 Go away (2 Pet. 3:10)
39 "The Lord is faithful, who shall ___ you" (2 Thess. 3:3)
40 Strike (1 Sam. 31:3)
42 Where river meets sea
45 Candy
46 Eighth month (abbr.)
47 To visit (1 Thess. 3:6)
49 To perceive (Neh. 8:8)
50 Russian ruler (var.)
51 "___ believe me for the very works' sake" (John 14:11)
52 Timothy's grandmother (2 Tim. 1:5)
53 Predatory bird (Job 39:26)
54 Mend socks
55 "That the ___ men be sober, grave" (Titus 2:2)
56 Tableland
59 Western Indian summer wind
61 Cow sound

85 2 THESSALONIANS

by Mary A. Hake

• • • • • •

ACROSS

1 Grease (Sp.)
6 Flavor
10 Window
14 Notched
15 Smell
16 Solemn promise (Num. 21:2) (2 wds.)
17 "___ _____ is in thine own eye" (Matt. 7:4) (2 wds.)
18 Corn syrup
19 Religious ceremony
20 Northeastern state (abbr.)
21 "Set him ____ the works of thy hands" (Heb. 2:7)
23 Puts aside
25 Forthwith
26 Time
27 "I will fasten him as a ___" (Isa. 22:23)
28 "Meditate on thee in the night _____" (Ps. 63:6)
32 Dutch colonists
34 Industrial arts school (abbr.)
35 Snooze
37 Beginning of the Hebrew alphabet
38 Edible grain
39 This queen came to see Solomon
41 Free (Ex. 6:6)
42 The one who commits sin does this
43 "The ___ and the seasons" (1 Thess. 5:1)
44 Royal family line
47 "___ shall dance there" (Isa. 13:21)
48 "Taken ___ of the way" (2 Thess. 2:7)
49 Biological weapon
50 Central Indian language
53 Jacob grasped Esau's (Gen. 25:26)
54 Animal mother (Ex. 22:30)
57 Plod
58 Alda of MASH
60 We are made in God's _____
62 Thessalonica's continent
63 Temple had four ____ of pillars (1 Kings 7:2)
64 Dogs licked those of the beggar (Luke 16:21)
65 "You who are troubled ___ with us" (2 Thess. 1:7)
66 "As many servants as are under the ___" (1 Tim. 6:1)
67 Japanese motor company

DOWN

1 Joyful (1 Pet. 4:13)
2 "They put on him a purple ____" (John 19:2)
3 Eve's second son
4 "Like a wave of the ____" (James 1:6)
5 "___ him as a brother" (2 Thess. 3:15)
6 "Manifest ___ of the righteous judgment" (2 Thess. 1:5)
7 The twelfth Jewish month (Est. 3:7)
8 "Neither by spirit, ___ by word" (2 Thess. 2:2)
9 "Your faith ____ exceedingly" (2 Thess. 1:3)
10 A leper is one
11 Tel ___ (city in Israel)
12 Be aware of (2 Thess. 3:14)
13 Female sheep (Ps. 78:71) (pl.)
22 Volcano (abbr.)
24 Circle part
25 Retirees' group
27 The virtuous woman helps them (Prov. 31)

28 Petrol
30 "He ___ there two days" (John 4:40)
31 Colorless
33 Keepsake
34 Monotonous tone
35 Cubic centimeter (abbr.)
36 Scoundrel
38 Morning moisture (Prov. 3:20)
40 Electroencephalograph
43 "___ hold on eternal life" (1 Tim. 6:12)
44 5th day of work week (abbr.)
48 Data (abbr.)
50 "____ that which is evil" (Rom. 12:9)
51 Computer key (abbr.)
53 Soggy (Ex. 12:9)
56 Greek sandwiches
58 "Be at peace ___ yourselves" (1 Thess. 5:13)
59 "As small as the ____ frost" (Ex. 16:14)
60 Patmos (Rev. 1:9)
61 "I will be ____ in the LORD" (Ps. 104:34)
62 Negative (prefix)
63 Paul went this way from Berea
64 Hawkeye State
65 Vegetable and meat dish
66 Unclean animal (Deut. 14:7)
69 "Onesiphorus. . .___ refreshed me" (2 Tim. 1:16)

84 1 Thessalonians

by Mary A. Hake

• • • • • •

ACROSS

1 "No man can serve ___ masters" (Matt. 6:24)
4 Middle Eastern headgear (pl.)
10 Touching the ___ of Jesus' garment brought healing
13 Main island of Hawaii
15 Paul was gentle as one (1 Thess. 2:7)
16 Pretty
17 Travel
18 "Nor a ____ of covetousness" (1 Thess. 2:5)
19 Water (Sp.)
20 Early church leaders (Acts 2:42)
22 "Our exhortation was not of ___" (1 Thess. 2:3)
24 As 15 Across "cherisheth ___ children"
25 Bible affirmation
26 Heroic tale
29 Beheld (Rev. 1:17)
32 Jesus Christ
35 Of Moses
37 "Whether it be good or ____" (2 Cor. 5:10)
39 "How long will it be ___ they believe" (Num. 14:11)
41 Wading bird
42 "Good to be left at Athens ____" (1 Thess. 3:1)
44 Floating sea ice
45 "As many as are ____ by the Spirit of God" (Rom. 8:14)
46 Father
47 Electrical channel
49 "This epistle be ___ unto all" (1 Thess. 5:27)
52 Not no (Rom. 10:18)
54 Pleasant
55 "To ___ I am ashamed" (Luke 16:3)
57 Lout
59 "Esteem them very ___ in love" (1 Thess. 5:13)
62 Those who are over us in the Lord are to do this (1 Thess. 5:12)
67 Norway's capital
68 Repeated musical piece
70 Wine bottle
71 Like a wing
72 "I have told you ___" (Phil. 3:18)
73 Pitcher
74 "He rebuked the ___ sea also" (Ps. 106:9)
75 In scorpions' tails (Rev. 9:10)
76 We stand in this before God

DOWN

1 Grivet
2 Lengthwise thread in weaving (Lev. 13:48)
3 Buckeye State
5 Ner to Saul (1 Sam. 14:50)
6 Monarchs
7 Male siblings (abbr.)
8 "Whatsoever we ___, we receive of him" (1 John 3:22)
9 "Plead the cause of the poor and ____" (Prov. 31:9)
10 Ethiopians and the Lubims are a ____ host (2 Chron. 16:8)
11 Decorative needle case
12 Esau sold his birthright for a morsel of ____ (Heb. 12:16)
14 Positive feelings
16 Seed used for cocoa
21 Siamese
23 Moray
26 Watch and remain ____ (1 Thess. 5:6)
27 "Wherefore laying ____ all malice" (1 Pet. 2:1)

28 Customs
30 Hen's product (Job 6:6)
31 Wing-like structure
32 Thief's hideout (Jer. 7:11)
34 Animal doctor (abbr.)
36 Metric weight (abbr.)
37 Fermented drink
38 Not pro
39 "The ministry which thou hast ___" (Col. 4:17)
40 A believer's is in heaven (Col. 1:5)
42 The same as (Phil. 3:21)
43 "He hath ___, I will never leave thee" (Heb. 13:5)
45 They'd been told not to touch or this (Col. 2:21)
47 Imagine
48 Type of gasoline
50 He sent greetings (Col. 4:14)
52 Green shampoo
53 "For this ___ is mount Sinai" (Gal. 4:25)
54 Chinese desert
55 Selves
57 Type of pasta
58 Demonstrate
60 Mother of Cain
62 Doctorate degree

83

Colossians

by Mary A. Hake

• • • • • •

ACROSS

1 "Surety for a stranger shall ___ for it" (Prov. 11:15)
6 Motor's rate
9 Makes ill
13 Prohibited
14 Epoch
15 Inordinate
16 Willfully burning
17 "Take thou unto thee an iron ____" (Ezek. 4:3)
18 Ladies' hosiery (sing.)
19 Chilled
20 Dismiss employee (2 wds.)
22 Atlantic Coast time
23 "Called Oshea the son of ___ Jehoshua" (Num. 13:16)
24 It opens locks (Rev. 3:7)
25 "Then ___ one of the seraphims" (Isa. 6:6)
27 Dazes
29 "Dwelleth all the fulness of the ___" (Col. 2:9)
33 "__ your affection on things above" (Col. 3:2)
34 Promise (Eccl. 5:4)
35 Gawk
36 Parrot
39 Dragon's color (Rev. 12:3)
40 Indian lodge
41 Obstruct
42 "___ the word of Christ dwell in you" (Col. 3:16)
43 Signal for help
44 Inherited
46 Plant pest
49 "For which things' ___ the wrath of God cometh" (Col. 3:6)
50 Perish (Phil. 1:21)
51 "Let him ___ his foot in oil" (Deut. 33:24)
53 Time span (Heb. 11:11)
56 Grabbed
58 Foreteller (2 Sam. 24:11)
59 "___, ___ thee unto the house of Israel" (Ezek. 3:4) (2 wds.)
61 Vitality
62 Cycle
63 Set affection on things ____ (Col. 3:2)
64 7th Greek letter
65 Lodge
66 Come to life like Jesus did
67 Underworld
68 "Let the word of Christ ____ in you" (Col. 3:16)

DOWN

1 Blemish (Isa. 63:3)
2 "Sister's son to Barnabas" (Col. 4:10)
3 Not present (Col. 2:5)
4 1/4 acre
5 2,000 pounds
6 "Vengeance is mine; I will ____" (Rom. 12:19)
7 Talk to God
8 Paul called Timothy this (1 Tim. 6:11) (3 wds.)
9 "If ___ man have a quarrel against ___" (Col. 3:13) (same wd.)
10 Not working (1 Tim. 5:13)
11 Kenya natives
12 Paul ___ Tychicus there (Col. 4:8)
15 Opposite of 1 Cor. 3:2
20 "Beware ___ any man spoil you" (Col. 2:8)
21 "Shall ____ rivers of living water" (John 7:38)
24 "___ the grace of God in truth" (Col. 1:6)
26 Rushing sound

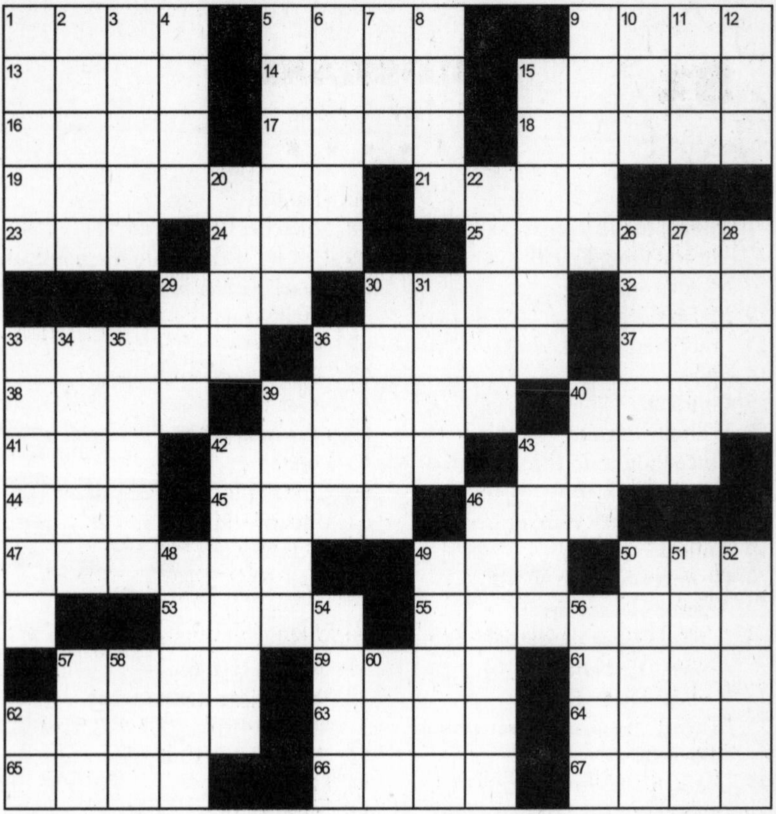

28 "____ with zeal" (Isa. 59:17)
29 Mid-U.S. time zone
30 Browned bread
31 "____ the souls" (Ezek. 13:18)
33 "Convey them. . .in ____ unto the place" (1 Kings 5:9)
34 "Wherefore did Sarah ____" (Gen. 18:13)
35 Acid + alcohol - water
36 Jericho's walls fell ___
39 A feeling of boredom or dissatisfaction
40 "The power of ___ resurrection" (Phil. 3:10)
42 Whether present or ____, Paul cared
43 "___ to speak the word without fear" (Phil. 1:14)
46 All these salute the Philippians (Phil. 4:22)
48 "To ___ in the flesh is more needful" (Phil. 1:24)
49 Many are enemies of this (Phil. 3:18)
50 Swivel
51 "Over all the power of the ____" (Luke 10:19)
52 "If two of you shall ____" (Matt. 18:19)
54 "Now ___ you even weeping" (Phil. 3:18)
56 Gamaliel and Luke (Acts 5:34) (pl.) (abbr.)
57 River (Sp.)
58 "Go to the ___" (Prov. 6:6)
60 Lion constellation
62 Military rank (abbr.)

82

PHILIPPIANS

by Mary A. Hake

ACROSS

1 "But for you it is ____" (Phil. 3:1)
5 Froglike amphibian
9 Musical conclusion
13 Journey
14 "Ye sent ___ and again" (Phil. 4:16)
15 Hunter constellation (Job 9:9)
16 Uncommon (Dan. 2:11)
17 "Good works for necessary ____" (Titus 3:14)
18 Some have this as their god (Phil. 3:19)
19 "Now much more in my ____" (Phil. 2:12)
21 Peace "shall ___ your hearts and minds" (Phil. 4:7)
23 West Coast time
24 Cereal grain
25 Fabled
29 "I ___ do all things" (Phil. 4:13)
30 Biblical "you"
32 Love never causes this to another (Rom. 13:10)
33 Paul said not to put confidence in this (Phil. 3:3)
36 "Being ___ in fashion as a man" (Phil. 2:8)
37 Auto manufacturer
38 "At the ___ your care of me" (Phil. 4:10)
39 Flavorless
40 Christ is the ____ of the Church
41 "Work ___ your own salvation" (Phil. 2:12)
42 An end (2 wds.)
43 "A ____ from the hand of the fowler" (Prov. 6:5)
44 "Mine ___ is as nothing before thee" (Ps. 39:5)
45 Sheet of matted cotton
46 Distress signal
47 Beat up
49 Gold Rush State (abbr.)
50 Pod vegetable
53 Covet these gifts (1 Cor. 12:31)
55 Twice the psalmist pleads for this and delivering for himself (Ps. 144)
57 "Early and latter ____" (James 5:7)
59 Judge from Zebulon (Judg. 12:11)
61 "The earth shall rejoice ____ them" (Rev. 11:10)
62 Premium chocolate brand
63 "___ I should have sorrow" (Phil. 2:27)
64 "None evil can ___ upon us" (Mic. 3:11)
65 Carry
66 Paul counted everything as this
67 Infected eyelid (var.)

DOWN

1 Leather cord
2 Promised-land town inherited by Judah (Josh. 15:52)
3 "From the ___ day until now" (Phil. 1:5)
4 Dueling sword
5 Bird with huge bill
6 Start
7 Genius
8 School furniture
9 "___ in unawares" (Jude 1:4)
10 A strange woman's mouth is smoother than this (Prov. 5:3)
11 Federal agency overseeing work
12 Some
15 "As ye have always ___" (Phil. 2:12)
20 Japheth's father (Gen. 6:10)
22 Improve
26 Mountain climber
27 Homer's epic

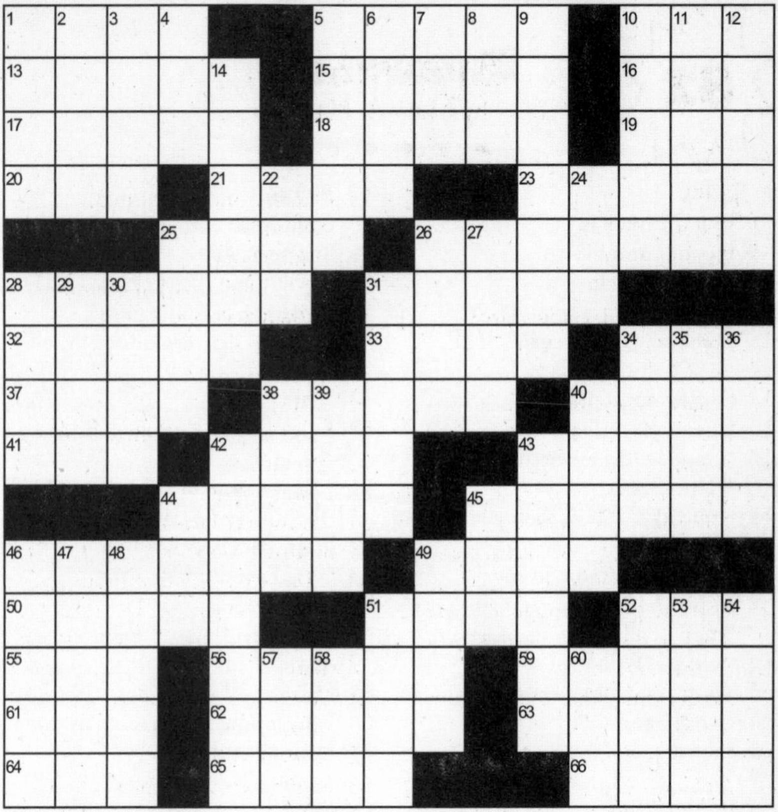

31 "We should be holy and without ___" (Eph. 1:4)
34 Jesus told us to be ___ to one another
35 Carved image of worship
36 Leaf bud
38 Abrasive in sandpaper
39 Jesus said that our praises ____ to him
40 Tinter
42 Horizontal measurement (Eph. 3:18)
43 "Ye were ___ with that holy Spirit" (Eph. 1:13)
44 Liturgical vestment
45 Packers' assoc.
46 Flowering plant
47 "Neither is ____ respect of persons" (Eph. 6:9)
48 "I ___ of your faith in the Lord" (Eph. 1:15)
49 "She is thine ___" (Lev. 18:14)
51 Minneapolis's state (abbr.)
52 Continent Paul traveled
53 Makes stuffy
54 Coin
57 Beam of light
58 Point at target
60 Put on this man (Eph. 4:24)

81

EPHESIANS

by Mary A. Hake

• • • • • •

ACROSS

1 Easter bonnets
5 Venomous snake
10 Sharp tool
13 "___ with thine adversary quickly" (Matt. 5:25)
15 Detached (Ps. 38:11)
16 Chief Information Officer
17 Fish with large net
18 Hoax
19 "___ the oppressed" (Isa. 1:17) (abbr.)
20 "Touch the ___ of his garment" (Matt. 14:36)
21 Glory to Jesus through all these (Eph. 3:21)
23 By the way
25 Satan is the father of this (John 8:44)
26 "___ together for an habitation of God" (Eph. 2:22)
28 Be this in the Lord (Eph. 6:10)
31 Fruit of olive tree (James 3:12) (sing.)
32 "For this ___ I bow my knees" (Eph. 3:14)
33 "___ than the least of all saints" (Eph. 3:8)
34 "But for his ___, that is near unto him" (Lev. 21:2)
37 Am not
38 Give (Eph 3:16)
40 Antic
41 Type of sandwich
42 Jesus said to fill the pots to the ____ (John 2:7)
43 Council
44 Come back to life as Jesus did
45 "Camel to go through the eye of a ____" (Mark 10:25)
46 Sports participant
49 Not near (Eph. 2:17)
50 Queen from here visited Solomon
51 Think about
52 Pro football division (abbr.)
55 Brewed beverage
56 Flow off
59 "Seek peace, and ___ it" (1 Pet. 3:11)
61 Make a mistake (James 1:16)
62 Contaminate
63 Lower oneself
64 Crimson (Matt. 16:3)
65 Spiritual song
66 "Who told thee that thou ____ naked?" (Gen. 3:11)

DOWN

1 "You ___ he quickened" (Eph. 2:1)
2 Clan in India
3 Overhead conveyance
4 Stitch together (Eccl. 3:7)
5 Microwave laser
6 Swiss mountains
7 Cow's cry
8 Scary greeting
9 Things to be done (Eph. 6:22)
10 Bitter smelling
11 Irish playwright
12 "Christ also ___ the church" (Eph. 5:25)
14 City in Arkansas
22 Muzzle
24 Tricky
25 Jesus came to save these
26 "Have ___ taught by him" (Eph. 4:21)
27 Urban Studies
28 Healing sore (Lev. 14:56)
29 "Make thee the head, and not the ____" (Deut. 28:13)
30 Smallest of litter

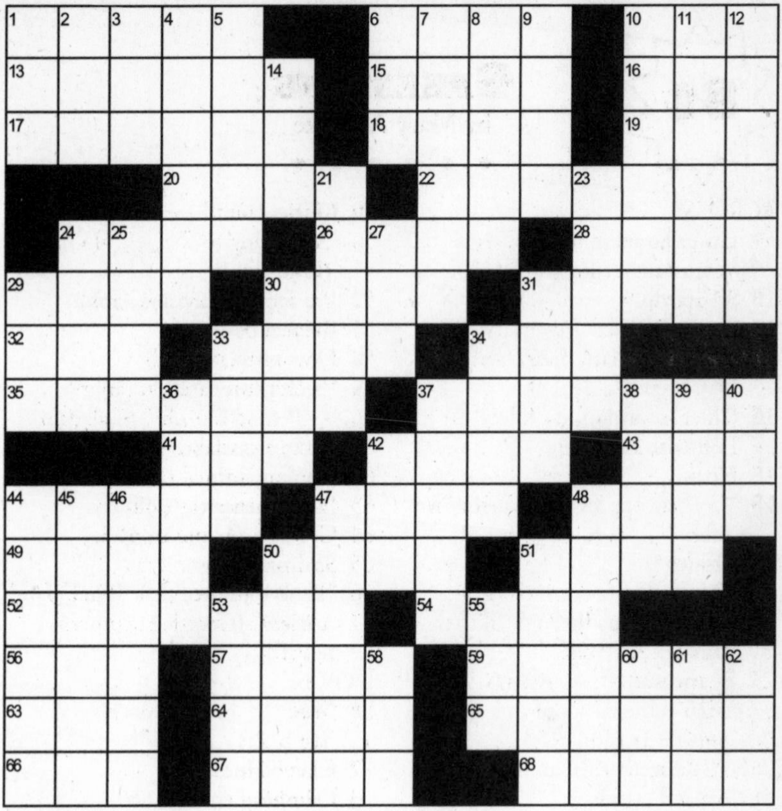

30 Slash
31 31 Across (sing.)
33 Mists
34 "Ye are so ___ removed from him" (Gal. 1:6)
36 Region in Israel
37 Paul says this present one is evil (Gal. 1:4)
38 Vigorous enthusiasm
39 "Violently turn and ____ thee" (Isa. 22:18)
40 "The anger of the LORD was ___" (Judg. 10:7)
42 Epistle addressed to multiple churches (abbr.)
44 Author of Galatians (2 wds.)
45 Rough
46 The Bible should never be ____
47 This or that
48 Soup
50 Be not this in well doing (Gal. 6:9)
51 "Gladly spend and be ____ for you" (2 Cor. 12:15)
53 There was one of these at Siloam
55 Wool bearer
58 "___ not liberty for an occasion" (Gal. 5:13)
60 We are all under ____ (Gal. 3:22)
61 From Corinth to Galatia
62 "___ us also walk in the Spirit" (Gal. 5:25)

80

GALATIANS

by Mary A. Hake

• • • • • •

ACROSS

1 God wanted to make all Israel one of these (Ezek. 37:17)
6 Appear to be
10 Youth farming club
13 Noah numbered clean beasts by this (Gen. 7:2)
15 Wheel shaft
16 Long time
17 12th U.S. president
18 "Our Father: To ___ be glory for ever" (Gal. 1:4–5)
19 Pull
20 What an eagle cropped (Ezek. 17:4) (sing.)
22 Paul was one (Gal. 1:1)
24 Glory not to be desired (Gal. 5:26)
26 "Walk according to this ___" (Gal. 6:16)
28 Pare
29 CD or DVD
30 "Jesus. . .suffered without the ____" (Heb. 13:12)
31 "Look well to thy ____" (Prov. 27:23)
32 "Which groweth of ___ own accord" (Lev. 25:5)
33 Moses put a veil over this
34 Paul often traveled by ____
35 City named for Jesus' earthly father (2 wds.)
37 "Faith which ___ by love" (Gal. 5:6)
41 Expression of disgust
42 "Let us do ____ unto all men" (Gal. 6:10)
43 Water closet
44 Wind-driven clouds or water (pl)
47 Merit
48 "As I have also told you in time ____" (Gal. 5:21)
49 Musical pitch
50 "According to the ___ of God" (Gal. 1:4)
51 We are adopted as God's (Gal. 4:5)
52 Low protective wall
54 Variety store section (abbr.)
56 "___ ye so foolish?" (Gal. 3:3)
57 Hawaiian island
59 Unclean animal (Lev. 11:29)
63 North American country
64 Gold, silver, and iron (pl.)
65 Railroad locomotive
66 "Be ___ of the Spirit" (Gal. 5:18)
67 Ancient stringed instrument
68 Belief

DOWN

1 Fast plane
2 Steeped beverage
3 Climbing vine
4 Gaelic
5 "Ye have ___ God. . .are ___ of God" (Gal 4:9) (Same wd.)
6 Beheld
7 Breathe out
8 Run away and marry
9 Brief note
10 "Often bound with ____ and chains" (Mark 5:4) (sing.)
11 Made dirty (Ezek. 34:19)
12 "It was ordained by ___" (Gal. 3:19)
14 Title of respect in India
21 One of the book of Galatians' primary themes
23 Paul did not do this like other men (Gal. 3:15)
24 Short autobiographical account
25 An organization (abbr.)
27 Southwestern Indian
29 Show disrespect (slang)

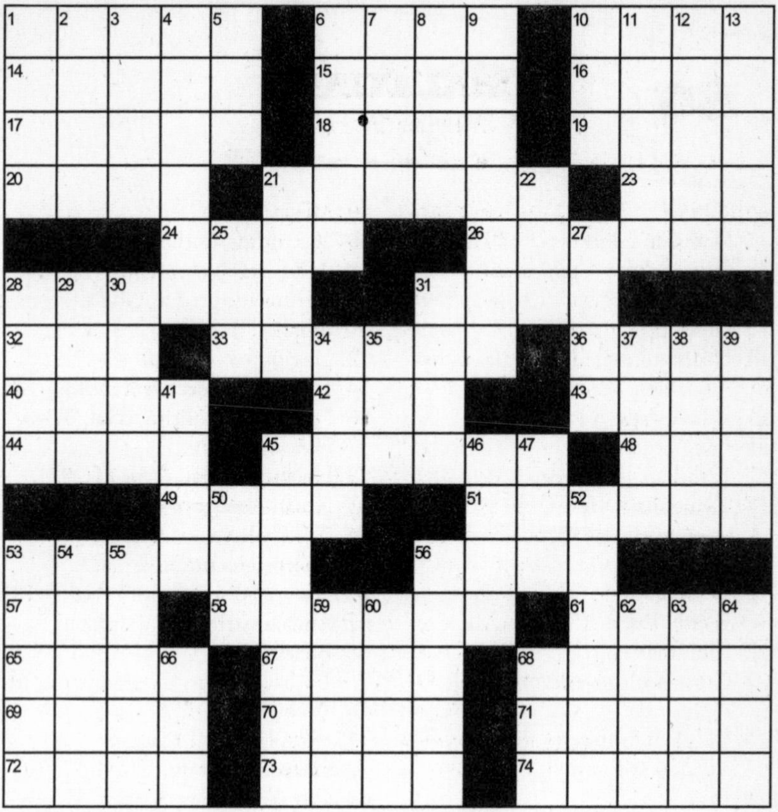

30 Paul prayed they would not do this (2 Cor. 13:7)
31 Christ will one day sit here to judge (2 Cor. 5:10)
34 Man's were opened after sin
35 "In Christ, he is a ___ creature" (2 Cor. 5:17)
37 People gathered manna at a daily ___ (Ex. 16:4)
38 Distinct place
39 Most northern of 48 states (abbr.)
41 Job's never turned out of the way (Job 31:7)
45 Enoch's testimony: "He ___ God" (Heb. 11:5)
46 Relieve
47 Repeat an exercise (abbr.)
50 Building addition
52 Rodent
53 "Turn to the Lord, the vail shall be ___ away" (2 Cor. 3:16)
54 Expatriate
55 Intellectuals' organization
56 "Not that other men be ___, and ye burdened" (2 Cor. 8:13)
59 "Because thou didst ___ on the LORD" (2 Chron. 16:8)
60 Siddim was in one (Gen. 14)
62 Spaghetti sauce brand
63 Pennsylvania's Great Lake port
64 Paul ___ Titus to Corinth
66 Acquire
68 Beginning of alphabet

79

2 Corinthians

by Mary A. Hake

• • • • • •

ACROSS

1 The Corinthians proved to be this (2 Cor. 7:11)
6 Our Father God invites us to call Him this
10 Drafting software
14 Cuban dance
15 Paul didn't handle God's deceitfully (2 Cor. 4:2)
16 "____ her nails" (Deut. 21:12)
17 Constellation (Job 9:9)
18 Healing plant (Ps. 45:8) (sing.)
19 "Though I be ___ in speech" (2 Cor. 11:6)
20 Country where Incas once ruled
21 Kills by submerging (1 Tim. 6:9) (pl.)
23 "Jacob ___ pottage" (Gen. 25:29)
24 "___ we. . .letters of commendation?" (2 Cor. 3:1)
26 Derrick hands
28 Large, heavy hammer
31 Trigonometric function
32 11th month (abbr.)
33 God did this to the door (2 Cor. 2:12)
36 Trolley
40 Portuguese city
42 "___, though we have known Christ" (2 Cor. 5:16)
43 Draped women's garment
44 Money (slang)
45 Tin alloy
48 Number of times Laban changed Jacob's wages (Gen. 31:7)
49 Snaky fish
51 The sea Paul traveled on from Berea to Corinth
53 "Ye are the ___ of the living God" (2 Cor. 6:16)
56 Sports programs 24/7
57 Used to cut trees (Luke 3:9)
58 Newly hatched insects
61 Verb used twice regarding comfort in 2 Cor. 1:4 (pl.)
65 Aretas's position (2 Cor. 11:32)
67 Paul had perils traveling these
68 "At an hour when he is not ____" (Luke 12:46)
69 Otherwise (1 Cor. 15:29)
70 English Language and Literacy
71 Commence (1 Pet. 4:17)
72 Orderly
73 Changed cloth's color (Isa. 63:1)
74 Small glass bottle

DOWN

1 Bird's gullet (Lev. 1:16)
2 Attract
3 Middle East chieftain
4 "God is able to make all grace ___" (2 Cor. 9:8)
5 "The brook that ____ through" (2 Chron. 32:4)
6 Honor
7 Western necktie
8 A crowd led Jesus to this part of a hill (Luke 4:29)
9 Lymphatic tissue in upper throat
10 Method of calculating cost
11 "For which ___ we faint not" (2 Cor. 4:16)
12 Fervor
13 Mighty ones were signs of an apostle (2 Cor. 12:12)
21 Paul spent a night and day there (2 Cor. 11:25)
22 Jesus was made this for us (2 Cor. 5:21)
25 Self
27 Permits
28 Obstacle
29 Christ's constraineth (2 Cor. 5:14)

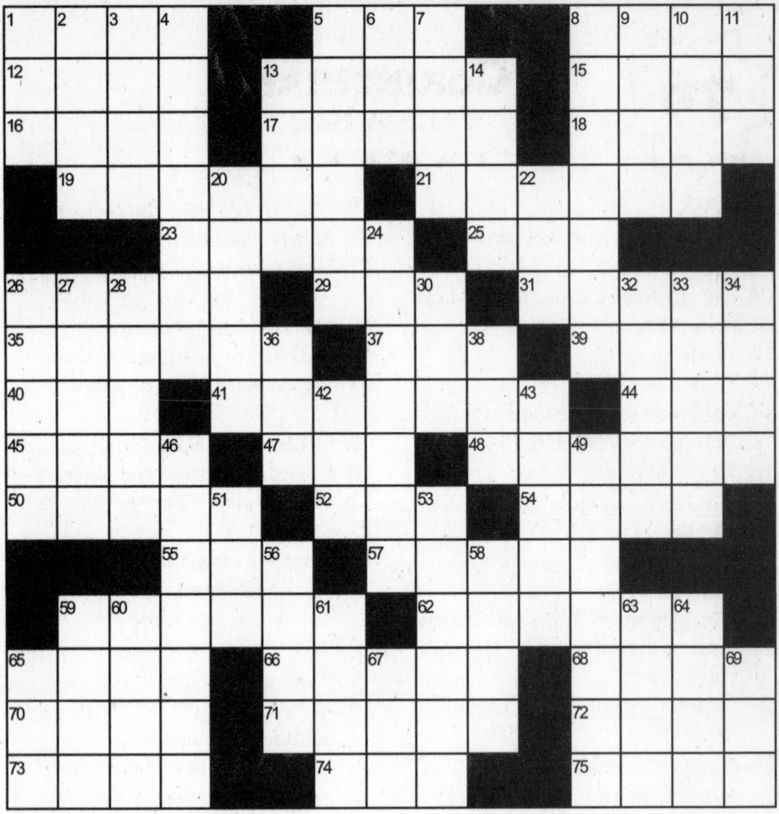

28 Ahasuerus reigned from here to Ethiopia (Est. 1:1)
30 Father of Moses' successor
32 A carpenter marks one (2 wds.)
33 This kept Paul from fainting (2 Cor. 4:1)
34 Job said his couch would do this (Job 7:13)
36 Ribbed fabric
38 Muscle spasm
42 Paul told Festus he was not (Acts 26:25)
43 Group of notes
46 Don't accept this Jesus or gospel (2 Cor. 11:4)
49 Remaineth (1 Cor. 13:13)
51 Drunk driver's charge
53 "___, now is the day of salvation" (2 Cor. 6:2)
56 Investment income
58 Pens' tips
59 Automated Office Systems Equipment
60 Situation
61 National Association of Disability Officers
63 Fencing sword
64 Columbus's ship
65 Doeg saw David there (1 Sam. 22:9)
67 Moses carried one of these
69 Texas's summer time

78 2 CORINTHIANS

by Mary A. Hake

• • • • • •

ACROSS

1 Christ is called this (John 1:29)
5 Wind direction
8 "At ___ in the body" (2 Cor. 5:6)
12 Bible plant (Ps. 45:8) (sing.)
13 Haste
15 Stork-like bird
16 God's desire and plan (2 Cor. 1:1)
17 What Pilate put on Christ's cross (John 19:19)
18 Mountain (Fr.)
19 Blossom (Ps. 103:15)
21 Decrease
23 Uninteresting
25 "In ___ time Christ died for the ungodly" (Rom. 5:6)
26 Foreign-born (Job 19:15)
29 "Though ye have ___ thousand instructers" (1 Cor. 4:15)
31 No one should do this to Paul (2 Cor. 8:20)
35 "___ therefore to all their dues" (Rom. 13:7)
37 "Not with fleshly wisdom, ___ by the grace of God" (2 Cor. 1:12)
39 Tiny insect pest
40 Excellent (slang)
41 Satanic
44 U.S. tax agency
45 Israel's continent
47 Standard or average
48 Time and ____ happen to all (Eccl. 9:11)
50 "By faith ye ____" (2 Cor. 1:24)
52 Small amount
54 God asks us to _____ His commandments
55 "___ sufficiency is of God" (2 Cor. 3:5)
57 American realistic painter
59 Movement
62 Paul renounced these things (2 Cor. 4:2)
65 Daughter of Zelophehad (Num. 36:11)
66 Chocolate substitute
68 Heroic
70 Prophetic utterance
71 False gods
72 "Thoughts of the diligent ___ only to plenteousness" (Prov. 21:5)
73 Jotham fled there (Judg. 9:21)
74 What number of them is redeemed? (Num. 3:48)
75 Sun's is burning (James 1:11)

DOWN

1 All the commandments comprise the ____
2 First letter of the Arabic alphabet
3 Gangster's female accomplice
4 Affectionate term Paul used for the believers
5 He lives in the heart (2 Cor. 1:22)
6 Wager
7 "Ye might ___ bear with him" (2 Cor. 11:4)
8 God reconciled us to whom? (2 Cor. 5:18)
9 Musical instrument
10 12th largest U.S. state (abbr.)
11 New York time
13 Only this stood between David and death (1 Sam. 20:3)
14 Paul said as he wrote so he'd be in this when present (2 Cor. 10:11)
20 Grew smaller
22 Underwater boat
24 Prophetess and judge (Judg. 4:4)
26 Wall hanging
27 Paul described himself as the _____ (1 Cor. 15:9)

26 God's not one of confusion (1 Cor. 14:33)
28 Dots above a vowel
30 Solomon compared a beloved to this (Song 2:9)
31 "___ thou called being a servant?" (1 Cor. 7:21)
32 "___ him glory in the Lord" (1 Cor. 1:31)
34 Call to come (1 Cor. 10:27)
36 Knock
37 Weather vane direction
38 Paul didn't fight as beating this (1 Cor. 9:26)
39 Representative
40 Color of horse
42 Admonish (1 Cor. 4:14)
43 "Now ___ I say" (1 Cor. 15:50)
45 "Will they not hear me, ___ the Lord" (1 Cor. 14:21)
47 Large African animals
48 Northern U.S. dweller
50 These places shall fall (Ezek. 38:20)
52 Leavening agent
53 Satisfy
54 Gone without permission
55 Author of this epistle
57 American Revolutionary politician
58 Girl superhero from *DC Universe*
60 Job asked where this came from (Job 38:29)
62 Measure of dove's dung (2 Kings 6:25)

77

1 Corinthians

by Mary A. Hake

• • • • • •

ACROSS

1 Death reigned after his transgression (Rom. 5:14) (poss.)
6 Spooky greeting
9 Double sulfate
13 Wealthy area of Istanbul
14 "Do they not ___ that devise evil?" (Prov. 14:22)
15 "The head of ___ man is Christ" (1 Cor. 11:3)
16 School assignment
17 "___ you with milk, and not with meat" (1 Cor. 3:2)
18 Paul claimed to be this of all apostles (1 Cor. 15:9)
19 Legal claim to property
20 Prescribed amount
22 Morse code dash
23 Sea eagle
24 Electroencephalograph
25 Quechuan peoples
27 Musical composition
29 This type of man is not spiritual (1 Cor. 2:14)
33 If everyone spoke in tongues at once they'd seem this (1 Cor. 14:23)
34 Wager
35 Mourners did this to clothes
36 Kingdom (Dan. 6:3)
39 Accomplished
40 Scarlett's Mr. Butler
41 Israel's continent
42 Marry
43 "Ye are ___ superstitious" (Acts 17:22)
44 Careful reading
46 Harass
49 "Devil threw him down, and ___ him" (Luke 9:42)
50 Death's sting (1 Cor. 15:56)
51 This material will be burned (1 Cor. 3:12–13)
53 "The trees of the LORD are full of ___" (Ps. 104:16)
56 Bars of metal
58 Cattle (Gen. 41:2)
59 "Their laying ___ was known" (Acts 9:24)
61 John did this with angel's book (Rev. 10:10)
62 Inca manager
63 "Good for a man not to ___ a woman" (1 Cor. 7:1)
64 "___ them about thy neck" (Prov. 6:21)
65 Used with myrrh to anoint the dead (Ps. 45:8)
66 Women's magazine
67 Clairvoyance
68 "Sin which doth so easily ___ us" (Heb. 12:1)

DOWN

1 White poplar
2 "___ spiritual gifts" (1 Cor. 14:1)
3 "____ in body, but present in spirit" (1 Cor. 5:3)
4 "Know therefore what these things ___" (Acts 17:20)
5 "Thou with him spread out the ____" (Job 37:18)
6 Confuse
7 Job 28:2 lists two types (pl.)
8 Decreed (1 Cor. 2:7)
9 Latin greeting
10 The Lamb. . .shall ____ them" (Rev. 7:17)
11 One of the bear constellations
12 Fable
15 God's chosen
20 Action (1 Cor. 5:3)
21 Jesus said Pharisees strained at this (Matt. 23:24)
24 Type of cheese

26 Excavate
28 Paul had sown and hoped to ___ spiritually (1 Cor. 9:11)
29 Sorcerer's work
30 First Hebrew letter
31 Paul often stated, "For this ___"
32 "Every man ___ receive his own reward" (1 Cor. 3:8)
33 Fragrant shrub
34 Ezekiel sought a man to stand in it
36 One point east of due south
38 Paul said Gentiles were ___ to worship idols
39 Root vegetable
41 The Spirit searches these things of God (1 Cor. 2:10)
43 Jeremiah said the hurt was healed this much (Jer. 6:14)
46 "___ ye the church of God" (1 Cor. 11:22)
48 Joshua was one
51 One-third were posted at this gate (2 Kings 11:6)
53 Intellectual property rights
56 Powder
57 Plant often listed with myrrh
58 Typesetting measurement
60 Tide recedes
61 Region
62 Jesus rode on one
64 "Fashion of this world passeth ___" (1 Cor. 7:31)
65 Christians should have the same for all (1 Cor. 12:25)
66 Paul's were blinded (Acts 9:9)
68 Public transportation
70 Female pronoun used often in 1 Cor. 7

76 1 Corinthians

by Mary A. Hake

ACROSS

1 Day of week (abbr.)
4 "Not under bondage in such ___" (1 Cor. 7:15)
9 Social class
14 Overnight lodging
15 If any man's work does this, he will receive a reward (1 Cor. 3:14)
16 Dramatic musical production
17 "___ the Holy One of Israel" (Ps. 78:41) (abbr.)
18 Do this with the old leaven (1 Cor. 5:7)
19 Job asks God why he does this (Job 19:2) (pl.)
20 If man's work fails he will suffer this (1 Cor. 3:15)
22 Jesus spoke of a camel going through its eye (Mark 10:25)
24 "Many members, ___ but one body" (1 Cor. 12:20)
25 Not an even number
27 Not knowing the Bible causes one to do this (Heb. 3:10)
29 Madman
32 Strong bows were made of this
34 Ninth NT book (abbr.)
35 Grind the teeth (Ps. 112:10)
37 Paul said he died to self this frequently
40 "___ men be sober" (Titus 2:2)
42 Large musical instruments
44 Entreat
45 Paul mentioned sounds harped or this (1 Cor. 14:7)
47 Elisha told the widow she'll survive when she does this with the oil (2 Kings 4:7)
49 High naval rank (abbr.)
50 Curdled milk product
52 Pertaining to fat
54 Primary Support Unit
55 Cheat
56 Spigot
59 "We ___ Christ crucified" (1 Cor. 1:23)
63 All run in this (1 Cor. 9:24)
67 Excuse
69 Gideon put some in a pot (Judg. 6:19)
71 Paul showed a more excellent one (1 Cor. 12:31)
72 Place
73 Star of the ball
74 "Tempted above that ye ___ able" (1 Cor. 10:13)
75 Come to an end (1 Cor. 13:8)
76 This beast "shall cry to his fellow" (Isa. 34:14)
77 Affirmative reply

DOWN

1 "Shew the Lord's death ___ he come" (1 Cor. 11:26)
2 "Grace be ___ you" (1 Cor. 1:3)
3 "___ of the world" (1 Cor. 10:11)
4 Hat
5 Paul desired to see this much grace (2 Cor. 4:15)
6 Male parent
7 The sword's kills (Luke 21:24)
8 What is sown
9 Praying women's heads should be
10 Ships from Tarshish brought Solomon this primate
11 Proverbs warns against this type of woman
12 Tall leafy plant
13 Jesus said lightning comes from this direction (Matt. 24:27)
21 Jesus' relation to the Father
23 "___ a man examine himself" (1 Cor. 11:28)

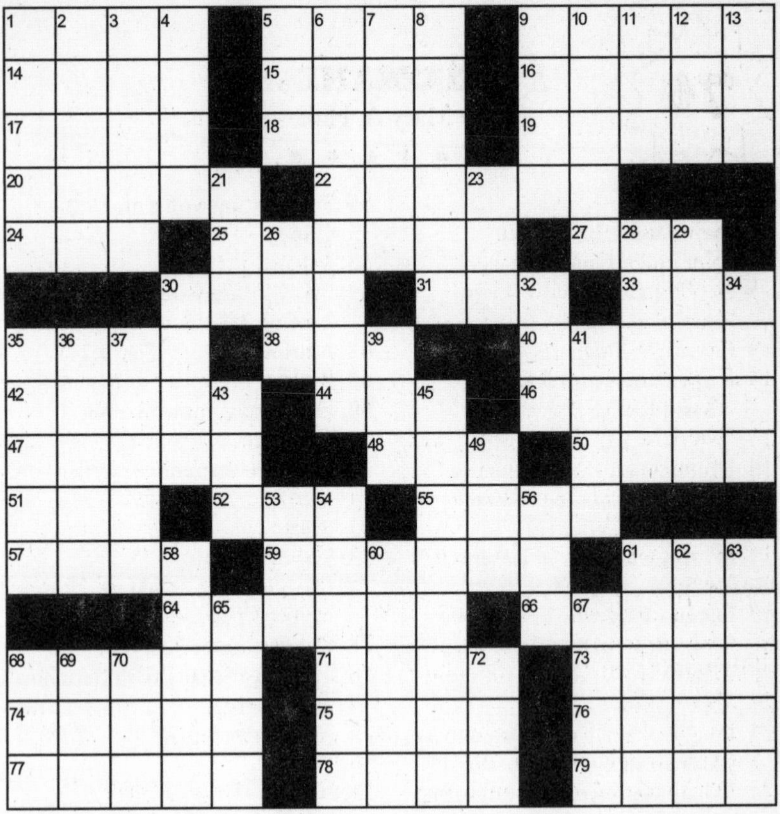

21 Kilometers per hour
23 Not cooked
26 Pagan goddess
28 Sporty make of car
29 Tally
30 "For conscience ___" (Rom. 13:5)
32 "Cast ___ the works of darkness" (Rom. 13:12)
34 "Continuance in ___ doing" (Rom. 2:7)
35 Informed (Matt. 24:50)
36 Suit
37 Concrete left unfinished (Fr.)
39 "While we were ___ sinners" (Rom. 5:8)
41 "I am ___ alone" (Rom. 11:3)
43 __ Lanka
45 Cigarette ingredient
49 Brand of cooking spray
53 Professional players' group
54 Silver State
56 "We hope for that we ___ not" (Rom. 8:25)
58 Peaks
60 Game played on wood board
61 Assisted
62 "He had ___ prepared unto glory" (Rom. 9:23)
63 Synthetic fiber
65 Ascend (Rom. 15:12)
67 Eat
68 Compass direction
69 Battle
70 Has a pseudonym
72 Lair

75

ROMANS

by Mary A. Hake

• • • • • •

ACROSS

1 Men sought to ___ Paul (Acts 9:29)
5 Jael brought butter in a lordly one (Judg. 5:25)
9 Former Nigerian capital
14 By faith the just do this (Rom. 1:17)
15 "Baptized ___ Jesus Christ" (Rom. 6:3)
16 Paul ____ with Peter 15 days (Gal. 1:18)
17 International Board of Advisors
18 Mop
19 "Thou shalt not ___" (Rom. 7:7)
20 Give one to a thirsty enemy (Rom. 12:20)
22 Shorten (abbr.)
24 Encoded Archival Description
25 Cyrus's kingdom (Dan. 10)
27 Don't make anyone stumble by what you ___ (Rom. 14:21)
30 "Feet ____ with the preparation of the gospel" (Eph. 6:15)
31 Pair
33 This will feed with a bear (Isa. 11:7)
35 We can call God this (Rom. 8:15)
38 Crafty
40 One instrument from Dan. 3
42 Israelite feast (Ex. 34:22)
44 Japanese money
46 Wild
47 "Walk not ___ the flesh" (Rom. 8:1)
48 Part of ear anointed (Lev. 14)
50 Don't cause a brother to do this (Rom. 14:13)
51 Nickname for Brazilian city
52 Had no room for Jesus' parents
55 "___ off the works of darkness" (Rom. 13:12)
57 Italian volcano
59 "___ servants to God" (Rom. 6:22)
61 American Academy of Neurology
64 Necktie
66 Build up another (Rom. 14:19)
68 Hindu religious teacher
71 Dry like a desert
73 Graven image
74 "Beloved for the father's ___" (Rom. 11:28)
75 Unborn children have not "___ any good or evil" (Rom. 9:11)
76 Emperor who had Paul killed
77 Rub out
78 So be it! (Rom. 1:25)
79 God's garden

DOWN

1 "None of his steps shall ___" (Ps. 37:31)
2 Constellation
3 ___ those who cause division (Rom. 16:17)
4 To bear young
5 Treat with disrespect or contempt (slang)
6 A true Jew is one this way (Rom. 2:29)
7 Pokes with knife
8 Bilbo Baggins
9 A blue one tied the rings of the ephod (Ex. 28:28)
10 "Esteemeth one day ___ another" (Rom. 14:5)
11 Jesus would have this on His shoulder (Isa. 9:6) (abbr.)
12 Lyric poem
13 "___ forth to be a propitiation" (Rom. 3:25)

26 "Instructed ___ of the law" (Rom. 2:18)
28 Jesus was from Jesse's (Rom. 15:12)
29 Worries (Ps. 34:4)
30 Regal
31 Armed robbery
32 Merge
33 Nettle plant
34 Chief Warrant Officer
36 "____ I would not have you ignorant" (Rom. 1:13)
37 Spanish for Mrs. (abbr.)
39 Lower limb
41 Sin deceived and ___ Paul (Rom. 7:11)
43 Offspring (Rom. 9:26)
46 "Thou ___ not the root" (Rom. 11:18)
48 Paul's affirmation
51 Pressure unit
53 Change color
56 Performing (abbr.)
57 Make a whizzing sound
58 Italian money
60 "Provide yourselves ____" (Luke 12:33)
61 Big, fuzzy hair
62 In ___ of (instead of)
64 Solomon had some of linen (1 Kings 10:28)
65 Great Lake
66 "Not reckoned of grace, but of ___" (Rom. 4:4)
68 "Live peaceably with all ___" (Rom. 12:18)
70 "To the ___ ye may be established" (Rom. 1:11)

74

Romans

by Mary A. Hake

ACROSS

1 Gut muscles (abbr.)
4 Caravan animal (Luke 18:25)
9 Plant louse
14 Jesus said not to resist those who do this (Matt. 5:40)
15 White poplar
16 Doctrine
17 Love does not work this to his neighbor (Rom. 13:10)
18 "___ not against the branches" (Rom. 11:18)
19 Put these on enemy's head (Rom. 12:20)
20 "God is ___ to make him stand" (Rom. 14:4)
22 UN agency promoting education and culture
24 Cat or dog
25 Those led by the Spirit are God's ___ (Rom. 8:14)
27 Belonging to us
29 Scam
31 A potter makes a vessel for this (Rom. 9:21)
34 Business leader
35 Tight
38 Relating to quality of musical sound
40 God's are past finding out (Rom. 11:33)
42 Greek column style
44 "In due ___ Christ died" (Rom. 5:6)
45 Toothbrush brand
47 Wishy ___
49 Jesus talked about this fruit tree
50 "Time to awake out of ___" (Rom. 13:11)
52 Colorful hippie clothes
54 "Foolish heart ___ darkened" (Rom. 1:21)
55 "Behold, I ___ in Sion" (Rom. 9:33)
56 Hole-punching tool
59 Off-color
63 "Leah was tender ___" (Gen. 29:17)
67 Wind's instrument
69 It's kindled (2 wds.)
71 "Such things ___ worthy of death" (Rom. 1:32)
72 "Round ___ like the moon" (Isa. 3:18)
73 Plant color
74 Adam's bone given to Eve
75 "God. . .___ you to be likeminded" (Rom. 15:5)
76 This went into all the earth (Rom. 10:18)
77 Disciples used one to fish

DOWN

1 Paul preached throughout this area
2 Flower start
3 Opposite of buy (Luke 12:33)
4 Taxi
5 "Where sin ___, grace did much more" (Rom. 5:20)
6 Paul desired to save by any ___ (Rom. 11:14)
7 "Accusing or ___ excusing" (Rom. 2:15)
8 "___ do evil" (Rom. 3:8) (contr.)
9 Everyone must give one (Rom. 14:12)
10 Not amateur
11 How you place 19 Across
12 Not busy (1 Tim. 5:13)
13 "Why ___ thou judge thy brother?" (Rom. 14:10)
21 Rare species habitat (abbr.)
23 Dove sound

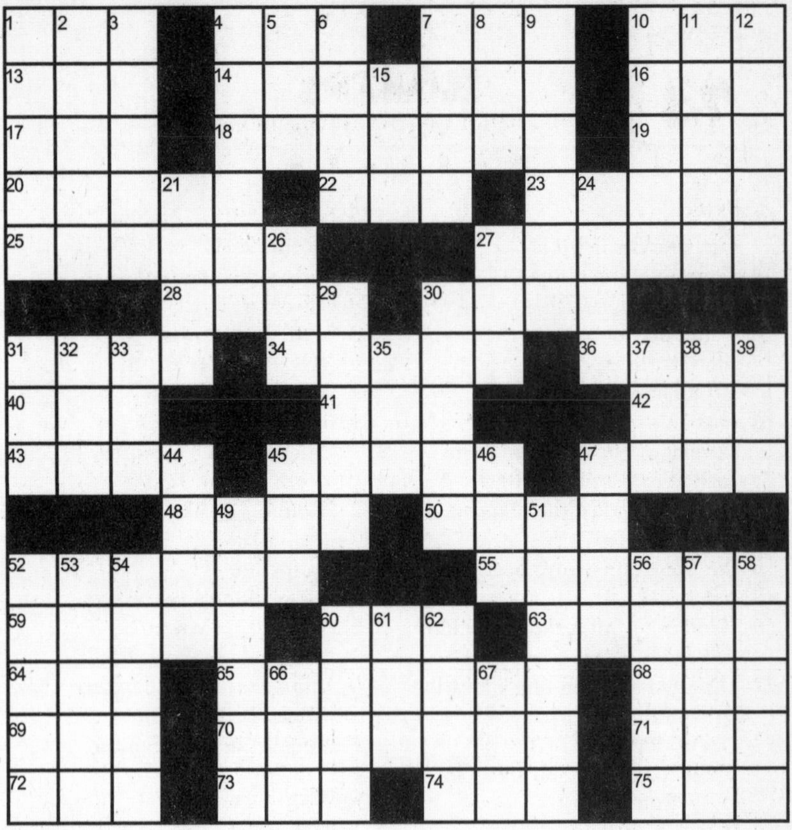

29 "As I ___ to speak" (Acts 11:15)
30 ___ days (long ago)
31 "Smote them ___ and thigh" (Judg. 15:8)
32 Miner's goal
33 Shelter
35 "The ___ fell upon Matthias" (Acts 1:26)
37 Whiz
38 Droop
39 "Bound with ___ chains" (Acts 21:33)
44 "Unto the uttermost ___ of the earth" (Acts 1:8)
45 "Feed thy people with thy ___" (Mic. 7:14)
46 "Priest shall see the ___ flesh" (Lev. 13:15)
47 Together
49 Japanese entertaining girl
51 "He saw in a ___" (Acts 10:3)
52 Break
53 Oklahoma city
54 Back street
56 Capital of Delaware
57 "All come in the ___ of the faith" (Eph. 4:13)
58 "Preaching ___ by Jesus Christ" (Acts 10:36)
60 "___ her nails" (Deut. 21:12)
61 "___, she is broken" (Ezek. 26:2)
62 "Received the word ___ all readiness" (Acts 17:11)
66 Great!
67 "Satan filled thine heart to ___" (Acts 5:3)

73

Acts

by Sarah Lagerquist Simmons

ACROSS

1 Accountant
4 Watch chain
7 Tuesday was Creation's ___ day (abbr.)
10 Danish krone
13 "And the ___ of oil" (Lev. 14:24)
14 "Now ___ feared the LORD greatly" (1 Kings 18:3)
16 Beersheba to Hebron dir.
17 Our eighth month (abbr.)
18 Rice dish
19 "To the right!"
20 Leave now!
22 "Abraham set seven ___ lambs of the flock" (Gen. 21:28)
23 "What ___ we do to these men?" (Acts 4:16)
25 "God before had ___ by the mouth" (Acts 3:18) (var.)
27 Rip-offs
28 A little (2 wds.)
30 Squeal
31 "Anointed Jesus of Nazareth with the ___ Ghost" (Acts 10:38)
34 Screams
36 Nazareth lies ___ of Mt. Carmel
40 Wrath
41 "Was zealous toward ___" (Acts 22:3)
42 Crow's cry
43 "Unto wizards that ___" (Isa. 8:19)
45 Ranker
47 Type of lily
48 Competition at the Greek games
50 "Hiram sent in the ___ his servants" (1 Kings 9:27)
52 David ___ at Bathsheba
55 Not battery operated
59 Many (prefix)
60 "Delivered me out of the ___ of the lion" (1 Sam. 17:37)
63 Quick bread
64 "Having a good report of ___ the Jews" (Acts 22:12)
65 African language
68 Travel term
69 Tyre to Jezreel dir.
70 ___ Hornblower
71 And so forth (abbr.)
72 "The ___ appeareth and the tender grass" (Prov. 27:25)
73 "Stand in ___, and sin not" (Ps. 4:4)
74 "As a ___ gathereth her chickens" (Matt. 23:37)
75 "Appointed barley and the ___" (Isa. 28:25) (var.)

DOWN

1 Caste
2 Judas carried money ___
3 Irritation
4 "God himself that ___ the earth" (Isa. 45:18)
5 Kimono sash
6 "Set there upon her own ___" (Zech. 5:11)
7 Jerusalem is ___ of temple
8 "Neither ___ nor drink till they have killed him" (Acts 23:21)
9 "Shew whether of these two thou hast ___" (Acts 1:24)
10 Impressionist painter
11 Jesus ___ in the garden
12 Pulls in
15 ___ Jones Industrial Average
21 "Peter went ___ with them" (Acts 10:23)
24 Elijah did ___ to mountain cave (1 Kings 19:9)
26 "If we this ___ be examined" (Acts 4:9)
27 "Ananias, with Sapphira ___ wife" (Acts 5:1)

33 Uses as a reference
34 David's son (abbr.)
35 "Continued by the space of ___ years" (Acts 19:10)
36 Records brain's electrical activity
37 "To this ___ was I born" (John 18:37)
39 Transportation
44 "Here is ___; what doth hinder me" (Acts 8:36)
45 Haze
46 Loose gown worn at mass
47 "Tithe mint and ___" (Luke 11:42)
48 "Some of them were ___ of Cyprus" (Acts 11:20)
50 Swiss city (Fr.)
52 Capital of Vietnam
53 Paul was ___ at making tents
54 Dye by hand
55 Dents
57 Show for a score
58 Syllables used in songs (2 wds.)
60 "The hinder ___ was broken" (Acts 27:41)
62 "The ___ shall overflow" (Joel 2:24) (sing.)
63 Daniel stayed here overnight
65 "___ down in that place to sleep" (Gen. 28:11)
66 Silent
67 Prodigal son worked here

72

Acts

by Sarah Lagerquist Simmons

● ● ● ● ● ● ● ● ● ●

ACROSS

1 "___ besought us" (Acts 16:15)
4 Subatomic particle
9 Embarrass
14 Samaritan did ___ robbing victim
15 Sporty car brand
16 Radiuses
17 "Paul was long ___" (Acts 20:9)
19 Stuck up people
20 Very large truck
21 "They rushed with ___ accord" (Acts 19:29)
22 "Holy offerings ___ they in pots" (2 Chron. 35:13)
23 "Be not ___ with thy mouth" (Eccl. 5:2)
25 "In this we ___, earnestly desiring" (2 Cor. 5:2)
27 "Arise, lift up the ___" (Gen. 21:18)
30 Kind of soul made fat (Prov. 11:25) (abbr.)
32 Root vegetable
33 Soda
34 Not found on NT churches
38 Implicitly
40 "___ no man" (Rom. 13:8)
41 ___ voyage
42 Relative of mouse
43 Dye type
45 Rifle
49 "Watched the gates day ___ night" (Acts 9:24)
50 "For they ___ not the land" (Ps. 44:3)
51 Swerve
52 "World cannot ___ you" (John 7:7)
54 "He ___ to speak boldly" (Acts 18:26)
56 Inventor Franklin
57 "He ___ havock of the church" (Acts 8:3)
58 "Whose ___ is in his hand" (Matt. 3:12)
59 Clip
61 Debilitated
64 God's peace ___ our fears
68 "Lord. . .shall ___ the bough" (Isa. 10:33)
69 "Brought the young man ___" (Acts 20:12)
70 Cabbage dish
71 Telegraphic signal
72 "He was ___ up" (Acts 1:9)
73 Hinder (var.)

DOWN

1 Drains sap
2 Employer
3 Swelling
4 Computer
5 Repeat
6 Taking to court
7 Irascible
8 Bother
9 Malicious burning
10 "A centurion of the ___" (Acts 10:1)
11 Hubbub
12 Esau was Jacob's ___ (abbr.)
13 "Against the Lord, and against ___ Christ" (Acts 4:26)
18 Passageway
22 "Thou art a ___, and hast a devil" (John 8:48)
24 Jacob's ___ was never the same (Gen. 32:32)
26 Cereal
27 "Neither part nor ___ in this matter" (Acts 8:21)
28 "They were ___ scattered abroad" (Acts 8:1)
29 "The next ___ he shewed himself" (Acts 7:26)
31 "And the moon into ___" (Acts 2:20)

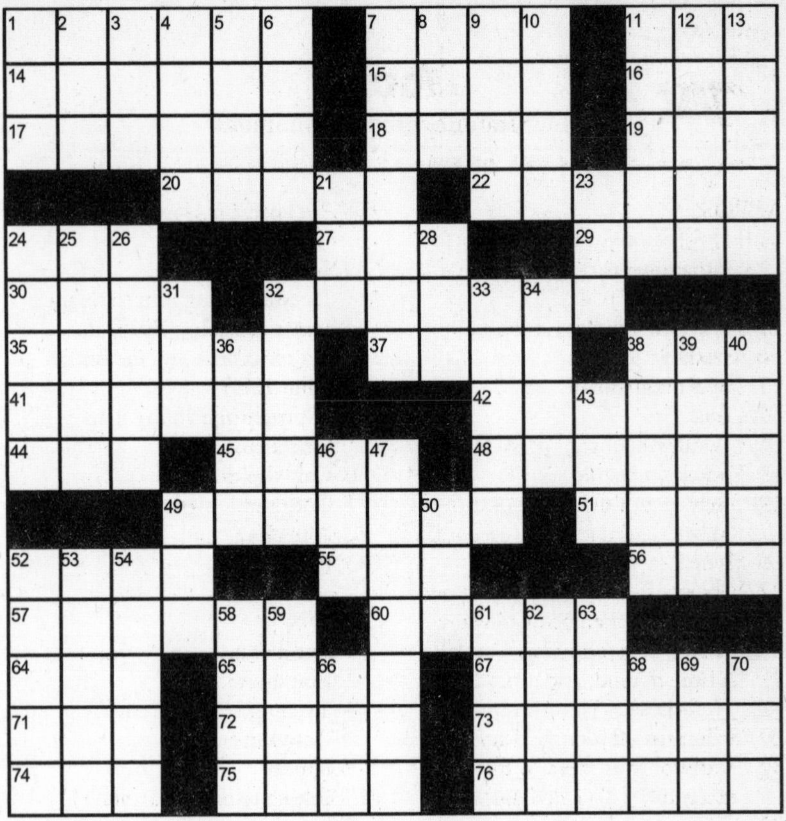

31 "Thy pound hath gained ___ pounds" (Luke 19:16)
32 Prodigal son squandered every ___
33 Potter's needs
34 Polish
36 "As the partridge sitteth on ___" (Jer. 17:11)
38 "For this man is a ___" (Acts 22:26)
39 Philosopher
40 Impressionist painter
43 "The word of ___ came" (John 10:35)
46 Chart
47 "Go out quickly into the ___" (Luke 14:21)
49 "Do alway ___ in their heart" (Heb. 3:10)
50 Moray
52 Analyze
53 City
54 Semi-aquatic mammal
58 Wager
59 Genghis ___
61 "I ___ record of myself" (John 8:14)
62 Cookie
63 "The ___ that I have spoken" (John 12:48)
66 "Have I need of ___ men" (1 Sam. 21:15)
68 "Shall be seven days under the ___" (Lev. 22:27)
69 Arrival
70 "When he came to the ___" (Dan. 6:20)

71

John

by Sarah Lagerquist Simmons

ACROSS

1 Flatfish
7 "Also one of this ___ disciples?" (John 18:17)
11 Radiation dose (abbr.)
14 Messianic prophet
15 Lotion ingredient
16 Lager
17 Mescal
18 Dell
19 Biblical 10th or 11th month (abbr.)
20 Shine
22 Vapors
24 "How can a man be born when he is ___?" (John 3:4)
27 "A time to rend, and a time to ___" (Eccl. 3:7)
29 "So he drew off his ___" (Ruth 4:8)
30 "Run not with them to the same excess of ___" (1 Pet. 4:4)
32 Assistant
35 Spirit ___ with water and blood (1 John 5:8)
37 Capital of Norway
38 Turns per minute
41 "These ___ understood not his disciples" (John 12:16)
42 African nation
44 And so forth (abbr.)
45 Placed in ephod
48 Royal officer
49 Lands
51 Go out with
52 "The ___ always ye have with you" (John 12:8)
55 ___ Trib or Post Trib
56 "I will ___ leave you comfortless" (John 14:18)
57 Commuter train
60 Nudge
64 Rodent
65 "Ask any thing in my ___" (John 14:14)
67 Worn
71 "___, supposing him to be the gardener" (John 20:15)
72 "___ this is the Son of God" (John 1:34)
73 Supply oxygen
74 "He touched his ___, and healed him" (Luke 22:51)
75 "Unto the ___ of the earth" (Mic. 5:4)
76 NBA's Dennis

DOWN

1 "Upon the ___ of the right ear" (Lev. 14:28)
2 "To ___ them despitefully" (Acts 14:5)
3 Light
4 Bible contains many men's ___ (abbr.)
5 "God had sworn with an ___ to him" (Acts 2:30)
6 "Now come I to ___" (John 17:13)
7 Professor X's nemesis
8 "Committed ___ judgment unto the Son" (John 5:22)
9 Biblical nays
10 "I ___ you to reap" (John 4:38)
11 Indian prince
12 "Remember the ___"
13 Compressed
21 Atlantic Coast time
23 Samaria to Shiloh dir.
24 Speak in public
25 "That was the true ___" (John 1:9)
26 Style of Greek column
28 "Jesus ___ not come to them" (John 6:17)

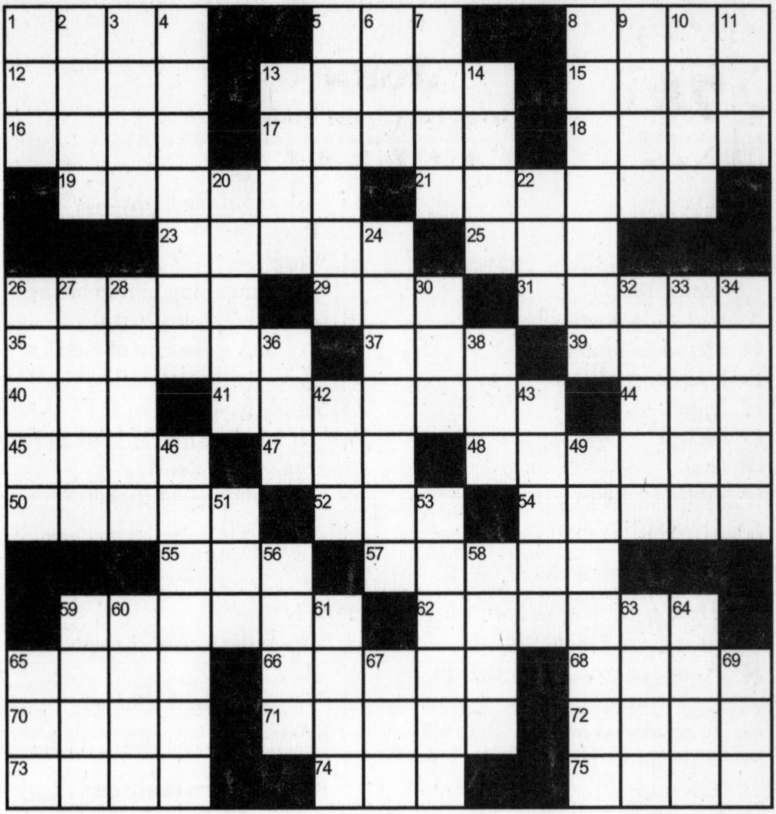

26 Animal skin disease
27 Love
28 Quoter
30 "Cut off his right ___" (John 18:10)
32 Cleans a hole
33 Acclaim
34 Twit
36 Distress call
38 Male cat
42 "___ art thou?" (John 1:22)
43 "Sir, give me this ___" (John 4:15)
46 "The same came for a ___" (John 1:7)
49 Many disciples became ___
51 "That they might ___ the passover" (John 18:28)
53 Hit some pins
56 Restaurant
58 "The streets. . .shall be full of ___" (Zech. 8:5)
59 "Ye cannot hear my ___" (John 8:43)
60 "Ishbosheth, who lay on ___ ___" (2 Sam. 4:5) (2 wds.)
61 "Descending from heaven like a ___" (John 1:32)
63 "Cast a ___, and take up the fish" (Matt. 17:27)
64 Christmas
65 W.C.
67 "That I may ___ Christ" (Phil. 3:8)
69 "And a ___ of cedar beams" (1 Kings 7:12)

70

JOHN

by Sarah Lagerquist Simmons

ACROSS

1 Puff
5 Hovel
8 "With the scab, and with the ___" (Deut. 28:27)
12 "Went ___ the sea" (John 6:17)
13 "Sin which doth so easily ___ us" (Heb. 12:1)
15 We are ___ mortals
16 "Men shall ___ with me at noon" (Gen. 43:16)
17 "___ hither thy finger" John 20:27)
18 "Ye also shall ___ witness" (John 15:27)
19 City in Minnesota (2 wds.)
21 Cutting down
23 "___ these things Jesus walked in Galilee" (John 7:1)
25 Angel did ___ Jacob (Gen. 32)
26 Big
29 "Render unto the wife ___ benevolence" (2 Cor. 7:3)
31 Dried up
35 Good-byes
37 "The heron after her kind. . .and the ___" (Deut. 14:18)
39 Ten (prefix)
40 "His own received him ___" (John 1:11)
41 Unrefined person
44 "He told me ___ that ever I did" (John 4:39)
45 "People ___ and multiplied in Egypt" (Acts 7:17)
47 "___ said, No man, Lord" (John 8:11)
48 Animal group created on 6th day
50 Uncanny
52 Shape of Earth
54 Palatable
55 Little bit
57 "___, just, holy, temperate" (Titus 1:8)
59 "We have ___ all things" (Jer. 44:18)
62 "I am not ___ to unloose" (John 1:27)
65 Ear part
66 "Of an humble spirit with the ___" (Prov. 16:19)
68 "Lift up ___ eyes" (John 4:35)
70 Metals
71 Plants
72 Rolled chocolate candy brand
73 Chances of winning
74 "He loved them unto the ___" (John 13:1)
75 Alter

DOWN

1 "Cry mightily unto ___" (Jonah 3:8)
2 Car rental agency
3 "Father which hath ___ me" (John 5:30)
4 "I go to ___ a place for you" (John 14:2)
5 Many people ___ Jesus
6 America
7 Industrial (abbr.)
8 Consumed
9 Adolescent
10 "Upon the ___ of the rock" (Job 39:28)
11 "Jesus saith unto ___" (John 20:17)
13 Very dry wine
14 "Whence ___ hast thou that living water?" (John 4:11)
20 Out of bounds
22 "Barabbas ___ a robber" (John 18:40)
24 Gum elastics

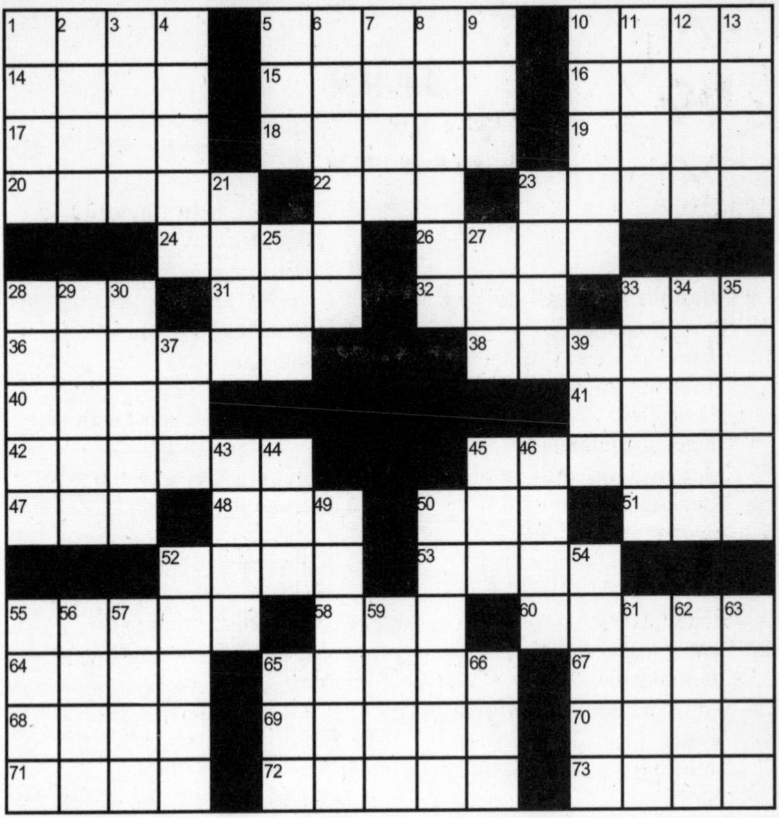

23 State (abbr.)
25 Death in battle
27 Garden tool
28 Birthmark
29 Pickle juice
30 "And ___, saying, His name is John" (Luke 1:63)
33 Literature category
34 Organic compound
35 "All I have is ___" (Luke 15:31)
37 Fighter
39 "They ___ my path" (Job 30:13)
43 "First took a wife, and ___ without children" (Luke 20:29)
44 Yang's partner
45 "I will break also the ___ of Damascus" (Amos 1:5)
46 Also written to Theophilus
49 Adam did ___ forbidden fruit
50 Drive nuts
52 "___ porridge hot. . ."
54 Destroy
55 "New ___ must be put into new bottles" (Luke 5:38)
56 "Offered sacrifice unto the ___" (Acts 7:41)
57 "___ to and fro, and stagger" (Ps. 107:27)
59 Christ was put ___ the cross
61 "___ them that have the rule over you" (Heb. 13:17)
62 "He was exceeding ___" (Luke 23:8)
63 Dried-up
65 "Be thou planted in the ___" (Luke 17:6)
66 Shiloh to Jericho dir.

69

LUKE

by Sarah Lagerquist Simmons

ACROSS
1 Isaac's brother's line
5 Marry on the run
10 Attention problem
14 "Put it on a blue ___" (Ex. 28:37)
15 "When he was twelve ___" (Luke 2:42)
16 Camping equipment
17 Baseball glove
18 Moral principles
19 Magma
20 "Zacharias said unto the ___" (Luke 1:18)
22 Second day of Creation (abbr.)
23 "The ___, because he cheweth the cud" (Lev. 11:5)
24 Wrote Luke
26 "Lord, ____ us the Father" (John 14:8)
28 Direction
31 "___, thou hast nothing to draw with" (John 4:11)
32 2,000 pounds
33 "___ thee out" (Luke 13:31)
36 List of errors
38 Pharisees tried to ___ Jesus
40 "The harp, and the ___" (Isa. 5:12)
41 Not for (prefix)
42 Scruffy
45 "Blessed are the ___" (Luke 23:29)
47 "Seeing they might not ___" (Luke 8:10)
48 Traditional number of wise men (Rom. num.)
50 McDonald's "Big ___"
51 "How long will it be ___ they believe me" (Num. 14:11)
52 Eastern state (abbr.)
53 "Many of them also which used curious ___" (Acts 19:19)
55 Cabled
58 "Art thou then the Son of ___?" (Luke 22:70)
60 Hazes
64 God gave Noah ___ of ark
65 God ___ angels as messengers
67 "Is not ___ to finish it" (Luke 14:29)
68 Opp. of yeses
69 Painter Richard
70 Do not ___ your conscience (1 Tim. 4:2)
71 Women's magazine
72 Jesus did ___ for our sin
73 Jekyll's "partner"

DOWN
1 Quebec town
2 "The ___ descended" (Matt. 7:27)
3 Sarah was ____ as Abraham's sister (Gen. 20:2) (abbr.)
4 Pepper plant
5 "When thine ___ is evil" (Luke 11:34)
6 Luke written as ___ to Theophilus
7 Hawaiian island
8 "There came down a certain ___" (Luke 10:31)
9 "To ___ all these things" (Luke 21:36) (abbr.)
10 Moses' face was ___
11 College head
12 "Ye ___ made it a den of thieves" (Luke 19:46)
13 Cart
21 "___ not after her beauty" (Prov. 6:25)

28 Elisabeth's ___ was John
29 "Adversaries shall not be ___ to gainsay" (Luke 21:15)
30 Gideon did ___ the Midianites
31 "___ his flesh in water" (Num. 19:8)
34 Actor Alda
35 "Two men ___ up into the temple" (Luke 18:10)
36 Author of Luke
38 Drudge
39 Luke wrote this book
40 "___ out all mine iniquities" (Ps. 51:9)
42 "In the watering ___" (Gen. 30:38)
43 Zacharias was a ___
44 "___ unto you!" (Luke 11:47)
45 "And the lapwing, and the ___" (Lev. 11:19)
46 Popular condiment
47 "Women ___ themselves in modest apparel" (1 Tim. 2:9)
48 Fat
49 Hand dye
51 Pater
52 "Thou shalt be ___" (Luke 1:20)
53 Cain's brother
54 Elisabeth's cousin
57 Rive
58 Hebron to Jerusalem dir.
60 Intelligence group

68

LUKE

by Sarah Lagerquist Simmons

ACROSS

1 Cuts
5 Worship of Baal was ___
10 "Any taste in the white of an ___?" (Job 6:6)
13 Regions
15 "___ him that is high" (Ezek. 21:26)
16 "Enter in at ___ strait gate" (Luke 13:24)
17 Lithuanian capital
18 Japanese dish
19 "Lest a more ___ man than thou" (Luke 14:8) (abbr.)
20 Moray
21 Saclike structure
23 "To shew thee __ glad tidings" (Luke 1:19)
25 "I pray ___ therefore" (Luke 16:27)
26 Pastor ___ his congregation
28 "Elisabeth was ___" (Luke 1:7)
31 Hat
32 "I must be ___ my Father's business" (Luke 2:49)
33 Like a wing
34 "Take an ___, and thrust it" (Deut. 15:17) (var.)
37 "Made the vail of ___, and purple" (2 Chron. 3:14)
38 Easily cheated
40 Color of Mordecai's apparel (Est. 8:15) (Fr.)
41 "___ because this widow troubleth me" (Luke 18:5)
42 Technician
43 Lumber
44 "Moses ___ unto us" (Luke 20:28)
45 Author of *Wuthering Heights*
46 Pubs
49 Entice
50 Goodbye (Fr.)
51 Woo
52 "Let the ___ go, and take the young" (Deut. 22:7)
55 Cut
56 "Your reward is ___ in heaven" (Luke 6:23)
59 Breathing device
61 Hindu Mr.
62 Sanskrit language
63 Kitchen timepiece
64 "Jesus answered ___ said" (Luke 22:51)
65 "All men shall ___ well of you" (Luke 6:26)
66 Efficiently

DOWN

1 "___ thou authority over ten cities" (Luke 19:17)
2 Lake
3 "___, thou good servant" (Luke 19:17)
4 ___ Francisco
5 Out of style
6 Adjoin
7 Car fuel
8 "Planteth an ___" (Isa. 44:14)
9 "___ accuse any falsely" (Luke 3:14)
10 "Libner, and ___, and Ashan" (Josh. 15:42)
11 "Baptize you with the Holy ___" (Luke 3:16)
12 Genetic makeup
14 Potpourri bag
22 Desire
24 "___ as an oven" (Hos. 7:7)
25 "Commit to your trust the ___ riches?" (Luke 16:11)
26 Snaky fish
27 Doctor's picture

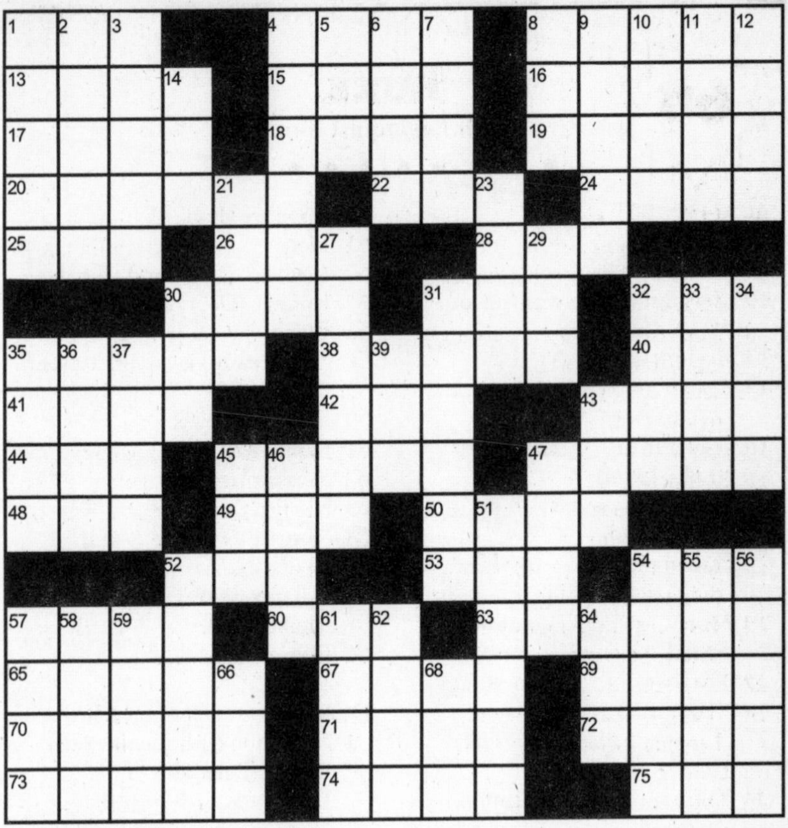

23 "All things are possible unto ___" (Mark 14:36)
27 Commotion
29 Poem of praise
30 "Broth in a ___" (Judg. 6:19)
31 Lullaby composer
32 Jacob was Rachel's ___
33 Sports channel
34 "Lord hath ___ of him" (Mark 11:3)
35 "Am I ___ ___" (Job 7:12) (2 wds.)
36 "Thou shalt ___ up the tabernacle" (Ex. 26:30)
37 Wrote book of Mark
39 "Archers ___ him" (1 Chron. 10:3)
43 "The mystery of the kingdom of ___" (Mark 4:11)
45 Investigation group
46 "He denied with an ___" (Matt. 26:72)
47 "To cover his ___" (Mark 14:65)
51 Baby eagle
52 "Ran through that ___ region" (Mark 6:55)
54 "The centurion, which ___ over against him, saw" (Mark 15:39)
55 Bird's "thumb"
56 W. Australian capital
57 God's love is ___ not fiction
58 Rebekah's ___ was to deceive Isaac
59 "Her clothing is ___ and purple" (Prov. 31:22)
61 Ishmael's descendant
62 Comedian Jay
64 Big Apple
66 "The ___ of man indeed goeth" (Mark 14:21)
68 Arrival

67

Mark

by Sarah Lagerquist Simmons

ACROSS

1 Float up and down
4 "Then shall he ___ his angels" (Mark 13:27)
8 "This man hath done nothing ___" (Luke 23:41)
13 "Jesus sat ___ against the treasury" (Mark 12:41)
15 Canal
16 Recipient
17 "___ and sound" (Luke 15:27)
18 Compass point
19 "Cast him into ___ darkness" (Matt. 22:13)
20 "Bethany, at the mount of ___" (Mark 11:1)
22 Fast plane
24 "Thy ___ is as the tower of Lebanon" (Song 7:4)
25 Clock time
26 Abraham's servant did ___ Rebekah
28 "The brass of it may be ___" (Ezek. 24:11)
30 South American country
31 "Her daughter laid upon the ___" (Mark 7:30)
32 Joseph's brother's nickname
35 David could not wear Saul's ___
38 "For ___ things the earth is disquieted" (Prov. 30:21)
40 Lydia to Emmaus dir.
41 "Moses' ___" (Matt. 23:2)
42 Government intelligence
43 Open wide
44 "Cut off his ___" (Mark 14:47)
45 "She went ___" (Mark 6:24)
47 "He ___ them asleep again" (Mark 14:40)
48 Noah "entered into the ___" (Matt. 24:38)
49 "From the ___ that looketh southward" (Josh. 15:2)
50 Brew
52 "To ___, that God was in Christ" (2 Cor. 5:19)
53 Pocket
54 "Trees of the Lord are full of ___" (Ps. 104:16)
57 "Take up the ___ that first cometh up" (Matt. 17:27)
60 Movie *2001*'s talking computer
63 "We were ___ among you" (1 Thess. 2:7)
65 Cheerio (Sp.)
67 "Earth shall ___" (Isa. 24:20)
69 "If it be ___ minds" (2 Kings 9:15)
70 Stringed instrument
71 Parlay
72 "Find a ___ tied" (Mark 11:2)
73 "When he had ___ the five loaves" (Mark 6:41)
74 "Let down the ___ into the sea" (Acts 27:30)
75 Morse code dash

DOWN

1 "Carry them in his ___" (Isa. 40:11)
2 Squashed circles
3 Correspond
4 Detector
5 "But ___ the messenger came to him" (2 King 6:32)
6 Small licorice treats
7 "___ which are in the mountains" (Judg. 6:2)
8 "Why make ye this ___?" (Mark 5:39)
9 "___ of Olives" (Mark 14:26)
10 "Get ___ the ship" (Mark 6:45)
11 Perceives with eye
12 Ecological communities
14 Minister (abbr.)
21 Vessel

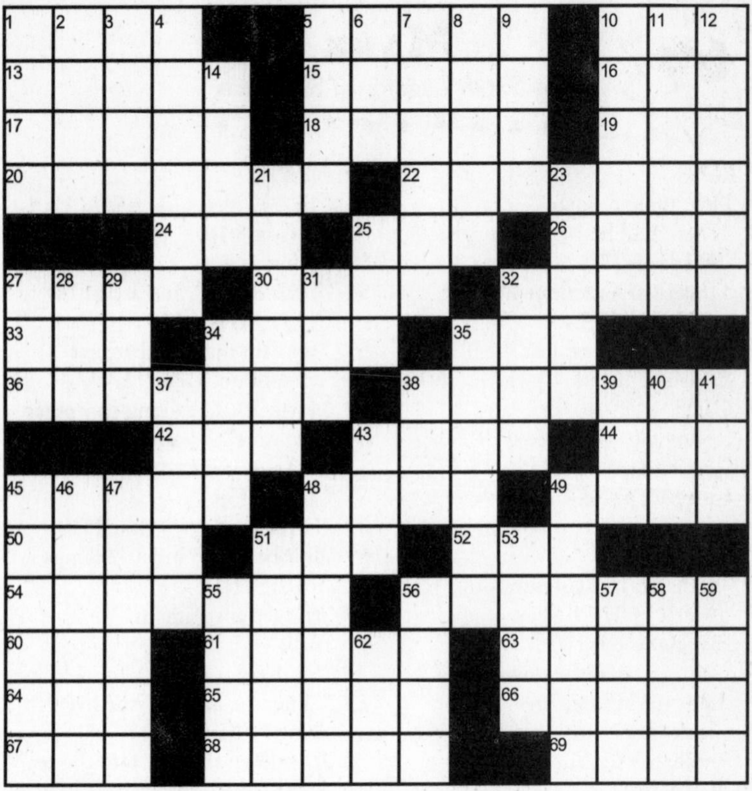

27 Weight per inch
28 Cation
29 Nervous system
31 Street (abbr.)
32 "Perceiving that he had answered them ___" (Mark 12:28)
34 Carpe ___
35 Obtainer
37 Plasma
38 Corporate top dog
39 "He casteth forth his ___ like morsels" (Ps. 147:17)
40 Not (prefix)
41 "Son of the living ___" (Matt. 16:16)
43 Ex-serviceman
45 "Beginning of the ___ of Jesus Christ" (Mark 1:1)
46 Metric units
47 Ran away and married
48 Analyzes
49 David did not behave ___ (1 Sam. 21:13)
51 "___ saith unto them" (Mark 14:27)
53 Baby powder
55 Alternate meaning of Abba
56 Penny
57 God gave Noah ___ to build ark
58 Seaweed substance
59 "If ye ___ to them" (Luke 6:34)
62 "If I should ___ with thee" (Mark 14:31)

66

MARK

by Sarah Lagerquist Simmons

• • • • • • • • • •

ACROSS

1 Sham
5 Wild sheep
10 Ship initials
13 Programming language
15 Control system
16 Car speed
17 Planet's shadow
18 Crawling vines
19 "Satan filled thine heart to ___" (Acts 5:3)
20 Central American xylophone
22 "___ ye the way of the Lord" (Mark 1:3)
24 Nazareth to Tyre dir.
25 "Given to hospitality, ___ to teach" (1 Tim. 3:2)
26 "A ___ of apparel" (Judg. 17:10)
27 Typesetting measurement
30 "To cover his ___" (Mark 14:65)
32 Units of electric power
33 "Jesus, thou ___ of the most high" (Mark 5:7)
34 "Spirit like a ___ descending" (Mark 1:10)
35 Hair stuff
36 Jesus did ___ many to good
38 Jesus had a ___ effect on storms
42 Downwind
43 "The ___ of the temple was rent" (Mark 15:38)
44 Murmur
45 Temple's gold did ___ brightly
48 Long time
49 "He would not ___ them away" (Mark 5:10)
50 Aaron was anointed with ___ (Ex. 29:21) (pl.)
51 Extrusion
52 Approximate destination time
54 Pounded feet
56 From the cranium
60 High school club
61 "He took him ___ from the multitude" (Mark 7:33)
63 Ridge
64 "How long will it be ___ thou be quiet?" (Jer. 47:6)
65 "John was ___ __ prison" (Mark 1:14) (2 wds.)
66 "That the outside of them may be ___ also" (Matt. 23:26)
67 Mind-altering substance
68 Disciples were an ___ to Jesus' ministry
69 A cubit is about half a ___

DOWN

1 "Whose ___ is therein" (Ezek. 24:6)
2 Jairus's daughter wasn't in a ___
3 Reduce (abbr.)
4 Boat dock
5 "They which dwelt in ___ heard" (Acts 19:10)
6 "___ is his name" (Ps. 111:9) (abbr.)
7 Influenza
8 Christians should ___ their eyes from evil
9 "He shall not ___ his reward" (Mark 9:41)
10 German letter topper
11 "He hath an unclean ___" (Mark 3:30)
12 Samson demanded thirty ___ (Judg. 14:13)
14 "Behold the ___ of God" (John 1:29)
21 "They did set them ___ the people" (Mark 8:6)
23 "David delivered first this ___" (1 Chron. 16:7)
25 Peter was an ___ fisherman

26 Priest
27 Alaskan Island resident
29 Tears
30 Witless
31 "Peter took him, and ___ to rebuke him" (Matt. 16:22)
32 Upturned lips
33 Whitens
34 Concerning
36 "Be not, as the hypocrites, of a ___ countenance" (Matt. 6:16)
39 American Indian
44 "___ for a camel to go through the eye of a needle" (Matt. 19:24)
46 "He ___ their sick" (Matt. 14:14)
49 "They ___ the people" (Num. 21:6)
50 "At midnight there was a ___ made" (Matt. 25:6)
52 "Shave her head, and ___ her nails" (Deut. 21:12)
54 "He that cometh in the ___ of the Lord" (Matt. 23:39)
55 Prick
56 "But ___ ye pray, use not vain repetitions" (Matt. 6:7)
57 "He shall save his people from their ___" (Matt. 1:21)
58 "Where Christ should be ___" (Matt. 2:4)
59 "The lame ___" (Matt. 11:5)
60 Location
61 Fall month (abbr.)
63 Abraham's servant did ___ Rebekah
65 Fall behind

65 MATTHEW

by Sarah Lagerquist Simmons

ACROSS

1 "Take up thy ___, and go" (Matt. 9:6)
4 "Cast the ___ away" (Matt. 13:48)
7 Governs food
10 We shouldn't be ___ anyone (Rom. 13:8)
13 "___ no man any thing" (Rom. 13:8)
14 Ache
16 "To be tempted of the ___" (Matt. 4:1)
17 "Darkness over ___ the land" (Matt. 27:45)
18 "Biteth the horse ___" (Gen. 49:17)
19 Jesus, his disciples shared final ___
21 "Go into the land of ___" (Matt. 2:20)
23 Tyre to Cana dir.
24 "They did all ___" (Matt. 15:37)
25 Government agency
28 "The ___ and Pharisees sit" (Matt. 23:2)
32 Resort hotel
35 "A man sick of the ___" (Matt. 9:2)
37 Bethany to Jericho dir.
38 Man
40 Thought
41 Henpeck
42 "Take thee a ___, and lay it" (Ezek. 4:1)
43 Unskillful
45 Genetic code
46 ___ MacInnes, author
47 "A city that is ___ on a hill" (Matt. 5:14)
48 "In the ___ of the multitude" (Luke 22:6)
51 Atlantic Coast time
52 Weight per inch
53 "Herd of swine ___ violently down" (Matt. 8:32)
55 The Church ___ Christ's return
58 ___ govern how churches work
61 Orange-yellow (var.)
62 The other half of Jima
64 Electronic communication
66 "Be of good ___; it is I" (Matt. 14:27)
67 "___ by the earth; for it is his footstool" (Matt. 5:35)
68 Triangle-shaped Greek letter
69 "When the ___ heard it, they were moved" (Matt. 20:24)
70 "This is my beloved ___" (Matt. 3:17)
71 Barrel

DOWN

1 Physique
2 Vessel
3 Plunge
4 "There was none other ___ there" (John 6:22)
5 "Bore his ear through with an ___" (Ex. 21:6) (var.)
6 Cafe
7 "Then are the children ___" (Matt. 17:26)
8 Child's toy
9 Muscle group (abbr.)
11 Pinches
12 Vacant
14 Flail
15 "They should ___ the furnace" (Dan. 3:19)
20 Abel was the ___ son (abbr.)
22 "Righteous men have desired to ___" (Matt. 13:17)
25 Grand stories

27 "To ___ out the land" (Josh. 14:7)
28 Leave
29 Automobile
30 Northeastern state
31 "Which used curious ___" (Acts 19:19)
32 "His brethren ___ without" (Matt. 12:46)
33 ___ Gras
35 Tiny branch
37 Loch ___ monster
40 "Gave heed unto them, ___ to receive" (Acts 3:5) (var.)
41 "___ weather" (Matt. 16:3)
43 "Declare unto us this ___" (Matt. 15:15)
46 Shoveled
47 "Yet I ___ unto you" (Matt. 6:29)
48 "The ___ of Man came not to be ministered unto" (Matt. 20:28)
50 "Go work ___ ___" (Matt. 21:28) (2 wds.)
51 Cups
52 "Preach the word in ___" (Acts 16:6)
53 Israel's son
54 "Went their ways, one to his ___" (Matt. 22:5)
55 Fill
56 Garner
57 Pros
60 Edge
62 Possible nickname for David's son

64

MATTHEW

by Sarah Lagerquist Simmons

ACROSS

1 "In the ___ of his son" (Gen. 22:13)

6 "Heart lifteth thee up to ___" (2 Chron. 25:19) (var.)

10 "Have ye not fulfilled your ___" (Ex. 5:14)

14 Cola

15 Satan did try to ___ Jesus (Matt. 4:10)

16 "And the burning ___" (Lev. 26:16)

17 Anonym

18 Law student (abbr.)

19 "He shall baptize you with the ___ Ghost" (Matt. 3:11)

20 Care

21 Peter found ___ in fish's mouth (Matt. 17:27)

23 Self-righteousness ___ to God

25 "Man shall not ___ by bread alone" (Matt. 4:4)

26 "They did all ___" (Matt. 15:37)

27 'How can ye ___ the damnation" (Matt. 23:33)

30 Communism parent philosophy

34 Frown angrily

35 Sticky black substances

36 Change color

38 "Thou shalt ___ thy vineyard" (Lev. 25:3)

39 "To ___, for the prophet" (1 Kings 13:23)

40 "He had promised ___ by his prophets" (Rom. 1:2)

42 Talk

43 "Their ___, and their cords" (Num. 4:32)

44 "Sleep in the ___" (Ezek. 34:25)

45 "In the LORD's ___ unto the people" (Hag. 1:13)

48 Ishmael's descendants

49 Average work performance

50 "They ___ not, neither do they spin" (Matt. 6:28)

51 Malay Peninsula

54 Type

55 "Jesus, walking by the ___" (Matt. 4:18)

58 "They ___ helps" (Acts 27:17)

59 Nail

61 Jesus' ancestor

63 "Will he ___ him a stone?" (Matt. 7:9)

64 Italian currency

65 ___ Dame

66 "And ___ unto it, Let no fruit grow" (Matt. 21:19)

67 TV award

68 Dales

DOWN

1 "He ___ on the ground" (John 9:6)

2 "___ ye the daughter of Sion" (Matt. 21:5)

3 Heroic

4 "Then ___ took all the silver" (1 Kings 15:18)

5 "The ___ is not above his master" (Matt. 10:24)

6 Cool

7 Woman in Jesus' family tree

8 "Thou also ___ one of them" (Matt. 26:73)

9 Fountains

10 Favorite vacation island

11 Competition at the Greek games

12 Pout

13 "Will give unto thee the ___" (Matt. 16:19)

22 Boulevard (abbr.)

24 Matthew was a ___ collector

25 Grass

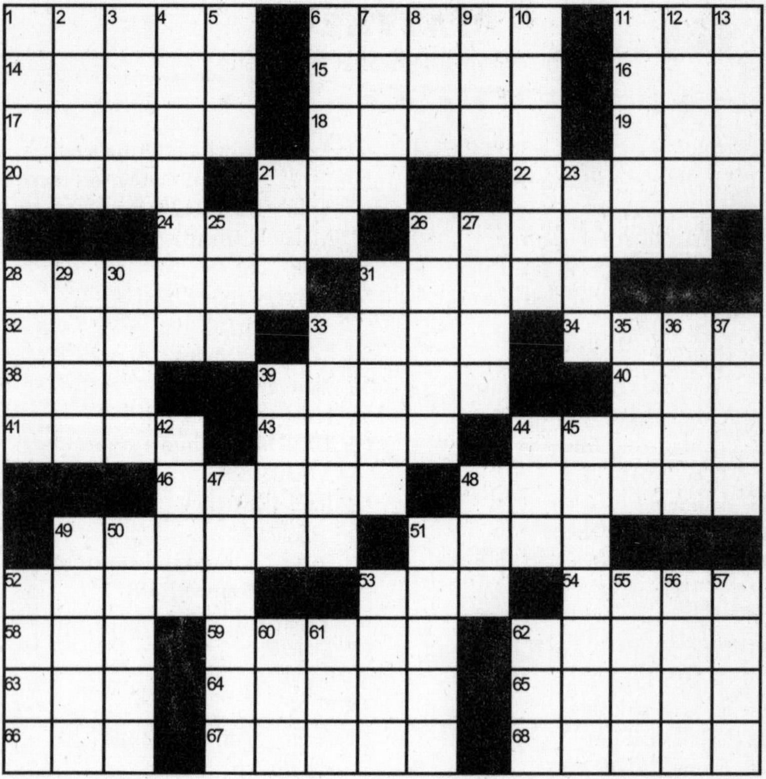

23 Lie in the sun
25 "Fear ___ me, saith the Lord" (Mal. 3:5)
26 "He is the messenger of the Lord of ___" (Mal. 2:7)
27 "Curious ___" (Acts 19:19)
28 Tribe
29 Air (prefix)
30 "My ___ shall be great" (Mal. 1:11)
31 "He walked with me in ___" (Mal. 2:6)
33 "Not many ___" (1 Cor. 1:26)
35 Snaky fish
36 Fencing sword
37 "The heavens shall ___ away" (2 Pet. 3:10)
39 Data transmission rate
42 "I am the ___, I change not" (Mal. 3:6)
44 Where Daniel's lions lived
45 Not at present
47 Largely
48 "The ___ of truth was in his mouth" (Mal. 2:6)
49 Artery
50 "Ye offer polluted ___ upon mine altar" (Mal. 1:7)
51 Pertaining to manner or form
52 "Jesus ___" (John 11:35)
53 What Moses did not have to do at the Red Sea
55 Affirm
56 ___ ex machina
57 Swirl
60 River (Sp.)
61 "I am. . .the beginning and the ___" (Rev. 22:13)
62 Licensed nurse

63

MALACHI

by Vicki J. Kuyper

ACROSS

1 Moses' food
6 "I am a ___ King, saith the Lord of hosts" (Mal. 1:14)
11 Fall month (abbr.)
14 Palestine and Persia, e.g.
15 Movie "king"
16 Boxer Muhammad
17 Under (poet.)
18 Crooked
19 "A ___ honoureth his father" (Mal. 1:6)
20 Dress from India
21 Medical org.
22 "Who may ___ the day of his coming?" (Mal. 3:2)
24 "It is appointed unto men ___ to die" (Heb. 9:27)
26 What some Pharisees would do to Jesus
28 "God ___ be tempted" (James 1:13)
31 Caesarea, Tyre, and Miletus, e.g.
32 "I am the ___ of the apostles" (1 Cor. 15:9)
33 "Thou set thy ___ among the stars" (Obad. 1:4)
34 "The priest's lips should ___ knowledge" (Mal. 2:7)
38 "On mine ___ shall they trust" (Isa. 51:5)
39 "There came other ___ from Tiberias" (John 6:23)
40 Environmental advocate
41 Christmas refrain
43 Alphabet
44 Dells
46 Plant seed
48 Telescope viewers
49 Rub down
51 "Ye have caused ___ to stumble" (Mal. 2:8)
52 "Wearied the Lord with your ___" (Mal. 2:17)
53 What Adam must have said seeing Eve
54 "Have I also ___ you contemptible" (Mal. 2:9)
58 "Sir, come down ___ my child die" (John 4:49)
59 "Ye shall ___ down the wicked" (Mal. 4:3)
62 "I have ___ you, saith the Lord" (Mal. 1:2)
63 School group
64 Singer Ronstadt
65 "Now we call the ___ happy" (Mal. 3:15)
66 Measure of faith needed to move mountains
67 Warble
68 Chatty

DOWN

1 "A ___ pride shall bring him low" (Prov. 29:23)
2 Domain
3 "I will come ___ to you to judgment" (Mal. 3:5)
4 "All ___ shall call you blessed" (Mal. 3:12)
5 Goes with sackcloth
6 "By ___ are ye saved" (Eph. 2:8)
7 Grating sound
8 Antlered animal
9 One of God's creations
10 Frustrate
11 Fertile desert area
12 "Flesh is clothed with worms and ___ of dust" (Job 7:5)
13 Fork prong
21 "The ___ of violence is in their hands" (Isa. 59:6)

27 "Thou, O God, hast heard my ___" (Ps. 61:5)
28 "The Lord God shall ___ the trumpet" (Zech. 9:14)
29 Skim
30 Saudi citizen
31 "Joshua. . .stood before the ___" (Zech. 3:3)
34 Billings' state (abbr.)
35 Recommend
36 KJV "roes"
38 "___ my people" (Zech. 8:7)
39 Inkling
40 Temple, e.g.
42 "I made thee. . .a ___ to all countries" (Ezek. 22:4)
43 The ones Zechariah saw were red, speckled, and white (Zech. 1:8)
44 Movie 2001's talking computer
45 "I have sent forth thy prisoners out of the ___" (Zech. 9:11)
46 Sacred song
47 Where Jonah had time to think (2 wds.)
48 Isaiah's state for three years (Isa. 20:3)
49 Egypt did not keep the ___ of tabernacles (Zech. 14:19)
51 One of Columbus's ships
52 Zechariah's grandfather (Zech. 1:1)
53 Chocolate and caramel candy brand
54 Pitcher
57 "Not by might, ___ by power" (Zech. 4:6)
58 Deserved
60 Tweak

62

ZECHARIAH

by Vicki J. Kuyper

• • • • • •

ACROSS

1 "Set there upon her own ___" (Zech. 5:11)
5 Coastal state (abbr.)
10 McDonald's "Big ___"
13 Bird's "thumb"
15 Swelling
16 "He that remaineth. . .shall be for ___ God" (Zech 9:7)
17 "___ of myrrh" (Ps. 45:8)
18 Mordecai did this for his cousin, Esther (Est. 2:7)
19 "In that day shall there be ___ Lord" (Zech. 14:9)
20 "Shall be as though I ___ not cast them off" (Zech. 10:6)
21 "Caused thine iniquity to ___ from thee" (Zech. 3:4)
23 "The Lord of ___" (Zech. 2:11)
25 "Displeased with the heathen that are at ___" (Zech. 1:15)
26 29,028 ft. mountain
28 A name for Jesus (Zech. 6:12)
31 Worship
32 Worm-like stage
33 "Good ___" (Prov. 25:25)
34 By-product of the flood
37 Affirmative
38 "We see not our ___" (Ps. 74:9)
40 "Lord hath been ___ displeased" (Zech. 1:2)
41 Samson's hair was woven with this (Judg. 16:13)
42 "Yea, they ___ their hearts" (Zech. 7:12)
43 Flexible joint
44 Shanty
45 "Cast it unto the ___: a goodly price" (Zech. 11:13)
46 Cure for disease, evil, hardship
49 God promised to be a wall of ___ around Jerusalem (Zech. 2:5)
50 "It hath no ___" (Hos. 8:7)
51 "They straightway left their ___" (Matt. 4:20)
52 What God felt against Jerusalem
55 "___ ye of the Lord rain" (Zech. 10:1)
56 Ahasuerus ruled from Ethiopia to here (Est. 1:1)
59 "He shall surely ___ her to be his wife" (Ex. 22:16)
61 Downwind
62 Urim and Thummim, e.g.
63 Move up to
64 "Surely oppression maketh a wise man ___" (Eccl. 7:7)
65 "How ___ is his goodness" (Zech. 9:17)
66 "Oppress not. . .the ___" (Zech. 7:10)

DOWN

1 Hit
2 __ mater
3 Took to court
4 Annex
5 "___ from anger, and forsake wrath" (Ps. 37:8)
6 Totals
7 Constellation
8 Rascal
9 "Your ___, where are they?" (Zech. 1:5)
10 Elk-like animal
11 Father's sisters
12 Top of wave
14 S. American llama
22 Offering remains
24 Miner's goal
25 "Let not thine heart ___ sinners" (Prov. 23:17)
26 Temporary home to Adam and Eve

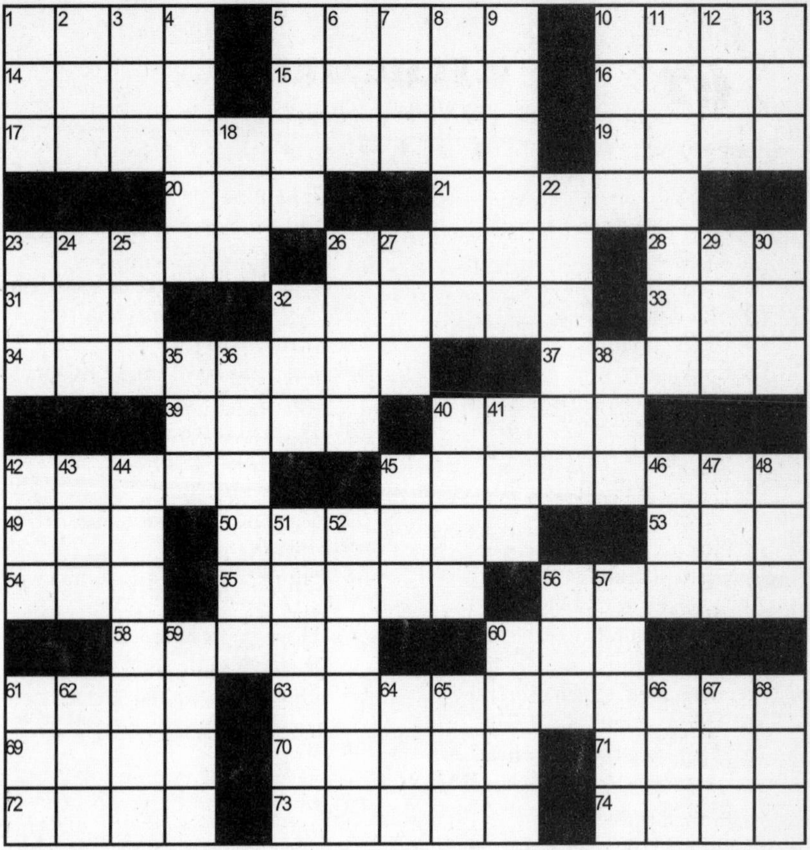

36 "Spikenard, very ___" (John 12:3)
38 Morse code dot
40 "'The gold is ___,' saith the Lord" (Hag. 2:8)
41 Gorilla
42 Center of chariot wheel
43 North American country
44 Sovereign's substitutes
45 "As a ___ returneth to his vomit" (Prov. 26:11)
46 David unintentionally provokes this in Saul
47 Mongrel dog
48 "The ___ of the house of David will I lay" (Isa. 22:22)
51 Large zoo animals
52 Reply
56 Alphabet
57 What God promises in His new temple
59 Nerd
60 Month Haggai spoke final prophecy
61 What Jesus once was
62 "Every ___ by the sword" (Hag. 2:22)
64 Haman, from the book of Esther, had a big one
65 What Simon did for work (Acts 9:43)
66 Abraham's nephew
67 Nurse
68 "Is the seed yet in the barn? ___" (Hag. 2:19)

61

HAGGAI

by Vicki J. Kuyper

ACROSS

1 Local government in ancient Greece
5 Isaiah is a ___ prophet
10 "The children's teeth are set on ___" (Ezek. 18:2)
14 Spoken
15 Tree not bearing fruit for Haggai's people
16 Rank
17 The governor Haggai spoke to (Hag. 1:1)
19 Exploiter
20 Judah, after God calls for a drought
21 Boom box
23 Asian nation
26 Current name for Melita, Paul's "shipwreck" island
28 Nickname for one of Israel's tribes
31 Roman three
32 Tom ___
33 Pixie
34 Tuna
37 Romantic interlude
39 Animals Haggai's people raised
40 One of Hawaii's islands
42 Aches
45 Oil level tester
49 "___ hospitality one to another without grudging" (1 Pet. 4:9)
50 What Darius sat on
53 "Woe unto you, Pharisees! For ye tithe mint and ___" (Luke 11:42)
54 "Ye. . .earneth wages to put it into a ___ with holes" (Hag. 1:6)
55 Feudal superior
56 Impersonation
58 "I covenanted with you when ye came out of ___" (Hag. 2:5)
60 North by east
61 Isolated
63 How Psalms are written
69 Stake
70 Jubal led those who played this instrument (Gen. 4:21)
71 Deal with
72 Office furniture
73 Temple foundation is built from this
74 Volcano in Italy

DOWN

1 Number of Israel's tribes (abbr.)
2 "And ___ the lamp of God went out" (1 Sam. 3:3)
3 "They ___ my path" (Job 30:13)
4 Avoid, as in building temple
5 Famous whale
6 Wing
7 Fore-and-aft sail
8 Excessively
9 Give an account of
10 Decorative needle case
11 What Haggai's people did to God
12 "To the right!"
13 "You do ___" (Matt. 22:29)
18 Lingerie item
22 King during Haggai's time
23 Korean car company
24 "I called for a drought. . .upon the ___" (Hag. 1:11)
25 Where Eve came from
26 God made this planet on the fourth day
27 "My heart standeth in ___ of thy word" (Ps. 119:161)
29 Annex
30 Football assoc.
32 What Haggai's people do with corn
35 "Taken in adultery, in the very ___" (John 8:4)

24 "Dust thou ___" (Gen. 3:19)
25 "Every one that passeth by her shall ___" (Zeph. 2:15)
26 "Surely thou wilt ___ me" (Zeph. 3:7)
27 Lawyer (abbr.)
28 Jericho to Jerusalem dir.
29 Aces
30 "___ in his love" (Zeph. 3:17)
31 Perhaps heard by Daniel (Dan. 3:5)
34 "In word or ___" (Col. 3:17)
35 Spoken
36 "___ shall make them afraid" (Zeph. 3:13)
38 "___, ye inhabitants of Maktesh" (Zeph. 1:11)
39 Canal
40 What Samson shouldn't have cut
42 Gideon's fleece was this the first morning (Judg. 6:38)
43 Examined
44 "___ not thine hands be slack" (Zeph. 3:16)
45 Scarf
46 Card game
47 One who despises
48 Writing
49 "Stretch forth thine hand. . .over the ___" (Ex. 8:5)
51 "Seek ye the LORD, all ye ___ of the earth" (Zeph. 2:3)
52 Eye
53 Valley
54 Prohibitionists
57 Lode yield
58 Sarah to Abraham
60 Bambi's mom

60

ZEPHANIAH

by Vicki J. Kuyper

ACROSS

1 "Be not ___ with thy mouth" (Eccl. 5:2)
5 Paul and shipmates were this before running aground (Acts 27:27) (2 wds.)
10 "He planteth an ___" (Isa. 44:14)
13 Earthy pigment
15 Bathsheba had this
16 "___ to her that is filthy and polluted" (Zeph. 3:1)
17 "The unjust knoweth no ___" (Zeph. 3:5)
18 Domestic fish
19 Wing
20 Brain wave recording
21 "A man plucked off his ___" (Ruth 4:7)
23 Leaf gatherer
25 "I will ___ them" (Zech. 13:9)
26 "O thou ___ among women?" (Song 6:1)
28 AT&T competitor
31 Reach (2 wds.)
32 "Every day they ___ my words" (Ps. 56:5)
33 "Swear not. . .neither by any other ___" (James 5:12)
34 Put on
37 Vineyard owner in Matt. 20:1
38 English king
40 David was considered this after fighting Goliath
41 Concorde, e.g.
42 Star Trek's humanoid drones
43 Eulogy
44 Author Carroll
45 "I will keep my mouth with a ___" (Ps. 39:1)
46 Coax
49 "An afflicted and ___ people" (Zeph. 3:12)
50 "I made ___, and delayed not" (Ps. 119:60)
51 "Surely ___ shall be as Sodom" (Zeph. 2:9)
52 "The ___ number of them is to be redeemed" (Num. 3:48)
55 "That which groweth of ___ own accord" (Lev. 25:5)
56 "Thy honourable ___" (Ps. 45:9)
59 Lawn tool
61 "Woe unto the inhabitants of the ___ coast" (Zeph. 2:5)
62 Sinned
63 Country singer, ___ Parton
64 "I. . .will ___ them as gold" (Zech. 13:9)
65 Writing tables
66 Snaky fish

DOWN

1 "They ___ early" (Zeph. 3:7)
2 Yearn
3 Thick carpet
4 Those who touched Jesus' were made whole (Matt. 14:36)
5 Mummer
6 "He will joy over ___ with singing" (Zeph. 3:17)
7 "I have not ___ with vain persons" (Ps. 26:4)
8 "Do they not ___ that devise evil?" (Prov. 14:22)
9 Zephaniah's great-grandfather (Zeph. 1:1)
10 "When I ___, I am still with thee" (Ps. 139:18)
11 "The ___ of your feet" (Deut. 11:24)
12 "Punish the men. . .that say in their ___, The LORD will not do good" (Zeph. 1:12)
14 Feel bitter about
22 Derby

25 One hundred of these makes a shekel in Greek marketplace
26 "Woe to him that buildeth a town with ___" (Hab. 2:12)
27 Long time
29 "Sanctuaries of Israel shall be laid ___" (Amos 7:9)
30 Self-esteem
32 North of the Beehive State
33 "My ___ is poured upon the earth" (Lam. 2:11)
34 Scamp
35 Describes Jacob
37 Bullring cheer
39 "If any man have an ___, let him hear" (Rev. 13:9)
42 Biblical "yea"
43 Type of partnership (abbr.)
47 Midwestern state
49 "Woe unto him that saith to the wood, ___" (Hab. 2:19)
50 Denver time zone
52 Biblical trumpet sounds
55 Roll
57 "Those that walk in pride he is able to ___" (Dan. 4:37)
58 Soft cheese
59 Jonah wished he had this
60 Snaky fish
61 "Walk. . .through the ___ of great waters" (Hab. 3:15)
62 Kilometer measure
63 "Give unto thee the ___ of the kingdom" (Matt. 16:19)
64 Unmake
65 "A name written, that no man ___" (Rev. 19:12)
68 Legume

59

HABAKKUK

by Vicki J. Kuyper

• • • • • •

ACROSS

1 Food laws org.
4 What Moses took across the desert (2 wds.)
9 First woman
12 Israel's son
14 Brides' headdresses
15 Balaam's donkey should have done this
16 "The Son abideth ___" (John 8:35)
17 How God supplied Israelites with manna
18 "His soul shall dwell at ___" (Ps. 25:13)
19 Blimps
21 "Jesus came into the ___ of Caesarea Philippi" (Matt. 16:13)
23 "Shall not ___ these take up a parable" (Hab. 2:6)
24 Attila the ___
25 Cain's brother
28 "Save one little ___ lamb" (2 Sam. 12:3)
31 "Lilies. . .___ not, neither do they spin" (Matt. 6:28)
34 Ice houses
36 "Hast thou not heard long ___" (2 Kings 19:25)
38 "We shall not ___" (Hab. 1:12)
40 "The sun and ___ stood still" (Hab. 3:11)
41 Household cleaner brand
43 Volcanic flow
44 For
45 "___ I will rejoice in the LORD" (Hab. 3:18)
46 "My father will do nothing ___ great or small" (1 Sam. 20:2)
48 First person
51 "Walk through the ___ with thine horses" (Hab. 3:15)
53 Incense gives off this
54 Babylon to Jerusalem direction
56 "The ___ is slacked" (Hab. 1:4)
58 What idols don't have (Hab. 2:19)
61 This book's prophet
66 What Lazarus did after four days
67 Aida
69 Pittsburgh's state (abbr.)
70 "An ___ soul shall suffer hunger" (Prov. 19:15)
71 Thousands of sheets of paper
72 Dr. Jekyll and Mr. ___
73 Aurora
74 Slipup
75 We reap what we ___

DOWN

1 "King of Israel is come out to seek a ___" (1 Sam. 26:20)
2 False deity worshipped by Hindus
3 Affirm
4 The prayer of the righteous will ___ much
5 "The LORD is in his holy ___" (Hab. 2:20)
6 Jesus death does this to temple's curtain
7 "Love worketh no ___ to his neighbour" (Rom. 13:10)
8 Figure out
9 Extremely long time periods
10 The variety of God's creation is this
11 "Thou art of purer ___ than to behold evil" (Hab. 1:13)
13 Tax agency
15 Board game
20 Angelic head gear
22 "They came ___ as a whirlwind" (Hab. 3:14)

28 Side dish
29 South of the border crazy
30 Off-Broadway award
31 "Who can ___ before his indignation?" (Nah. 1:6)
34 "___ thee with sackcloth" (Jer. 6:26)
35 "Men ___ to die" (Heb. 9:27)
36 "As ___ children" (Eph. 5:1)
38 Brood
39 Rahab "bound the scarlet ___ in the window" (Josh. 2:21)
40 "Thy shepherds slumber, O ___ of Assyria" (Nah. 3:18)
42 "They only ___ to cast him down" (Ps. 62:4)
43 Ravine
44 Pallid
45 State leader (abbr.)
46 "My covenant will I not break, nor ___" (Ps. 89:34)
47 Judas used this
48 Jesus did this with Peter after rising from the dead (John 21:15)
49 "The heart melteth, and the ___ smite together" (Nah. 2:10)
51 "I am the Lord, and there is none ___ " (Isa. 45:6)
52 Tropical island
53 Small freshwater fish
54 "The tongue can no man ___" (James 3:8)
57 "___ height, ___ depth, ___ any other creature" (Rom. 8:39) (same wd.)
58 Remind
60 Entrance rug

58

Nahum

by Vicki J. Kuyper

• • • • • •

ACROSS

1 "God shall wipe away all tears from their ___" (Rev. 21:4)
5 Name
10 "He knoweth them that trust in ___" (Nah. 1:7)
13 "Her maids shall lead her as with the voice of ___" (Nah. 2:7)
15 Type of acid
16 "There is ___ come out of thee, that imagineth evil" (Nah. 1:11)
17 BB player Olajuwon
18 Small Mediterranean boat (var.)
19 "No ___ gathereth" (Nah. 3:18)
20 "All her great ___ were bound in chains" (Nah. 3:10)
21 Adam's garden
23 Turn over
25 "___! for that day is great" (Jer. 30:7)
26 Guarantees
28 "We had sailed ___ many days" (Acts 27:7)
31 Francis ___ Key
32 Ear parts
33 Weight measurements
34 "___ is jealous, and the Lord revengeth" (Nah. 1:2)
37 Vinegary
38 Shaping tool
40 Cattle (arch.)
41 "___ to the bloody city!" (Nah. 3:1)
42 Peter paid taxes with this from a fish's mouth
43 Approximate date
44 "Thy ___ is grievous" (Nah. 3:19)
45 Goose
46 Moderate musical tempo
49 Gorilla "king"
50 "Make thy ___ strong" (Nah. 2:1)
51 "Let not thine heart ___ sinners" (Prov. 23:17)
52 Halloween month (abbr.)
55 Large weight unit
56 Abraham was Lot's
59 Neb. city
61 Babylon to Ur direction
62 Aphid
63 This puzzle's prophet
64 "The shield of his mighty men is made ___" (Nah. 2:3)
65 "The fir ___ shall be terribly shaken" (Nah. 2:3)
66 Small pipe

DOWN

1 Swiss-like cheese
2 "Now will I break his ___ from off thee" (Nah. 1:13)
3 "Where the lion, ___ the old lion, walked" (Nah. 2:11)
4 "Thou shalt ___ thy children's children" (Ps. 128:6)
5 Mopes about
6 Prayer ending
7 Baby's eating apparel
8 Bethlehem to Damascus direction
9 "Thy crowned are as the ___" (Nah. 3:17)
10 Greek author
11 Silly
12 What God does to broken hearts
14 Scents
22 "The Lord is good, a strong hold in the ___ of trouble" (Nah. 1:7)
24 "___ and Lubim were thy helpers" (Nah. 3:9)
25 Describes those who saw Jesus' miracles
26 College class (abbr.)
27 "___ shall look back" (Nah. 2:8)

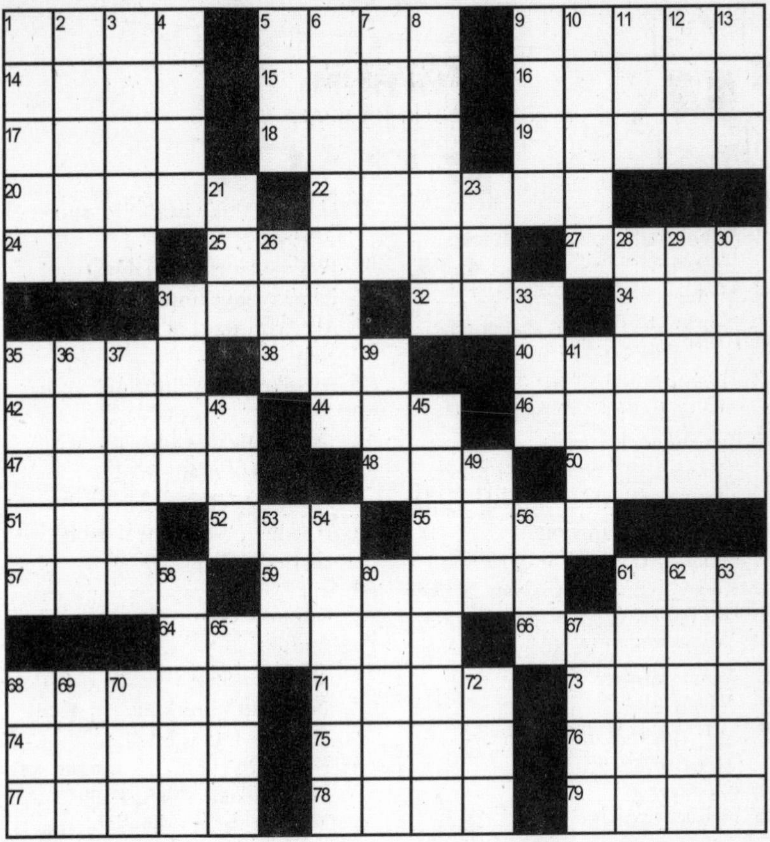

26 Choice (abbr.)
28 "I sent before thee Moses, ___, and Miriam" (Mic. 6:4)
29 Cornered
30 "Then shall the ___ be ashamed" (Mic. 3:7)
31 Malt liquor
33 "The ___ shall go forth of Zion" (Mic. 4:2)
35 Right angle to a ship's length
36 Guy (slang)
37 Everything and everywhere is God's
39 "Thou shalt ___, but not be satisfied" (Mic. 6:14)
41 Says (slang)
43 God told Moses, "Stretch out thine hand over the ____" (Ex. 14:16)
45 Noah's weather forecast
49 "They oppress a ___ and his house" (Mic. 2:2)
53 Acid drug
54 Arm muscles
56 Root vegetable
58 Much
60 "Enlarge thy baldness as the ___" (Mic. 1:16)
61 Water bird
62 Micah's prophecy
63 Tower
65 Business group (abbr.)
67 Flightless birds
68 Said to call attention
69 Former rib
70 Aspire
72 Haifa to Jerusalem dir.

57

Micah

by Vicki J. Kuyper

• • • • • •

ACROSS

1 Island nation
5 Hawaiian dance
9 "God created man in his own ___" (Gen. 1:27)
14 "This time is ___" (Mic. 2:3)
15 "Received the seed. . .and ___ with joy receiveth it" (Matt. 13:20)
16 Bleacher
17 "They shall lick the ___ like a serpent" (Mic. 7:17)
18 "He ___ on the ground, and made clay" (John 9:6)
19 Red pigment
20 "My lovers and my friends stand ___" (Ps. 38:11)
22 Athens' goddess
24 "The whole herd of swine ___ violently" (Matt. 8:32)
25 Rank
27 Bishops' miters
31 "___ humbly with thy God" (Mic. 6:8)
32 Bad (prefix)
34 "They ___ gone into captivity" (Mic. 1:16)
35 Hairstyle
38 Ball holder
40 "To this ___ the words of the prophets" (Acts 15:15)
42 Ales
44 Adam was this to Cain
46 Adorer
47 Excite
48 Doubting apostle's nickname
50 "Now shall he be great unto the ___ of the earth" (Mic. 5:4)
51 "___ the idols thereof will I lay desolate" (Mic. 1:7)
52 Loose gown worn at mass
55 "He will teach us of his ___" (Mic. 4:2)
57 Abel's nickname for Eve
59 Earthy pigment
61 Yarmulke
64 Wild
66 God wants us to love this (Mic. 6:8)
68 "Jerusalem shall become ___" (Mic. 3:12)
71 Id's counterparts
73 "A man that beareth false witness. . .is a ___" (Prov. 25:18)
74 "Innumerable ___ have compassed me" (Ps. 40:12)
75 Overplus in KJV
76 "Who is a God like ___ thee" (Mic. 7:18)
77 Asian country
78 Dried-up
79 "Have not ___, and yet have believed" (John 20:29)

DOWN

1 Biblical tree of Lebanon
2 Screamer's throat dangler
3 Herd animal
4 Singing voice
5 KJV "hath"
6 Done to a suitcase
7 Unwilling
8 Song
9 "I will make thine horn ___" (Mic.. 4:13)
10 Morasthite prophet
11 Pairs with sackcloth
12 "To the right!"
13 "The prophets that make my people ___" (Mic. 3:5)
21 Farm association
23 Airport information

27 Number of prophets God sent to Nineveh
29 "Arise, lift up the ___, and hold him in thine hand" (Gen. 21:18)
30 Ninevite men and beasts did this (Jonah 3:7)
31 What God keeps
33 Floats in sea, like Jonah's whale
34 False god
36 "Putteth a piece of new ___ unto an old garment" (Matt. 9:16)
37 Flying machine
38 Nineveh's king did this with sackcloth
39 Capital of Western Samoa
40 Sweet potato
42 "To the right!"
44 "Ye shall rise up from the ___" (Josh. 8:7)
45 "Ye shall make no ___ with the inhabitants" (Judg. 2:2)
46 Soap
47 Baseball's Jackson
48 Deviation
50 Rogue
51 Nineveh's king sat in these
53 Type of tea
55 Rainy month (abbr.)
58 God's people burned incense under this tree (Hos. 4:13)
60 Home to Jonah's great fish
61 "Is there any taste in the white of an ___?" (Job 6:6)
62 Jonah sat outside Nineveh to do this

56

Jonah

by Vicki J. Kuyper

• • • • • •

ACROSS
1 Approximate date
6 New Testament book
10 Fuel
13 "There is a generation, whose teeth are as ___" (Prov. 30:14)
15 "Jonah rose up to ____ unto Tarshish" (Jonah 1:3)
16 "This do ye, as ___ as ye drink it" (1 Cor. 11:25)
17 What Jonah needed once ashore
18 Part of a semester
19 What Jonah did by fleeing
20 Jonah doesn't care if he lives or ____
22 Jonah's father (Jonah 1:1)
24 Messy person
26 Convicts (slang)
28 Used to scourge Jesus
29 Country in SE Asia
30 Groupies
31 Wrapped around Jonah's head (Jonah 2:5)
32 "Thou ___ a gracious God" (Jonah 4:2)
33 "Find the ___ wrapped in swaddling clothes" (Luke 2:12)
34 Snake
35 What God and Jonah do together
37 Broad street
41 Abraham's nephew
42 "Jonah was exceeding ____ of the gourd" (Jonah 4:6)
43 Government agency
44 Brass
47 Concrete
48 What the Philistines did to Samson
49 "Every moving thing that liveth shall be ___ for you" (Gen. 9:3)
50 Mentally alert
51 Ambience
52 What Jonah was not doing in the sea
54 "God prepared a vehement ____ wind" (Jonah 4:8)
56 Expression
57 Animal house
59 Periods
63 Take to court
64 "They turned from their ____ way" (Jonah 3:10)
65 To Jonah's disappointment, God didn't do this on His promise to the Ninevites
66 "___ children arise up, and call ___ blessed" (Prov. 31:28) (same wd.)
67 Regard
68 Phase

DOWN
1 Missouri time zone
2 The other half of Jima
3 What sailors tried to do to save Jonah
4 Tenets
5 Speak without preparation
6 Back of a ship
7 Dusts
8 What is agreed on
9 Very large truck
10 Famous German author
11 "The mariners were _____" (Jonah 1:5)
12 Saul does this when prophesying in front of Samuel (1 Sam. 19:24)
14 Nineveh to Babylon dir.
21 Strike workers
23 Nip
24 Indian dress
25 Used to decide Jonah was responsible for storm

27 "Though thou set thy ___ among the stars" (Obad. 1:4)
28 Seaweed substance
29 Type of exercise
31 Teen disease
32 "They that eat thy bread have laid a ___ under thee" (Obad. 1:7)
34 Power system
36 What Moses did after crossing the Red Sea
38 Destroy
39 Israel's oppressor in the book of Obadiah
40 ___ Ranger
41 David did this to Goliath
46 Breaking sound
47 "Thou shalt be ___ off for ever" (Obad. 1:10)
48 Elders
52 Fifth tone of musical scale
54 How manna was on the second day
55 "How should one ___ a thousand" (Deut. 32:30)
56 Vice ___
58 "Thou exalt thyself as the ___" (Obad. 1:4)
60 First ___
62 "We have heard a rumour from the ___" (Obad. 1:1)
64 What Esther brings to King Xerxes for her people
65 "The LORD will ___ from Zion" (Amos 1:2)
66 Beers
67 Small particle
68 "The day of the LORD is ___" (Obad. 1:15)
70 Frosty

55

OBADIAH

by Vicki J. Kuyper

• • • • • •

ACROSS

1 Swiss mountains
5 Data, for short
10 "Entered into the ___ of my people" (Obad. 1:13)
14 The disciple Jesus loved
15 What the disciples did over who of them was greatest
16 "Where no ___ are, the crib is clean" (Prov. 14:4)
17 The 7 churches from Revelation are here
18 Stringed instrument
19 "___ yourselves, and lament" (Joel 1:13)
20 Different beliefs about God
22 "For thy violence against thy brother Jacob ___ shall cover thee" (Obad. 1:10)
23 Bathroom
24 "Thou ___ greatly despised" (Obad. 1:2)
26 Hallucinogen
27 "Let your yea be yea; and your ___, ___" (James 5:12) (same wd.)
30 "___ nigh unto my soul" (Ps. 69:18)
33 Summer month (abbr.)
35 Opposite of ids
37 What the Pharisees were at times
42 Epic
43 Catholic sister
44 Golden calf
45 Eternity does this to life on earth
49 "As though hast ___, it shall be ___ unto thee" (Obad. 1:15) (same wd.)
50 African antelope
51 Harts from Song of Solomon
53 Kitten's cry
54 Hovercraft
57 What Eve did with the forbidden fruit
59 Where Cain dwelt (Gen. 4:16)
61 "Judah is a lion's ___" (Gen. 49:9)
63 Brings May flowers (2 wds.)
69 Card game
70 Inuit house
71 Mixed with myrrh for burial use (John 19:39)
72 Soviet Union
73 "City was pure gold, like unto ___ glass" (Rev. 21:18)
74 Greek cheese
75 "A little child shall ___ them" (Isa. 11:6)
76 Adam lived 130 of them
77 Russian ruler (var.)

DOWN

1 Open
2 "Whosoever will ___ his life for my sake (Matt. 16:25)
3 Daytime TV doc
4 What melts in Psalm 58:8
5 What shall come up on mount Zion (Obad. 1:21) (var.)
6 Peter, Paul, and Mary
7 Competition at the Greek games
8 OK city
9 "Hurt not the earth, neither the ___" (Rev. 7:3)
10 Artist van __
11 Longitudinal
12 Conditions
13 "The words of Job are ___" (Job 31:40)
21 "Thus saith the Lord ___ concerning Edom" (Obad. 1:1)
22 Wall support
25 What Elijah did to beat King Ahab's chariot

29 Flower holder
30 Phone connection (abbr.)
32 Capacity (abbr.)
35 "The ___ of Carmel shall wither" (Amos 1:2)
36 ___ chi
37 Mexican food brand
38 Amos needed to keep this up
39 Make again
40 Ocean Spray's drink starters
41 "I brought up Israel ___ of the land of Egypt" (Amos 9:7)
42 "I ___ no prophet" (Amos 7:14)
43 "They shall run to and ___" (Amos 8:12)
45 "The people of Syria shall go into captivity unto ___" (Amos 1:5)
46 Location of Mount Sinai (Gal. 4:25)
48 Amos's was male
49 Carve into
50 "Their words ___ to them as idle tales" (Luke 24:11)
52 "The ___ of Amos" (Amos 1:1)
56 "Was ___ with the soul of David" (1 Sam. 18:1)
57 "Let the wicked fall into their own ___" (Ps. 141:10)
58 "Learn to maintain good works for necessary ___" (Titus 3:14)
59 Direction from Israel to Egypt
60 "Was ___ in heaven" (Rev. 12:7)
61 Quebec "yes"
63 Globe
64 "Woe unto you that desire the ___ of the Lord!" (Amos 5:18)

54

Amos

by Vicki J. Kuyper

ACROSS

1 ___ whiz!
4 Rub clean
9 Winter toys
14 "Let judgment ___ down as waters" (Amos 5:24)
15 "Testify in the ___ of Jacob, saith the Lord" (Amos 3:13)
16 "He will take you away with ___" (Amos 4:2)
17 "Taken in adultery, in the very ___" (John 8:4)
18 Eight
19 Passageway
20 Scream like you saw a mouse
22 Church song
24 CEO (abbr.)
25 "O Lord God, forgive, I beseech ___" (Amos 7:2)
27 "Wait on the Lord, and he shall ___ thee" (Prov. 20:22)
31 "O thou ___, go" (Amos 7:12)
32 "Pour out the ___ of the wrath of God upon the earth" (Rev. 16:1)
33 What people were with God's laws in Amos
34 God's tiny creations
36 Covenant
38 U.S. Gulf States dweller
40 John the Baptist's camel hair clothes were this
42 "Judah is a lion's ___" (Gen. 49:9)
43 Amos was a "gatherer of sycomore ___" (Amos 7:14)
44 Amos tried to offer this to God's people
45 Weight measurement
47 Protection (Gr.) (var.)
51 God turns sin as white as this
53 "Threshed Gilead with threshing instruments of ___" (Amos 1:3)
54 DNA component
55 Gumbo ingredient
57 Refinement
59 "The Lord God hath ___ by his holiness" (Amos 4:2)
62 Indicates
65 "Isaac was old, and his eyes were ___" (Gen. 27:1)
66 ___ Arabia
67 How Israel felt about Amos's words
68 Joppa to Jerusalem dir.
69 Arm part
70 Metaphor for hell
71 ___ Sea

DOWN

1 Clasps
2 Card game
3 Main dish
4 God told Isaiah to "put off thy ___ from thy foot" (Isa. 20:2)
5 Crowed three times for Peter
6 Chariot wheel ditch
7 "___ hospitality" (1 Pet. 4:9)
8 "Prophesy not again any more at ___" (Amos 7:13)
9 Scheme
10 "I will bring up sackcloth upon all ___" (Amos 8:10)
11 VW model
12 Metric measure (abbr.)
13 Direction from Bethel to Jerusalem
21 "___ shall surely be led away captive" (Amos 7:11)
23 KJV "Yea"
25 "The prudent shall keep silence in that ___" (Amos 5:13)
26 KJV "hath"
28 "Say in all the highways, ___! ___!" (Amos 5:16) (same wd.)

29 Tortilla chip topping
30 Sackcloth partners
31 Canned meat brand
33 "The LORD will be the ____ of his people" (Joel 3:16)
35 Vent (2 wds.)
36 "The LORD also shall ___ out of Zion" (Joel 3:16)
37 Eye infection (var.)
39 "Thrice was I beaten with ___" (2 Cor. 11:25)
40 Pros opposites
42 Father of Joel (Joel 1:1)
45 "The ___ tree languisheth" (Joel 1:12)
46 Took part in Jesus' triumphant entry into Jerusalem
47 Spouse was pillar of salt
48 Mined metals
49 What sinners gnash
51 Courage
53 Mister (Ger.)
54 ____ Minor (Little Dipper)
56 "I ___ up your pure minds" (2 Pet. 3:1)
57 "The ___ of my redeemed is come" (Isa. 63:4)
59 "___ them about thy neck" (Prov. 6:20–21)
61 BB association
62 Physician (abbr.)

53

Joel

by Vicki J. Kuyper

• • • • • •

ACROSS

1 "The vats shall overflow with wine and ___" (Joel 2:24)
4 "___, ye ministers of the altar" (Joel 1:13)
8 Margarine
12 One (Sp.)
13 Familiar name for God
14 "God hath endued me with a good ___" (Gen. 30:20)
16 Frowning angrily
18 American state
20 Nabs
21 "____ yourselves, and lament" (Joel 1:13)
23 Abraham's was 175 when he died
24 "With his face toward the east ___" (Joel 2:20)
25 Not kosher meat
26 Army division
27 Same citation as previous
29 Exceed
32 "Wake up the mighty ___" (Joel 3:9)
33 "The day of the Lord is at ____" (Joel 1:15)
34 "Beat your. . .pruninghooks into ___" (Joel 3:10)
38 What army does at night
40 Vehicle familiar to Joel
41 Crouches
42 Psalm
43 Sunbeam
44 Causes hearing loss
46 "___ hath devoured the pastures" (Joel 1:19)
47 Cast to make a decision
50 That (possessive)
51 What Joel was to Pethuel (Joel 1:1)
52 Miner's goal
53 Mr. Downs of 20/20
55 Sucker
58 Seesaw
60 Swing
63 "Thou that art full of ___, a tumultuous city" (Isa. 22:2)
64 Black (poet.)
65 Killed in battle
66 Juno
67 "If any of you ___ wisdom, let him ask of God" (James 1:5)
68 "Do they not ___ that devise evil?" (Prov. 14:22)

DOWN

1 What God promised to do to the locust
2 Ancient Indian
3 Checks (2 wds.)
4 Onetime shampoo brand
5 Kimono sash
6 West by north
7 One who's late
8 Martha warned Jesus Lazarus's body had this
9 Jehovah
10 "The poor man had nothing, save one little ___ lamb" (2 Sam. 12:3)
11 "Rejoice at the sound of the ___" (Job 21:12)
15 Jellystone's bear
17 Unwanted plant (Jonah 2:5) (sing.)
19 "The kingdom of heaven is like unto a ___" (Matt. 13:47)
22 Pixie
25 European Nomads
26 Exploiter
27 Demons
28 "___ your plowshares into swords" (Joel 3:10)

22 God asked Hosea to ___ a harlot
25 Adios
26 "As an oven heated by the ___" (Hos. 7:4)
27 Direction from Jerusalem to Assyria
29 Socially superior
30 Nickname for Paul's "adopted" son
32 "Abominations were according as they ___" (Hos. 9:10)
33 "Openest" in KJV
34 Time at prime meridian
35 Speed measure in Europe
37 Government agency
39 Dynamite
42 Steal
43 Unpaired
47 Tirade
49 Hosea's wife
50 Tree
52 "I found Israel like ___ in the wilderness" (Hos. 9:10)
55 Records
57 Churches often have a center one
58 "To do ___ or more" (Num. 22:18)
59 Margarine
60 British brews
61 Plant life
62 Son of Zephaniah (Zech. 6:14)
63 "The king of Israel is come out to seek a ___" (1 Sam. 26:20)
64 Former Russian republic
65 "___ I strip her" (Hos. 2:3)
68 Day of the week (abbr.)

52

Hosea

by Vicki J. Kuyper

• • • • • •

ACROSS

1 Take
4 Indian dwelling
9 Contagious disease
12 Israel would do this to God's anger
14 Book by Homer
15 Block
16 Cabbage salad
17 Hosea's dad (Hos. 1:1)
18 "Let us return unto the Lord. . . he will ___ us" (Hos. 6:1)
19 Cardiovascular training sessions
21 Textured clothing
23 "They sacrifice flesh for the sacrifices of mine offerings, and ___ it" (Hos. 8:13)
24 "___ to yourselves in righteousness" (Hos. 10:12)
25 Tabitha was this when Peter saw her (Acts 9:40)
28 "___ the trumpet to thy mouth" (Hos. 8:1)
31 Scandinavian capital
34 Polish city
36 "Make them to ___ down safely" (Hos. 2:18)
38 Choose
40 Archangel's nickname
41 Gomer probably did this
43 "They have made ready their heart like an ___" (Hos. 7:6)
44 Golf equipment
45 "They are all ___ as an oven" (Hos. 7:7)
46 Pharisees were this in 48 Across
48 "The Pharisees began to ___ him vehemently" (Luke 11:53)
51 "The sluggard will not plow . . .therefore shall he ___ in harvest" (Prov. 20:4)
53 Totals
54 "The beauty of ___ men is the grey head" (Prov. 20:29)
56 "Peter. . .___ unto the sepulchre" (Luke 24:12)
58 Hosea's third child (Hos. 1:9)
61 What Gomer, and God's people, were not
66 She (Fr.)
67 "The Lord directeth his ___" (Prov. 16:9)
69 "The Lord he is God; there is none ___" (Deut. 4:35)
70 Another term for Hosea
71 Hand lotion brand
72 Loch ___ monster
73 What Hosea tried to issue to God's people
74 Good ___
75 "Thou ___ my people" (Hos. 2:23)

DOWN

1 Spaceship builders
2 "___. . .to raise up" (Matt. 3:9)
3 "As a ___ that is bereaved of her whelps" (Hos. 13:8)
4 Item in Ezekiel's Valley of Dry Bones
5 "I endure all things for the ___ sakes" (2 Tim. 2:10)
6 Popular American desserts
7 "Give ye ___, O house of the king" (Hos. 5:1)
8 Blue-pencils
9 "Whither shall I ___ from thy presence?" (Ps. 139:7)
10 Heavy burden
11 Not pretty
13 Number of Gomer's sons
15 A cow does this to its cud
20 "They howled upon their ___" (Hos. 7:14)

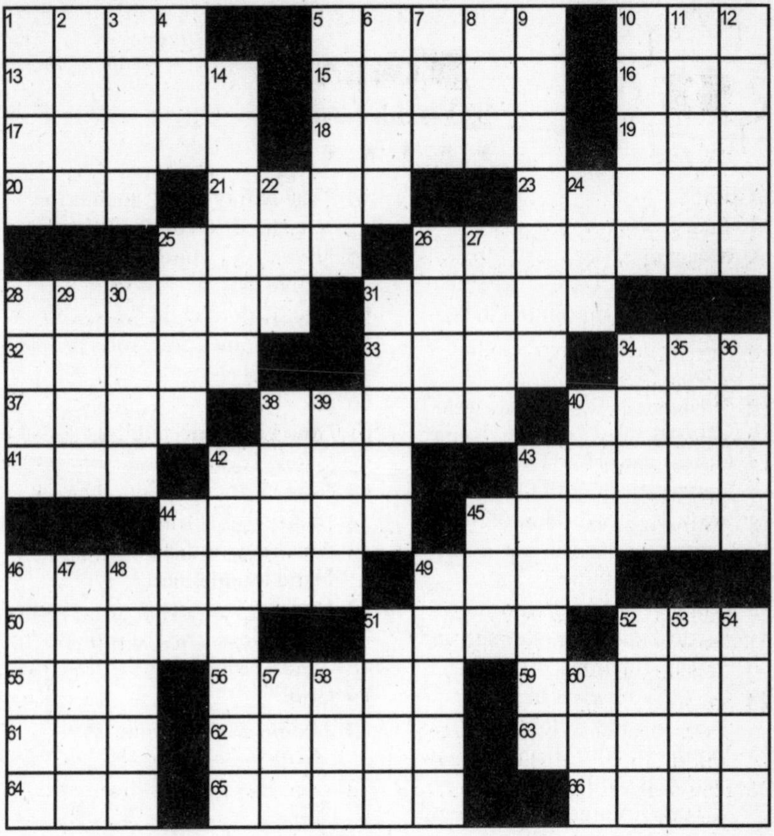

25 "No man shall ___ them away" (Deut. 28:26)
26 What Eve would do to the forbidden fruit
27 "I will ___ the writing unto the king" (Dan. 5:17)
28 Adam, Noah, and Abraham
29 European monetary unit
30 Ocean Spray's drink starters
31 Large cats
34 Father of biblical spy Gaddi (Num. 13:11)
35 Type of cheese
36 Shakespeare play: ___ *Well That Ends Well*
38 Call to worship king (Dan. 3:5)
39 Modern-day Persia
40 Astronomer, ___ Sagan
42 Bunkers
43 Fragrant wood
44 2,000 pounds
45 "Three times a ___, and prayed" (Dan. 6:10)
46 Antithesis of heaven
47 Mennonite neighbor
48 English sailor
49 Jonah's temporary home
51 Small bird
52 Dress
53 Fencing sword
54 Join metal
57 His wife turned to salt
58 "Darius. . .being about threescore and __" (Dan. 5:31)
60 "Is thy ___. . .able to deliver thee?" (Dan. 6:20)

51

DANIEL

by Vicki J. Kuyper

ACROSS
1 Type of palm in Sinai
5 What Daniel wanted the lions to do
10 Smaller than tbsp.
13 "___ yourselves unto God" (Rom. 6:13)
15 The kings of Daniel's day were this
16 Spring month (abbr.)
17 Swelling
18 "White ___ were given" (Rev. 6:11)
19 Hiss
20 Daniel's lions lived here
21 "Solomon made a ___ of ships" (1 Kings 9:26)
23 Spiral
25 "Four men loose, walking in the midst of the ___" (Dan. 3:25)
26 How Daniel's friends entered the furnace
28 "Hast made a ___" (Dan. 3:10)
31 "A ___ of new cloth" (Matt. 9:16)
32 Relating to the ear
33 Western state
34 Federal agency helping small businesses (abbr.)
37 Cart for hauling heavy things
38 Measured
40 Pick
41 "The fourth is like the ___ of God" (Dan. 3:25)
42 Where the king erected his statue (Dan. 3:1)
43 Swiss city
44 Canned meats
45 "Daniel prospered in the reign of ___" (Dan. 6:28)
46 Bromine
49 Where the hand wrote (Dan. 5:5)
50 Type of acid
51 Reasons
52 "A time to rend, and a time to ___" (Eccl. 3:7)
55 "Isaac was old, and his eyes were ___" (Gen. 27:1)
56 Radical
59 NT Greek word for love
61 Compass point
62 Shower need
63 Pitted mushroom
64 How Moses felt about speaking
65 What sealed the lions' den (Dan. 6:17)
66 Happened to Belshazzar the night he saw the hand (Dan. 5:30)

DOWN
1 "Cometh from Edom, with ___ garments" (Isa. 63:1)
2 Daniel was one of these to the king
3 Mary's life stage when she bore Jesus
4 Pagan incense was burned under this tree (Hos. 4:13)
5 "They ___ not thy gods" (Dan. 3:12)
6 Disgust with excess
7 Where Eve came from
8 What Daniel did with veggies
9 Mishael's Babylonian name (Dan. 1:7)
10 "They shall speak lies at one ___" (Dan. 11:27)
11 "Scatter among them the prey, and ___" (Dan. 11:24)
12 Fill-in
14 Hero of this book
22 "How mighty ___ his wonders!" (Dan. 4:3)
24 First woman

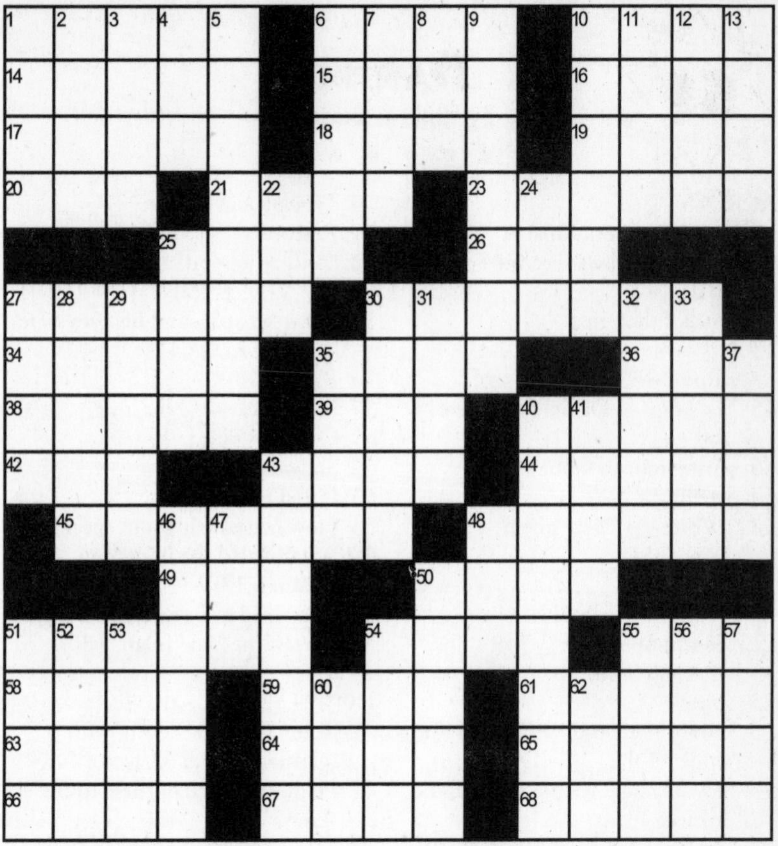

24 "Then Daniel. . .was astonied for ___ hour" (Dan. 4:19)
25 "This is the interpretation, O ___" (Dan. 4:24)
27 Pineapple brand
28 "After thee shall ___ another kingdom" (Dan. 2:39)
29 Girl detective
30 A la ___
31 The little horn of the beast had these (Dan.7:8)
32 Teacher
33 God's miracles do this
35 Glum
37 V.P.'s boss (abbr.)
40 Deny
41 "Play skilfully with a ___ noise" (Ps. 33:3)
43 Daniel's ability to interpret dreams was this
46 A way out
47 "Behold, one like the ___ of man" (Dan. 7:13)
48 Promissory note
50 How many times a day Daniel prayed (Dan. 6:10)
51 Baths
52 U.S. president
53 "By the river of ___" (Dan. 8:2)
54 "___ thy servants the dream" (Dan. 2:4)
55 Tree trunk
56 Little Mermaid's love
57 Division (abbr.)
60 By way of
62 Skin

50

Daniel

by Vicki J. Kuyper

ACROSS

1 Dardic language
6 "I was afraid, and fell upon my ___" (Dan. 8:17)
10 Mop
14 Fake chocolate
15 Actor Alda
16 "___ will I dwell; for I have desired it" (Ps. 132:14)
17 "I Daniel ___ saw the vision" (Dan. 10:7)
18 American state
19 Where Jonah was when on the ship
20 Number of days Daniel asked to eat veggies (Dan. 1:14)
21 "We have sinned, we have ___ wickedly" (Dan. 9:15)
23 "Thou shouldest bray a fool in a ___" (Prov. 27:22)
25 "Being ___ together in love" (Col. 2:2)
26 "How long shall it be to the ___ of these wonders?" (Dan. 12:6)
27 Dream interpreter
30 Small keyboard instrument
34 Great ape, for short
35 Ancient of ___
36 Sports official's nickname
38 Slang
39 Miner's goal
40 Lord's table
42 Abbr. for 100 Portuguese centavos
43 What Daniel needed to stand up to the king
44 Hooch
45 What Nebuchadnezzar was when afflicted
48 Habituates
49 "There is a ___ in heaven that revealeth secrets" (Dan. 2:28)
50 Moved with your foot
51 Scorns
54 Goliath
55 Where king dreamed
58 "Made a serpent of brass, and put it upon a ___" (Num. 21:9)
59 "O king, live for ___" (Dan. 2:4)
61 "It came to pass, ___ Isaiah was gone out" (2 Kings 20:4)
63 "___, ___ that great city Babylon" (Rev. 18:10) (same wd. both blanks)
64 Large African river turned to blood during plagues
65 Spring flower
66 Snow gliders
67 "The valley of Shaveh, which is the king's ___" (Gen. 14:17)
68 Build

DOWN

1 Beat it!
2 "___ thee to the judge" (Luke 12:58)
3 "It had great ___ teeth" (Dan. 7:7)
4 "___ his son, Jehoshuah his son" (1 Chron. 7:27)
5 Azariah's Babylonian name
6 What Daniel did after his vision of the ram (Dan. 8:27)
7 Lotion ingredient
8 Crow's cry
9 Metal paints
10 Broken pieces of pottery
11 First ram in Daniel's vision pushed this direction (Dan. 8:4)
12 Region
13 Second beast in Daniel's vision (Dan. 7:5)
22 "Thou anointest my head with ___" (Ps. 23:5)

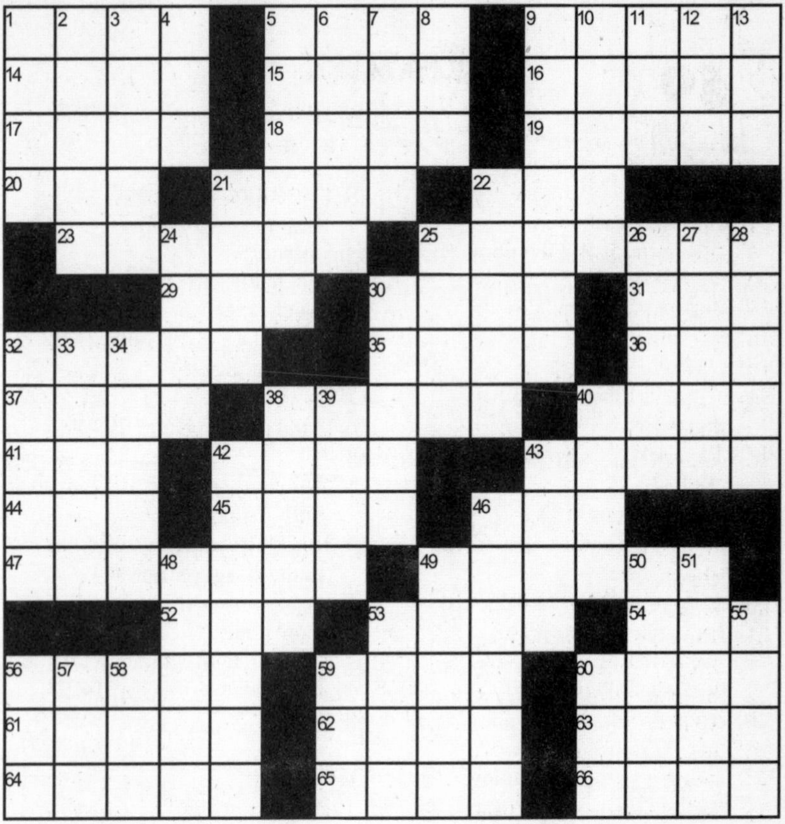

22 "Graven thee upon the ___ of my hands" (Isa. 49:16)
24 Christmas carol
25 ___ Sagan, astronomer
26 Pardon
27 Toothbrush brand
28 Live-in babysitter
30 "The ___ of hell gat hold upon me" (Ps. 116:3)
32 Something very small
33 Love intensely
34 Russian drink
38 "I spread my ___ over thee" (Ezek. 16:8)
39 Aaron is one to Moses
40 "___ me as the apple of the eye" (Ps. 17:8)
42 Disks
43 The king of Tyrus was covered in these (Ezek. 28:13)
46 "Full of wisdom, and perfect in ___" (Ezek. 28:12)
48 Jerusalem's "younger sister" (Ezek. 16:46)
49 Jeweled headdress
50 "A time to weep, and a time to ___" (Eccl. 3:4)
51 Spare
53 "Thy neck is an iron sinew, and thy ___ brass" (Isa. 48:4)
55 "Leah was tender ___" (Gen. 29:17)
56 College for doctors
57 Disapproval shout
58 Bullfight cheer
59 Kids' farming organization
60 Luke was this (abbr.)

49

Ezekiel

by Vicki J. Kuyper

• • • • • •

ACROSS
1 Soft mineral
5 Coastal university
9 "Ye shall have the passover, a ___ of seven days" (Ezek. 45:21)
14 Attention disorder
15 "I will ___ out my fury upon them" (Ezek. 20:8)
16 Color of fire in Ezekiel's 1st vision (Ezek. 1:27)
17 Superman's Ms. Lane
18 Thoughtfulness
19 Feisty
20 Wing
21 "Thou has despised mine ___ things" (Ezek. 22:8)
22 This symbolized an iron wall (Ezek. 4:3)
23 First covered dry bones (Ezek. 37:8)
25 "This city is the ___" (Ezek. 11:3)
29 "I have gathered them unto their ___ land" (Ezek. 39:28)
30 Satiate
31 Epoch
32 Expert
35 Dry bones become this (Ezek. 37:10)
36 God calls Ezekiel "Son of ___"
37 Anything worshipped falsely
38 Sailboat needs
40 Oven
41 Cain's home (Gen. 4:16)
42 Covered sinew on dry bones (Ezek. 37:8)
43 Manage (2 wds.)
44 Annoy
45 Hagar does this for Sarah, at first
46 "The Lord shall hiss for the fly. . . and for the ___" (Isa. 7:18)
47 Ezekiel did this to water before drinking (Ezek. 4:11)
49 God brought Ezekiel here via vision (Ezek. 41:1)
52 Fall mo.
53 Jews had this against Samaritans
54 Laid to tree roots in Luke 3:9
56 "He was a murderer from the beginning, and ___ not in the truth" (John 8:44)
59 German wife
60 Tax
61 The sky was the ___ of terrible crystal in Ezek. 1:22 (var.)
62 "He shall make a ___ against thee" (Ezek. 26:8)
63 Giant
64 Psalms
65 "The spirit lifted me up, and took me ___" (Ezek. 3:14)
66 African nation

DOWN
1 Ezekiel's gender
2 "Him that cometh according to the multitude of his ___" (Ezek. 14:4)
3 ___ con carne
4 Promos
5 North of downtown
6 "Living creatures. . .appearance was like burning ___ of fire" (Ezek. 1:13)
7 I Love ___
8 "Behold, thou ___ wiser than Daniel" (Ezek. 28:3)
9 ___ wounded
10 Make corrections to
11 Muscle group (abbr.)
12 "___ thine heart upon all that I shall shew thee" (Ezek. 40:4)
13 "Fire shall ___ every man's work" (1 Cor. 3:13)
21 "The four tables were of ___ stone" (Ezek. 40:42)

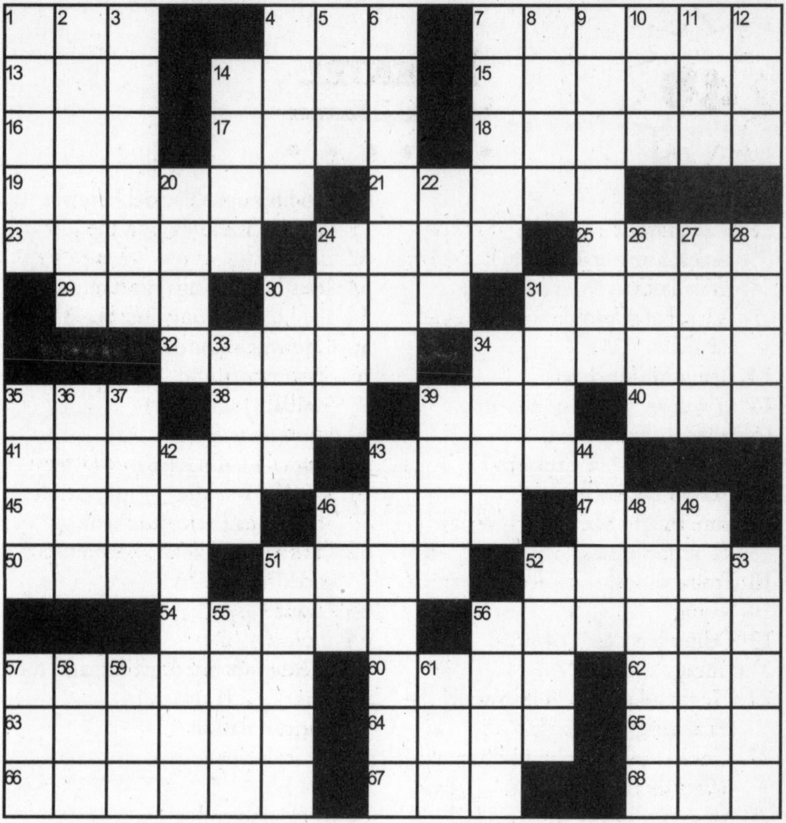

24 "The dead in Christ shall ___ first" (1 Thess. 4:16)
26 Spring flower
27 Loads
28 "I the LORD have brought down the high ___" (Ezek. 17:24)
30 Oils
31 When Ezekiel saw visions, he fell upon this
33 Ancient Germanic character
34 "All that have ___ and scales shall ye eat" (Deut. 14:9)
35 "They shall be ___ in their land" (Ezek. 34:27)
36 "There is but a ___ between me and death" (1 Sam. 20:3)
37 "Son of man, I send ___ to the children of Israel" (Ezek. 2:3)
39 God had Ezekiel do this with part of his hair (Ezek. 5:1–2)
42 Son of Buzi (Ezek. 1:3)
43 Noah saw much more than this
44 Visionary creatures had feet "like the ___ of a calf's foot" (Ezek. 1:7)
46 What God had Ezekiel do with a scroll
48 British noblemen
49 "Prophesy against the prophets of ___" (Ezek. 13:2)
51 Zacchaeus's stature
52 "To smite with the ___ of wickedness" (Isa. 58:4)
53 Rugged
55 Alley
56 Gasp
57 Stephen was stoned by this
58 Time period
59 Manager (abbr.)
61 Moray

48

EZEKIEL

by Vicki J. Kuyper

ACROSS

1 God forbade Ezekiel to do this when his wife died (Ezek. 24:16)
4 KJV "hath"
7 What neighbors thought Ezekiel was
13 Reduced, for short
14 "___ as a leaf" (Isa. 64:6)
15 Salt's companion
16 "___ this proverb in Israel" (Ezek. 18:3)
17 One face of Ezekiel's visionary creatures (Ezek 1:10)
18 Probable sound of dry bones rising
19 Duller
21 Guru
23 "These waters ___ out toward the east country" (Ezek. 47:8)
24 Ezekiel's prophecy said Pharaoh was like a cedar whose "___ was by great waters" (Ezek. 31:7)
25 Baseball glove
29 Alzheimer's casualty
30 "Take ___ from between the wheels" (Ezek. 10:6)
31 What God felt against people of Jerusalem
32 The feet of Ezekiel's visionary creatures sparkled like this (Ezek. 1:7)
34 One judgment against Jerusalem
35 Concorde, e.g.
38 Southwestern Indian
39 Pen brand
40 Direction from Tarshish to Jerusalem
41 Paul preached on Mars' hill in this city (Acts 17:22)
43 Sand hills
45 State of alarm (dial.)
46 Even a godly person does this
47 Kimono sash
50 Fencing sword
51 God "sendeth ___ on the just and on the unjust" (Matt. 5:45)
52 "Returned as the appearance of a ___ of lightning" (Ezek. 1:14)
54 Clumsy person
56 State capital
57 Medial
60 Jupiter
62 Abigail's Nabal was one (1 Sam. 25:25)
63 Traditional home to the Magi
64 Ezekiel spent 390 days on this side (Ezek. 4:4)
65 "I will spread my ___ upon him" (Ezek. 17:20)
66 Ezekiel's bread ingredient (Ezek. 4:9)
67 Sprite
68 Satan is this

DOWN

1 ___ Arabia
2 Preoccupy
3 Chicken serving
4 Ezekiel was pulled heavenward by this (Ezek. 8:3)
5 "Make ye this ___" (Mark 5:39)
6 Detectors
7 Small herring
8 Jesus' disciples were a spiritual one
9 Most favorable amount
10 Choose
11 Harden
12 "___ the lamp of God went out in the temple" (1 Sam. 3:3)
14 "My dearly beloved, ___ from idolatry" (1 Cor. 10:14)
20 God rendered Ezekiel this (Ezek. 3:26)
22 "Lamentations, and mourning, and ___" (Ezek. 2:10)

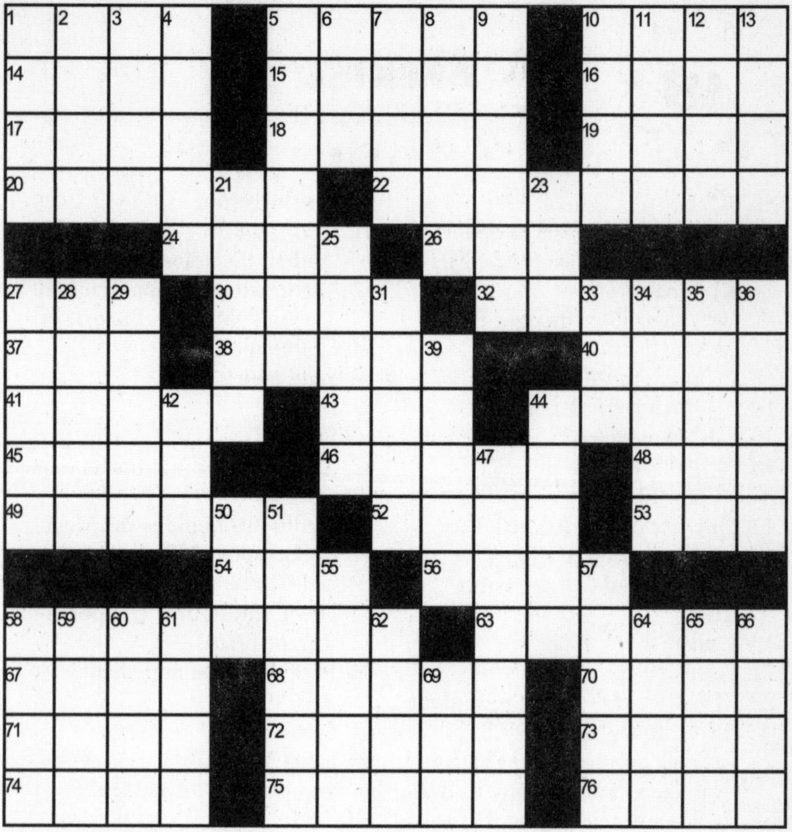

31 "___ our days" (Lam. 5:21)
33 Rie in KJV
34 A prophet does this with his garment
35 Desert pond
36 "Every day they ___ my words" (Ps. 56:5)
39 Potatoes pairing
42 "Mine ___ affecteth mine heart" (Lam. 3:51)
44 Chicken brand
47 Family rulers
50 "Let us lift up our heart with our hands unto ___" (Lam. 3:41)
51 What Jerusalem did to God's name
55 Neon fish
57 "He hath broken my ___" (Lam. 3:4)
58 River through France and Germany
59 "Be not ___ in thine own eyes" (Prov. 3:7)
60 Thought
61 "Thou drewest ___ in the day that I called upon thee" (Lam. 3:57)
62 "I AM the man that hath ___ affliction" (Lam. 3:1)
64 Idol recipient in Isa. 2:20
65 Where Paul was shipwrecked
66 "Mine ___ do fail with tears" (Lam. 2:11)
69 "It is good that a ___ should both hope and quietly wait for the salvation of the LORD" (Lam. 3:26)

47

Lamentations

by Vicki J. Kuyper

• • • • • •

ACROSS

1 "Thy brother is come; and thy father hath killed the fatted ___" (Luke 15:27)
5 Decree
10 Group of members (abbr.)
14 Open
15 Masculine
16 How Jeremiah felt delivering his prophecy
17 "I called upon thy ___, O Lord" (Lam. 3:55)
18 Thoughts
19 Hamburger rolls
20 Sell abroad
22 "Behold, O Lord, for I am in ___" (Lam. 1:20)
24 Jesus' apostles left these to follow
26 God's compassions are this (Lam. 3:22–23)
27 Part of body
30 "He was unto me as a ___ lying in wait" (Lam. 3:10)
32 "Behold my ___" (Lam. 1:18)
37 "A faithful witness will not ___" (Prov. 14:5)
38 The sword of the angel had two of these (Rev. 2:12)
40 Jesus' parents went to Jerusalem every ___ (Luke 2:41)
41 Delivered God's message to Mary
43 "Go to the ___" (Prov. 6:6)
44 How Jerusalem's people felt having heard this prophecy
45 "The Lord was my ___" (Ps. 18:18)
46 Run down
48 Insult (slang)
49 Mucus
52 "Let us search and try our ___" (Lam. 3:40)
53 Concorde, e.g.
54 Grain
56 Handle
58 What Jacob does to Esau
63 Describes Jerusalem's culture at this time
67 Military officer
68 Urim and Thummim
70 Curious
71 Afloat
72 "___ is thy faithfulness" (Lam. 3:23)
73 Women's magazine
74 "Go up, ___ an altar unto the Lord" (2 Sam. 24:18)
75 Rebekah had one (Gen. 24:59)
76 God does this in relation to everything

DOWN

1 "Thou hast brought me no sweet ___ with money" (Isa. 43:24)
2 Brand of surface cleaner
3 "Thy word is a ___ unto my feet" (Ps. 119:105)
4 Air-conditioning need
5 Gave off
6 Abraham was this to Isaac
7 Type of tea
8 "He hath made my ___ heavy" (Lam. 3:7)
9 Stirs up
10 To shorten, for short
11 Skid (var.)
12 Phoenix's BB team
13 Loch __ monster
21 What God's people did against Him
23 Number of the Sons of Thunder
25 Soap operas
27 Fix firmly
28 Galatians is this book in NT
29 George, plaster cast artist

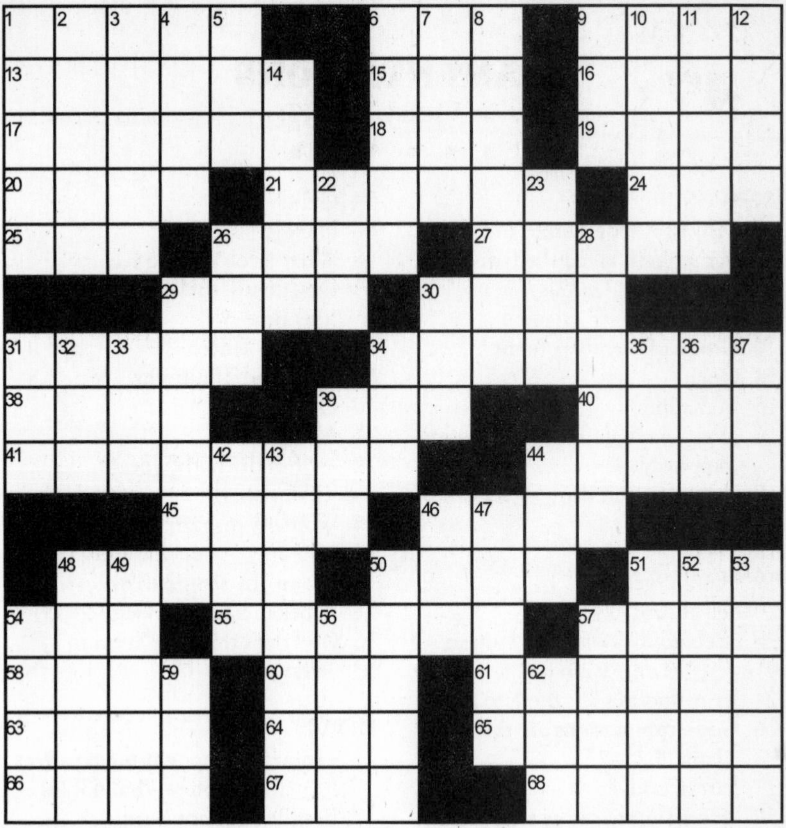

28 "The ___ tree shall flourish" (Eccl. 12:5)
29 Directionless
30 "No difference between the ___ and the Greek" (Rom. 10:12)
31 Muscles (abbr.)
32 Sandwich
33 "Let us search and try ___ ways, and turn again to the LORD" (Lam. 3:40)
34 Held perfume poured on Jesus' feet
35 No room for Jesus here
36 Whiz
37 "___ children are gone into captivity" (Lam. 1:5)
39 Downwind
42 "How doth the ___ sit solitary" (Lam. 1:1)
43 Sap (2 wds.)
44 Tax agency
46 "The young and the old ___ on the ground" (Lam. 2:21)
47 Type of mint
48 "Enemies have opened their ___ against thee" (Lam. 2:16)
49 Eagle's nest
50 What a dropped melon would do
51 "Jerusalem is as a menstruous ___ among them" (Lam. 1:17)
52 "Then Pashur ___ Jeremiah the prophet" (Jer. 20:2)
53 Got smaller, like a moon
54 "Thou ___ utterly rejected us" (Lam. 5:22)
56 "The ___ I be loved" (2 Cor. 12:15)
57 In ___
59 "He shall gather the lambs with his ___" (Is. 40:11)
62 British drink

46 LAMENTATIONS

by Vicki J. Kuyper

ACROSS
1 All of Jerusalem's are desolate (Lam. 1:4)
6 "The LORD hath cast off ___ altar" (Lam. 2:7)
9 Familiar name for God
13 Odors
15 Exit (abbr.)
16 "The ___ was as an enemy" (Lam. 2:5)
17 "From the daughter of Zion all her ___ is departed" (Lam. 1:6)
18 Boxer Muhammad
19 Palestine, e.g.
20 Young girl
21 Most uncommon
24 "Hide not thine ___ at my breathing" (Lam. 3:56)
25 Time zone
26 Am not
27 Splinter of glass
29 "He hath violently taken ___ his tabernacle" (Lam. 2:6)
30 Minor prophet
31 "His bow ___ in strength" (Gen. 49:24)
34 Probable author of book
38 What the blind man first saw when Jesus touched him (Mark 8:22–24)
39 "The ___ is no more" (Lam. 2:9)
40 "He that is perverse in his ways shall fall at ___" (Prov. 28:18)
41 More rigid
44 "By his Spirit in the ___ man" (Eph. 3:16)
45 "He burned against Jacob like a flaming ___" (Lam. 2:3)
46 Fat
48 Dull
50 "He will discover thy ___" (Lam. 4:22)
51 Direction from Israel to Egypt
54 Garden tool
55 Barked in pain
57 Cell body
58 Halo
60 Hair product
61 Earlier form of a word
63 "I ___ up your pure minds" (2 Pet. 3:1)
64 America
65 After Peter walked out of prison, "all the ___ of the children of Israel" were called together (Acts 5:21)
66 "The LORD is good unto ___ that wait for him" (Lam. 3:25)
67 Clock time
68 Pimpled

DOWN
1 Dormer
2 The South and Midwest
3 Browned bread
4 Flightless birds
5 "By the rivers of Babylon, there we ___ down" (Ps. 137:1)
6 "The joy of our ___ is ceased" (Lam. 5:15)
7 John wrote the book of Revelation on one
8 Cut with shears
9 ___ carte
10 Hole maker
11 "All her people sigh, they seek ___" (Lam. 1:11)
12 6th month (Jewish calendar)
14 Jesus was famous throughout this region (Matt. 4:24)
22 "No man hath seen God at ___ time" (1 John 4:12)
23 "Turn thou us unto ___, O LORD" (Lam. 5:21)
26 "My heart standeth in ___ of thy word" (Ps. 119:161)

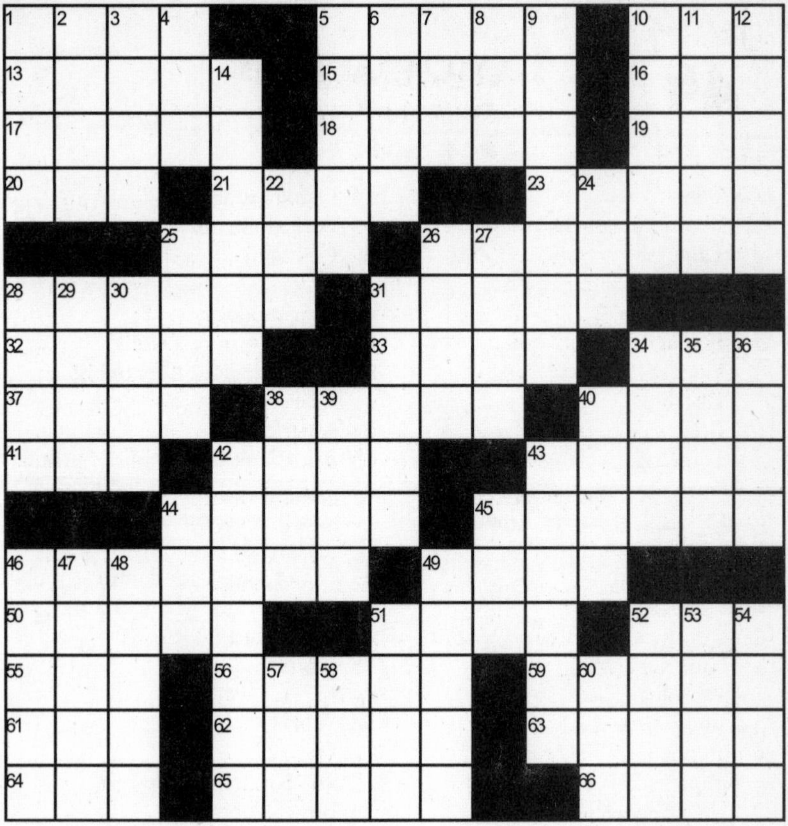

26 "___ thy people, the remnant of Israel" (Jer. 31:7)
27 "We are left but ___ ___of many" (Jer. 42:2) (2 wds.)
28 Good at crafts
29 "Jeremiah sunk in the ___" (Jer. 38:6)
30 Breastplate (var.)
31 "The heart of the wicked is little ___" (Prov. 10:20)
34 Judah burned incense to this god (Jer. 7:9)
35 Upon
36 "As far as the east is from the ___" (Ps. 103:12)
38 Ocean movement
39 "Oh that my ___ were waters" (Jer. 9:1)
40 Wine bottle cap
42 "Riches and honour are with me; yea, ___ riches and righteousness" (Prov. 8:18)
43 Pacific Ocean discoverer
44 What Mary may have carried ointment in (John 12:3)
45 Brother of Shem and Japheth (Gen. 5:32)
46 What the flood would do after 150 days (Gen. 8:3)
47 Slang for man
48 Build an altar, e.g.
49 "I will bring the ___ of the heathen" (Ezek. 7:24)
51 "My soul shall ___ in secret places" (Jer. 13:17)
52 Buckeye State
53 "Shall ___ no evil thing" (Eccl. 8:5)
54 "The Lord is the ___ God" (Jer. 10:10)
57 Scrap
58 Arctic condition
60 Discs

45

Jeremiah

by Vicki J. Kuyper

ACROSS

1 Financial whiz (abbr.)
5 "Behold, I cannot speak: for I am a ___" (Jer. 1:6)
10 Muscle group (abbr.)
13 What lay between Abraham's bosom and the rich man in Luke 16:26
15 Creepy
16 ___ whiz!
17 God created this on the sixth day
18 Fish basket
19 "Their widows ___ increased to me above the sand of the seas" (Jer. 15:8)
20 Jerusalem to Jeremiah's hometown dir. (Jer. 1:1)
21 "Cut off thine ___" (Jer. 7:29)
23 Colder
25 "___ unto me" (Jer. 33:3)
26 Pundits, e.g., Huldah, Nathan, and Agabus
28 Famous female pilot Earhart
31 Used by some churches for communion
32 Severity
33 "Set watchmen ___" (Jer. 6:17)
34 "They bend their tongues like their ___ for lies" (Jer. 9:3)
37 Stumble
38 "All Israel. . .___ down the high places" (2 Chron. 31:1)
40 "Thou hast bought me no sweet ___ with money" (Isa. 43:24)
41 "___ verily, their sound went into all the earth" (Rom. 10:18)
42 "A Continual ___ given him of the king of Babylon" (Jer. 52:34)
43 "___ from Tiberias" (John 6:23)
44 Israel's "treacherous sister" (Jer. 3:7)
45 "Thou hast played the ___ with many lovers" (Jer. 3:1)
46 Jeremiah's listeners were this (Jer. 5:22) (var.)
49 "___ therein, and ye shall find rest for your souls" (Jer. 6:16)
50 Baseball player Yogi
51 "Before thou camest forth out of the ___ I sanctified thee" (Jer. 1:5)
52 "As ___ as ye drink" (1 Cor. 11:25)
55 Brew
56 "The best of them is as a ___" (Mic. 7:4)
59 Iron ore used as pigment
61 What God gives
62 Shoe fasteners
63 Adios
64 "Thy words were found, and I did ___ them" (Jer. 15:16)
65 "Brought us up out of the land of ___" (Jer. 2:6)
66 "The dove found no rest for the ___ of her foot" (Gen. 8:9)

DOWN

1 What God does over His children's sorrow
2 Where Jeremiah's beard grew
3 Garment Elijah threw on Elisha (1 Kings 19:19)
4 Baking measure (abbr.)
5 ___ B. DeMille, movie director
6 German husband
7 Sin stirs this in God
8 "We ___ down in our shame" (Jer. 3:25)
9 "I am with thee, saith the Lord, to ___ thee" (Jer. 1:19)
10 "Return ___ to me" (Jer. 3:1)
11 Flat hat
12 People like Jeremiah
14 Angora hair fabric
22 Wing
24 Cab
25 Sound of camel hoof drop

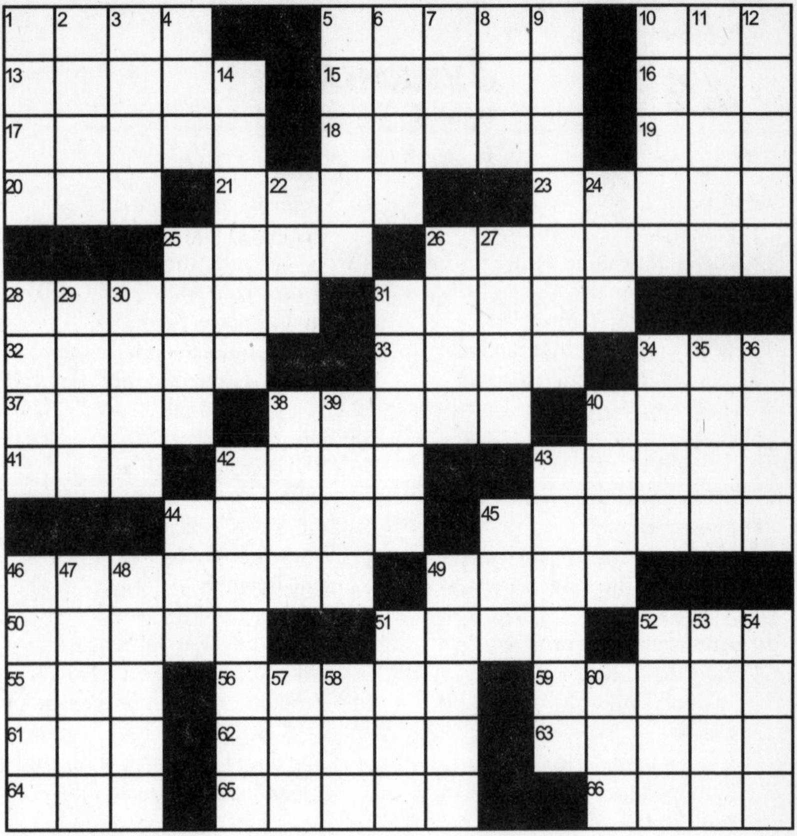

25 Cogged wheel
26 "There is but a ___ between me and death" (1 Sam. 20:3)
27 Tyre
28 Fifth book in NT
29 Podium
30 "They ___ up Jeremiah with cords" (Jer. 38:13)
31 "My people hath been lost ___" (Jer. 50:6)
34 List of meals
35 Back talk
36 "I see a rod of an almond ___" (Jer. 1:11)
38 Cut open
39 "To seek and to save that which was ___" (Luke 19:10)
40 "My people have forgotten me ___ without number" (Jer. 2:32)
42 Unraveling
43 Black and white bird
44 Tulsa time zone
45 Intelligence gatherer
46 Apostle's Creed
47 Relating to hearing
48 "Who is that shepherd that will ___ before me?" (Jer. 49:19)
49 "The ___ of the battle was against him" (2 Sam. 10:9)
51 Horse command
52 Fiddled while Rome burned
53 "No ___ in Gilead" (Jer. 8:22)
54 "God; there is none ___ beside him" (Deut. 4:35)
57 Tinge
58 Option (abbr.)
60 Audio recording

44

JEREMIAH

by Vicki J. Kuyper

ACROSS

1 Reverberate

5 Sound from 17 Across

10 "The heart is deceitful above ___ things" (Jer. 17:9)

13 "Can a maid forget her ornaments, or a ___ her attire?" (Jer. 2:32)

15 Onetime shampoo brand

16 Toilet

17 "As a cage is full of ___" (Jer. 5:27)

18 ___ of Chittim (Jer. 2:10)

19 Gedaliah's job (Jer. 40:7) (abbr.)

20 Compass point

21 Isn't able to

23 "In ___ days the house of Judah shall walk with the house of Israel" (Jer. 3:18)

25 "Hath a nation changed their ___, which are yet no ___?" (Jer. 2:11) (same wd. both blanks)

26 "My tabernacle is ___" (Jer. 10:20)

28 Common name for cockatrices (Jer. 8:17)

31 Jesus calmed one with words

32 Weight unit

33 "She is hardened against her young ones, as though they were not ___" (Job 39:16)

34 Boulder time zone

37 Step

38 Adam did this as God made Eve

40 "Be ye therefore followers of God, as ___ children" (Eph. 5:1)

41 Jerusalem to Egypt dir.

42 Ice sheet

43 Parsonage

44 New bill is this

45 Pony

46 Mary ____, artist

49 Good and bad fruit in Jeremiah's vision

50 Bumpy [road]

51 "So they ___ it up" (Mic. 7:3)

52 Bethlehem to Jerusalem dir.

55 Time period

56 Gem State

59 Perfect

61 One of twelve tribes

62 Synthetic fiber

63 Dukes

64 "Ask for the ___ paths. . .and walk therein" (Jer. 6:16)

65 Access (2 wds.)

66 Bible, e.g.

DOWN

1 A tide does this

2 Jesus' ____ was a manger

3 "Call the labourers, and give them their ___" (Matt. 20:8)

4 God's prophets are often considered this

5 Lower parts of faces

6 "Take the girdle that thou ___ got" (Jer. 13:4)

7 Annex

8 Athens to Jerusalem dir.

9 "The ___ are become brutish, and have not sought the LORD" (Jer. 10:21)

10 Double star

11 "Behold, I ___ thee this day from the chains which were upon thine hand" (Jer. 40:4)

12 "I have ___ thee with an everlasting love" (Jer. 31:3)

14 Accompany

22 Billboards

24 "The nations shall bless themselves in ___" (Jer. 4:2)

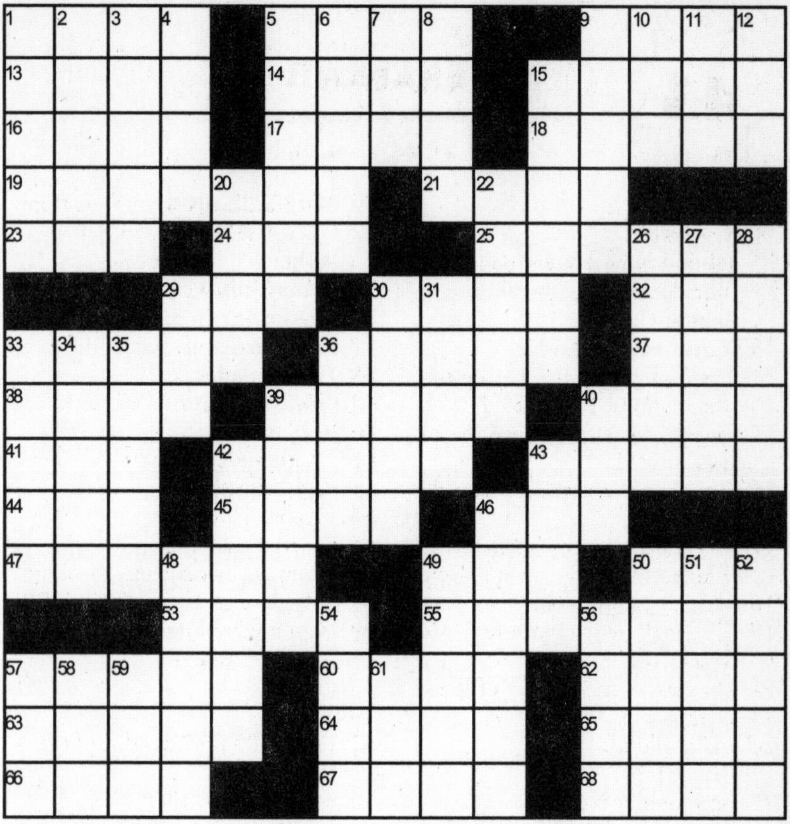

28 "The whole ___ is full of his glory" (Isa. 6:3)
29 "Bored a hole in the ___ of it" (2 Kings 12:9)
30 God's people weren't allowed to eat an animal that does this to a cud
31 God will "gently ___ those that are with young" (Isa. 40:11)
33 Growing older
34 Prima ___
35 "Thy ___ is thine husband; the LORD of hosts" (Isa. 54:5)
36 Dog breed
39 Those who do this need forgiveness
40 He had loaves and fishes (John 6:9)
42 "I ___ new heavens" (Isa. 65:17)
43 Pooch
46 The Savior would have "no ___ that we should desire him" (Isa. 53:2)
48 "In the garden. . .to ___ it" (Gen. 2:15)
49 Jacob tricked Isaac with these from a goat (Gen. 27:16)
50 Describes Eglon (Judg. 3:17)
51 Airplane parts
52 Spore plants
54 "By the way that he came, by the ___ shall he return" (Isa. 37:34)
56 First murder victim
57 "I will break also the ___ of Damascus" (Amos 1:5)
58 "___ the lamp of God went out in the temple" (1 Sam. 3:3)
59 Do this to "your heart, and not your garments" (Joel 2:13)
61 FBI cohort

43

Isaiah

by Vicki J. Kuyper

ACROSS

1 Knocks
5 Used to prepare Jesus' body for burial (John 19:39–40)
9 Assistant
13 Canal
14 "He hath sent me to ___ up the brokenhearted" (Isa. 61:1)
15 The churches mentioned in Rev. were this
16 "Shall ___ his name Immanuel" (Isa. 7:14)
17 Paul calls himself this in Philem. 1:9
18 "Arise, ___" (Isa. 60:1)
19 "The idols he shall utterly ___" (Isa. 2:18)
21 The feast of the nativity of Jesus
23 Oregon time
24 "As a wild bull in a ___" (Isa. 51:20)
25 Bun topping seed
29 Hallucinogenic drug
30 Indication
32 Constrictor snake
33 What we must do when we sin
36 The kind of sacrifice David refused to offer (2 Sam. 24:24)
37 "They have not known ___ understood" (Isa. 44:18)
38 "With an ox ___" (Judg. 3:31)
39 Wale
40 Fasting season
41 Jeremiah recorded his prophecies with this (Jer. 36:18)
42 What Jesus met when he entered Jerusalem (Matt. 21:8)
43 Swamp
44 Judah to Assyria dir.
45 "Thy cheeks are comely with ___ of jewels" (Song 1:10)
46 "Israel shall blossom and ___" (Isa. 27:6)
47 "Like a watered ___" (Isa. 58:11)
49 Ferret
50 "God will wipe away tears from ___ all faces" (Isa. 25:8)
53 "Filthy ___" (Isa. 64:6)
55 What God's words were to Ezekiel (Ezek. 3:3)
57 Francophile cap
60 Freedom assoc.
62 "He shall ___ their iniquities" (Isa. 53:11)
63 "With my dead body shall they ___" (Isa. 26:19)
64 Baseball glove
65 Sports channel
66 Company salespeople, for short
67 "My yoke is ___" (Matt. 11:30)
68 "Counted to him ___ than nothing" (Isa. 40:17)

DOWN

1 Psalm 106 provides this of the Exodus
2 Mideastern dwellers
3 Homophone for Pilate
4 "Jacob said, ___ me this day thy birthright" (Gen. 25:31)
5 "How to be ___" (Phil. 4:12)
6 "Let us walk in the ___ of the Lord" (Isa. 2:5)
7 "___ cried unto another, and said, Holy, holy, holy" (Isa. 6:3)
8 Swirl
9 God trades beauty for this (Isa. 61:3)
10 Roman three
11 One of twelve tribes
12 Jerusalem to Babylon dir.
15 During a great storm, Jesus was ___ (Matt. 8:24)
20 Association (abbr.)
22 Life did not go on as this during the exile
26 Cousin of Saul, commander of Israel's armies (1 Sam. 14:50)
27 "Your new ___ and your appointed feasts" (Isa. 1:14)

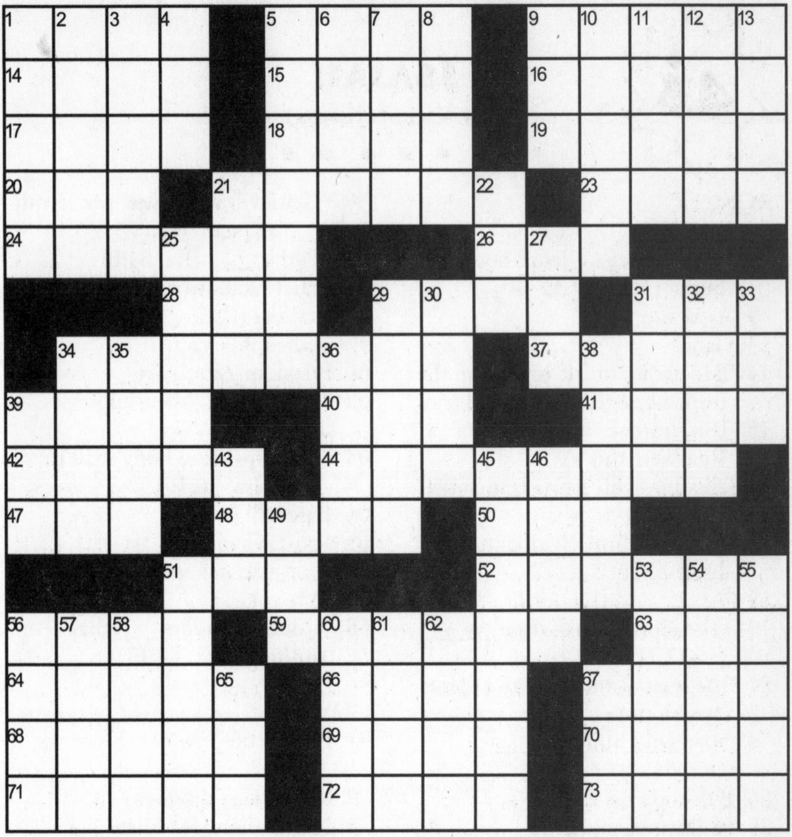

29 "Seek ye the LORD while he may be ___" (Isa. 55:6)
30 "They shall beat their swords ___ plowshares" (Isa. 2:4)
31 Skin lesion
32 "___ yourselves, and wonder" (Isa. 29:9)
33 "___ hast thou made us to err from thy ways" (Isa. 63:17)
34 "Come unto me: hear, and your ___ shall live" (Isa. 55:3)
35 Knitting stitch
36 Dunking cookie
38 An atheist says God doesn't do this
39 Agricultural financial org.
43 Pride
45 An atheist does this with God's Word
46 "The ___ shall be confounded" (Isa. 24:23)
49 Sphere
51 The lions Daniel faced were this
53 Hezekiah believed his was perfect (Isa. 38:3)
54 Jargon
55 Sloppy
56 Type of fish
57 ___ mater
58 "I will pour my spirit upon thy ___" (Isa. 44:3)
60 "Many of them also which used curious ___" (Acts 19:19)
61 "___ unto me, and be ye saved" (Isa. 45:22)
62 Decorative needle case
65 "Search me, O God. . .___ me" (Ps. 139:23)
67 Resort hotel

42

ISAIAH

by Vicki J. Kuyper

• • • • • •

ACROSS

1 Isaiah was a real person, e.g.
5 An ungodly person ___ up evil (Prov. 16:27)
9 Admonishes
14 Evils
15 Volcano
16 God's people do this for Jesus' return
17 "Shall ___ their hands" (Isa. 55:12)
18 New wine in old wineskins will do this (Matt. 9:17)
19 "They seek me ___, and delight to know my ways" (Isa. 58:2)
20 Pomegranates were around this on the priest's robe (Ex. 28:33)
21 Simpleton
23 "Unto me every ___ shall bow" (Isa. 45:23)
24 Disconnect from the socket
26 "Stand in ___" (Ps. 4:4)
28 What was left of Sodom
29 "When thou walkest through the ___" (Isa. 43:2)
31 Babylon to Jerusalem dir.
34 Tobacco chew destination
37 Hezekiah wanted God to spare him from this (Isa. 38:1–5)
39 Number of kings Isaiah prophesied under (Isa. 1:1)
40 Elijah dug this around the altar (1 Kings 18:32)
41 Doctor's picture
42 "Ye shall leave your name for a ___ unto my chosen" (Isa. 65:15)
44 Vastness
47 "The LORD hath laid on him the iniquity of us ___" (Isa. 53:6)
48 "The feet of him that bringeth ___ tidings" (Isa. 52:7)
50 VW car model
51 "___ ye shall be as an oak whose leaf fadeth" (Isa. 1:30)
52 King that Isaiah prophesied under (Isa. 1:1)
56 "The ___ against the honourable" (Isa. 3:5)
59 Whalebone
63 "The nobleman saith unto him, Sir, come down ___ my child die" (John 4:49)
64 Trumpet blast can do this (Ezek. 33:3)
66 Military division
67 A person's spirit often does this after hearing a prophet's words
68 Wipe
69 Isaiah does this with God's name
70 Not cons
71 "Wherefore look ye so ___ to day?" (Gen. 40:7)
72 Foot sleds
73 Lawyer (abbr.)

DOWN

1 Sheer, triangular scarf
2 Ethan ___, furniture brand
3 Holding device
4 Three make a tablespoon (abbr.)
5 "Then shalt thou ___ thyself in the LORD" (Isa. 58:14)
6 A temple candlestick, bowl, or lamp, e.g.
7 "They ___ not the bones till the morrow" (Zeph. 3:3)
8 Rice wine (var.)
9 Compact bundle
10 "___ and sing, ye that dwell in dust" (Isa. 26:19)
11 "I will also command the clouds that they ___ no ___" (Isa. 5:6) (same wd. both blanks)
12 River Moses' basket floated in
13 Eye infection (var.)
21 "Thy speech shall whisper out of the ___" (Isa. 29:4)
22 Sticky black substance
25 Dens
27 Esther and King Xerxes did this

24 "The wise took ___ in their vessels with their lamps" (Matt. 25:4)
25 Competition at the Greek games
27 What the seraphim did in Isaiah
28 Tag
29 King Solomon's was a palace
30 "I have ___ my honeycomb with my honey" (Song 5:1)
31 Bearing
32 Accepted practice
33 Bat GPS
35 What an angel supposedly wears
37 "From the lions' ___" (Song 4:8)
41 Loathe (var.)
43 Twisted
46 Illegal
47 Alcoholic beverage
48 "They all hold swords, being expert in ___" (Song 3:8)
50 Frequently
51 "To the ___ of spices" (Song 6:2)
52 Plant in the Bridegroom's garden
53 Church part
54 "They had ___ ___ small fishes: and he blessed" (Mark 8:7) (2 wds.)
55 Vinegary
56 Butter used in soap and candles
57 Mister (Ger.)
60 Government agency
62 "He casteth forth his ___ like morsels" (Ps. 147:17)

41 SONG OF SOLOMON

by Vicki J. Kuyper

ACROSS

1 Island Paul was shipwrecked on
6 "Lo, the winter is past, the ___ is over and gone" (Song 2:11)
10 Yarmulkes
14 In conflict with
15 Shaft
16 Opera solo
17 "Thy ___ is like a round goblet" (Song 7:2)
18 What God views sin as
19 "The angel Gabriel was ___ from God" (Luke 1:26)
20 "Sir, come down ___ my child die" (John 4:49)
21 The Bridegroom's are like doves by rivers of waters (Song 5:12)
23 Senility
25 Against (var.)
26 "Our rafters of ___" (Song 1:17)
27 Pitcher that brought comfort to Bridegroom (Song 2:5)
30 Eager to imitate
34 What Mary goes through giving birth to Jesus
35 "___, King of the Jews!" (John 19:3)
36 "The other holy offerings ___ they in pots" (2 Chron. 35:13)
38 "Horns of ivory and ___" (Ezek. 27:15)
39 "I took the little book out of the angel's hand, and ___ it up" (Rev. 10:10)
40 Level off
42 What brides and bridegrooms do
43 Dale
44 Boston airport
45 Tower that looks toward Damascus (Song 7:4)
48 "Many ___ cannot quench love" (Song 8:7)
49 ___ mode
50 "Swear not, neither by heaven. . . neither by any other ___" (James 5:12)
51 "His ___ over me was love" (Song 2:4)
54 Hairstyle
55 "He planteth an ___, and the rain doth nourish it" (Isa. 44:14)
58 Ardor
59 "His ___ hand is under my head" (Song 2:6)
61 Cleft in rock where dove hides
63 "Open to me, my sister, my love, my ___" (Song 5:2)
64 Fencing sword
65 Colder
66 "If ye had faith as a grain of mustard ___" (Luke 17:6)
67 "Until the day ___" (2 Peter 1:19)
68 "We will inclose her with boards of ___" (Song 8:9)

DOWN

1 Horse hair
2 "Thou understandest my thought ___ off" (Ps. 139:2)
3 Theme of Song of Solomon
4 Second day of work week (abbr.)
5 What Song of Solomon is often viewed as
6 "Black as a ___" (Song 5:11)
7 Center of rotation
8 How Maiden feels when not with her love
9 "One thing is ___" (Luke 10:42)
10 Cuban leader
11 Palestine, e.g.
12 ___ pong
13 Fill
22 Yang's partner

28 What Lazarus did before Jesus arrived
30 What disciples do as Jesus prays
31 "Breasts are like two young roes that are ___" (Song 7:3)
33 Minor prophet
34 Harts and hinds
35 "The waters were risen, waters to ___ in" (Ezek. 47:5)
36 What a little kid wants
37 The apostles hope Jesus ___ their faith (Luke 17:5)
39 "The time of the singing of ___ is come" (Song 2:12)
41 "___ . . .evil" (Rom. 12:9)
42 "My beloved is like a ___ or a young hart" (Song 2:9)
45 Vase
47 Ice crystals falling
50 "A bishop then must be. . .given," ___ to teach" (1 Tim. 3:2)
52 Big cigarette
53 "He brought me to the banqueting ___" (Song 2:4)
55 The Maiden is as black as the tents of ___ (Song 1:5)
56 Wear away
57 What the goat skin on Jacob's arm did to Isaac's judgment
58 Water carrier
60 Small fry (var.)
61 Luge
63 "___ skilfully with a loud noise" (Ps. 33:3)
65 "Thy belly is like a heap of wheat ___ about with lilies" (Song 7:2)
67 "Passed through the Red sea as by ___ land" (Heb. 11:29)

40 Song of Solomon

by Vicki J. Kuyper

• • • • • •

ACROSS

1 Where a flock is kept (2 Chron. 32:28)
5 One of baby's first words
10 Pros
14 "___ to me, my sister, my love" (Song 5:2)
15 What the Maiden did through the lattice
16 The Maiden without the Bridegroom
17 What the Maiden and Bridegroom struggle to do
18 "Let us ___ __ early to the vineyards" (Song 7:12) (2 wds.)
19 Cologne (Ger.)
20 "The ___ of the house, the inner doors" (2 Chron. 4:22)
22 Damply
24 Cask
25 "Thy teeth are like a flock of ___" (Song 4:2)
27 Listens
29 Concerning
32 What David did before shooting his slingshot
35 "Then did they ___ in his face, and buffeted him" (Matt. 26:67)
38 God delivered David from the ___ of a lion (1 Sam. 17:37)
39 Gentle wind
40 What the Bridegroom did with the Maiden's heart
41 Pain reliever
43 Be
44 Evil spirits
46 "Stir not up, ___ awake my love, until he please" (Song 8:4)
47 The Magi followed this
48 The Bridegroom's lips smell like this (Song 5:13)
49 Automobile
51 Cain's eldest son
54 What God did to create the world
57 Resort hotel
59 Public upheavals
62 Pest
64 "I would ___ thee" (Song 8:1)
66 Association
68 Golden calf
69 Dueling sword
70 Questioner
71 Nothing
72 "The children shall tremble from the ___" (Hos. 11:10)
73 Full of swamp grass
74 Color (var.)

DOWN

1 "Rise up, my love, my fair one, and ___ away" (Song 2:10)
2 Starts
3 Every one of the Maiden's has a twin
4 "I will cause the enemy to ___ thee well" (Jer. 15:11)
5 Chinese seasoning
6 God's grace offers us the chance to begin ___
7 "The ___ that is in thy brother's eye" (Matt. 7:3)
8 "His ___ is most sweet: yea, he is altogether lovely" (Song 5:16)
9 The Maiden's nose smells like one (Song 7:8)
10 "___, and ye shall receive" (John 16:24)
11 What Rebekah does to help deceive Isaac (2 wds.)
12 Women's magazine
13 Canticle (Ps. 149:1)
21 Japanese money
23 What the Maiden did for the Bridegroom
26 Coke's competitor

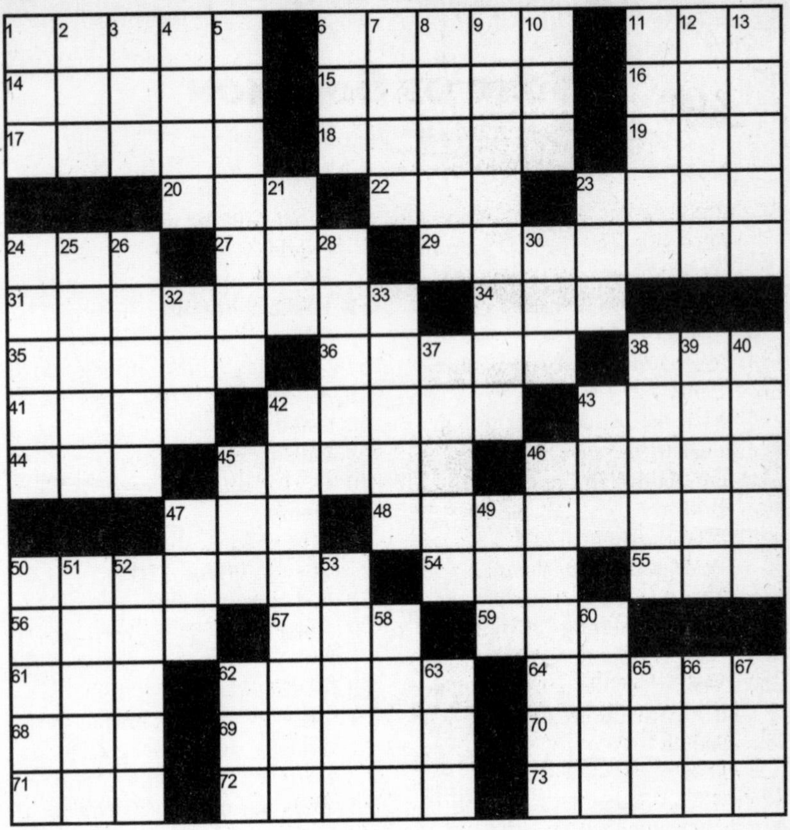

28 "Asked what these things ___" (Luke 15:26)
30 "Wise man's eyes are in ___ head" (Eccl. 2:14)
32 Adam lost this to Eve
33 Rehoboam's father ___ Ecclesiastes
37 "Fill his skin with barbed ___" (Job 41:7)
38 Relationship
39 Correct
40 Bound
42 Cabbage-like veggie
43 Football group
45 "Misery of ___ is great upon him" (Eccl. 8:6)
46 Gulf-like
47 Jesse was David's ___
49 "___ things are full of labour" (Eccl. 1:8)
50 "Seeing that ___ now is" (Eccl. 2:16)
51 David did ___ Saul (1 Sam. 18:7)
52 Littered
53 Warble
58 "Who ___ can hasten hereunto" (Eccl. 2:25)
60 Nineteenth century art philosophy
62 "Men shall ___ themselves" (Eccl. 12:3)
63 "___, of the Gentiles also" (Rom. 3:29)
65 "In the ___ of it" (2 Kings 12:9)
66 Ball holder
67 "I saw under the ___" (Eccl. 3:16)

39

ECCLESIASTES

by Sarah Lagerquist Simmons

ACROSS

1 Son of promise
6 "They have laid Jerusalem on ___" (Ps. 79:1)
11 Compass point
14 Opp. of macro
15 Aggressive
16 End of an ___
17 Clean feathers
18 Cop car topper
19 Tap
20 Disease fighting group
22 "Yet the ___ is not full" (Eccl. 1:7)
23 "I ___ my heart to know wisdom" (Eccl. 1:17)
24 "He that feareth __ shall come forth" (Eccl. 7:18)
27 "Be thou their ___ every morning" (Isa. 33:2)
29 The upper ___
31 Hebrews gives an ___ of Old Testament faith (Heb. 11)
34 "What shall be after ___?" (Eccl. 3:22)
35 Synthetic fabric
36 Sign of the zodiac
38 God's name is ___ (Ps. 111:9) (abbr.)
41 Fluent
42 Seasoner makers
43 "His ___ shall be covered with darkness" (Eccl. 6:4)
44 Time zone
45 Expression
46 "Thou shalt find it ___ many days" (Eccl. 11:1)
47 Telegraphic signal
48 Endowing
50 Proverbs 31 discusses ___ virtues
54 Satan is ___
55 Miriam sang an ___ (Ex. 15:21)
56 Joseph's coat was many ___ garment
57 "As a ___ from the hand of the hunter" (Prov. 6:5)
59 Drug
61 "Which groweth of ___ own accord" (Lev. 25:5)
62 Poorly
64 Adds flavoring
68 Discs
69 Eglon was ___ (Judg. 3:17)
70 Bye
71 Heavy freight barge
72 "They vex you with their ___" (Num. 25:18)
73 "A people ___ with iniquity" (Isa. 1:4)

DOWN

1 Rascal
2 "I go, ___" (Matt. 21:30)
3 David was a slingshot ___
4 Promised land is a small ___
5 Sunken
6 God ___ forgiven our sin
7 Aegis (var.)
8 "So did their witness ___" (Mark 14:59)
9 "I the ___ was king over Israel" (Eccl. 1:12)
10 "When thy king is the ___ of nobles" (Eccl. 10:17)
11 Forms flower calyx
12 Well done
13 "I have ___ my honeycomb" (Song 5:1)
21 Hindu title of respect
23 Pearl of great price
24 Stuff
25 Squashed circles
26 Resign

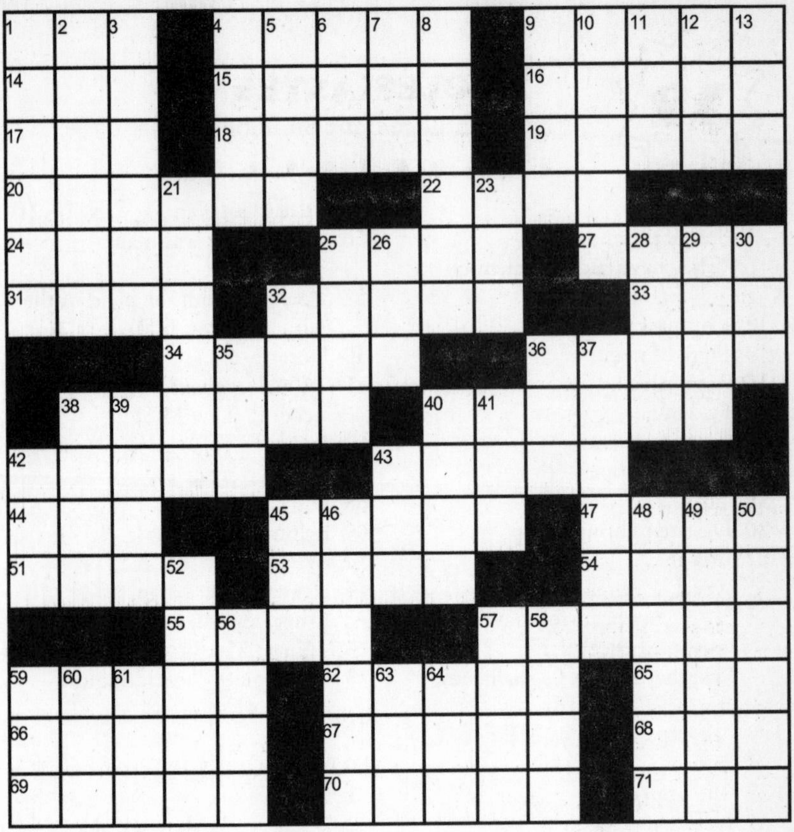

29 "The ___ himself is served by the field" (Eccl. 5:9)
30 Jerusalem to Peniel dir.
32 "My ___, be admonished" (Eccl. 12:12)
35 Exclamation
36 __ Lanka
37 "Their ___ made no lamentation" (Ps. 78:64)
38 "Their ears are ___ of hearing" (Matt. 13:15)
39 Capital of Norway
40 "God also ___ set the one" (Eccl. 7:14)
41 ___ league school
42 Talk
43 Dah's partner
45 Alphabet
46 Hairdo
48 "Took off their chariot ___" (Ex. 14:25)
49 Qualm
50 "Passing through the ___ near her corner" (Prov. 7:8)
52 "The ___ of a wise man's mouth" (Eccl. 10:12)
56 "Good works for necessary ___" (Titus 3:14)
57 Acts preacher (abbr.)
58 Mined metals
59 Caress
60 Condensed (abbr.)
61 Promissory note
63 5th day of Creation (abbr.)
64 Child

38

Ecclesiastes

by Sarah Lagerquist Simmons

ACROSS

1 "Fourth part of a ___ of dove's dung" (2 Kings 6:25)
4 Clomp
9 "Ye shall ___ down their altars" (Judg. 2:2)
14 "Ye tithe mint and ___ and all manner of herbs" (Luke 11:42)
15 Toil
16 Jesus still ___ the sick
17 And so forth
18 Type of acid
19 Pop (3 wds.)
20 "To be discreet, ___, keepers at home" (Titus 2:5)
22 "With her much ___ speech" (Prov. 7:21)
24 "Hide it there in a ___ of the rock" (Jer. 13:4)
25 Radar echo
27 "___ hold of this" (Eccl. 7:18)
31 Writer Bombeck
32 Large hotel room
33 "The man is near of ___ unto us" (Ruth 2:20)
34 River
36 Unclean animal (Deut. 14:8)
38 College teacher or lecturer
40 Parable about man ___ laborers (Matt. 20:1)
42 Sentimental
43 "Words of the Preacher, the son of ___" (Eccl. 1:1)
44 "___ the rivers run into the sea" (Eccl. 1:7)
45 Harmony
47 God ___ cattle of thousand hills (Ps. 50:10)
51 "Causeth his wind to ____" (Ps. 147:18)
53 "Discerneth ___ time and judgment" (Eccl. 8:5)
54 "For ___ hath man of all his labour" (Eccl. 2:22)
55 Owiee!
57 Acts to impress
59 Many ___ of animals on ark
62 "Clouds return ___ the rain" (Eccl. 12:2)
65 Samaria to Moab dir.
66 "He ___ with him the space of a month" (Gen. 29:14)
67 David's son ___ Ecclesiastes
68 Downwind
69 Tie
70 Flying toys
71 "I have not ___ with vain persons" (Ps. 26:4)

DOWN

1 Nativity scene
2 Solomon was an ___
3 Soothe
4 Strip
5 "Neither could any man ___ him" (Mark 5:4)
6 Kimono sash
7 First day of Creation (abbr.)
8 "There was no ___ under the sun" (Eccl. 2:11)
9 Siamese
10 "The ___ of the wise is in the house of mourning" (Eccl. 7:4)
11 "The living creatures ___ and returned" (Ezek. 1:14)
12 "A wise child than an ___ and foolish king" (Eccl. 4:13)
13 Jericho to Beersheba dir.
21 "Applied mine heart to know, and to ___" (Eccl. 7:25)
23 Hairy mammal
25 Baseball's short hit
26 "Highways ___ waste" (Isa. 33:8)
28 John was ___ to Jesus

24 Tortilla rollups
25 "___ decree justice" (Prov. 8:15)
26 Fish tank growth
27 "___ thyself to be a mourner" (2 Sam. 14:2)
28 Wooden projection
30 Something frightening
32 Proverbs has more than one ___
33 Combined
34 Rim of spoked wheel
37 Gibeon to Jerusalem dir.
38 Time zone
44 Naaman had to ___ seven times (pl.)
45 "She is not afraid of the ___" (Prov. 31:21)
48 Absalom tried to ___ David's throne
51 Haman did ___ law against Mordecai
53 "King had ___ ___ a navy" (1 Kings 10:22) (2 wds.)
55 Swimming mammal
56 Isaac had to ___ wood
57 "Tongue cleaved to the ___ of their mouth" (Job 29:10)
59 Opposite of yeses
60 Leaves
61 Average work performance
63 Pampering
64 "___ of it are the issues of life" (Prov. 4:23)
65 "Make ye this ___" (Mark 5:39)
67 Jerusalem to Shiloh dir.

37

PROVERBS

by Sarah Lagerquist Simmons

ACROSS

1 "He that speaketh lies shall not ___" (Prov. 19:5) (abbr.)
4 "She is like the merchants' ___" (Prov. 31:14)
9 Lemuel's ___ taught him (Prov. 31:1)
12 Baby powder
14 Asian capital
15 "Lest I ___ you in pieces" (Ps. 50:22)
16 Seaweed substance
17 Host
18 "Not good to ___ much honey" (Prov. 25:27) (pl.)
19 One-celled water animal (var.)
21 "Her candle ___ not out" (Prov. 31:18)
23 Wrangle
25 Enclosed
26 "I have longed ___ thy precepts" (Ps. 119:40)
29 Cut short (abbr.)
31 "What is the ___ to the wheat?" (Jer. 23:28)
35 Downwind
36 "She shall ___ in time to come" (Prov. 31:25)
39 "From them to whom it is ___" (Prov. 3:27)
40 "Where no ___ is for him" (Amos 3:5)
41 "They shewed his ___ among them" (Ps. 105:27)
42 Communication
43 "Had a great while ___ repented" (Luke 10:13)
44 Perceives by sight
46 Harden
47 Listlessness
49 "He saith, ___" (Matt. 17:25) (var.)
50 "She reacheth forth her hands to the ___" (Prov. 31:20)
52 Baths
54 "He that is ___ angry" (Prov. 14:17)
56 "Whoso putteth his ___ in the LORD" (Prov. 29:25)
58 Accent
61 "Stretcheth out her hand to the ___" (Prov. 31:20)
62 Ermine
66 Masked animal
68 Toy (2 wds.)
69 Avoid
70 Adolescent
71 Umpire
72 Ham
73 Samaria to Shiloh dir.

DOWN

1 Arrival
2 Adventure story
3 Shellfish
4 "He shall wave the ___" (Lev. 23:11)
5 Noah's son
6 Business title ending
7 Poet Edgar Allan
8 "Thou shalt lay ___ against it" (Ezek. 4:3)
9 "She. . .giveth ___ to her household" (Prov. 31:15)
10 "That I may perform the ___" (Jer. 11:5)
11 Proverbs 31 woman was a ___ (abbr.)
13 "They sailed close by ___" (Acts 27:13)
15 "Whose ___ are as swords" (Prov. 30:14)
20 Vigor
22 "Shall fall at ___" (Prov. 28:18)

27 God's provision is ___ ___ (2 wds.)
29 Pumpernickel made from this
30 Spots
31 Wrote most of New Testament (2 wds.)
32 Sarah was Isaac's
33 Similar
34 Cipher
35 Lad
36 "He that hath no ___" (Prov. 25:28)
37 Discharge
39 Official
43 "___, I am warm" (Isa. 44:16)
45 Measure (abbr.)
46 Excuse me
47 Israel celebrated David with ___ (1 Sam. 18:6)
51 Zero
52 "The rod of his ___ shall fail" (Prov. 22:8)
54 Gets up
55 "The ___ of the sea" (Est. 10:1)
56 "Oh that I had given up the ___" (Job 10:18)
57 Animal stomach
58 "A ___ look, and a proud heart" (Prov. 21:4)
59 "___ soul shall suffer" (Prov. 19:15)
61 Drop heavily
62 Bum
64 "___ not the poor" (Prov. 22:22)
66 "The ___ that mocketh at his father" (Prov. 30:17)
68 "Things which are ___ wonderful" (Prov. 30:18)

36

PROVERBS

by Sarah Lagerquist Simmons

ACROSS

1 10 grams (abbr.)
4 Pop
8 "Thou art as a ___ in the seas" (Ezek. 32:2)
13 Theatrical part
15 Boy's name
16 Brown
17 "Mine ___ hath done them" (Isa. 48:5)
18 To incite
19 Bees' cousins
20 Heavy coats
22 Expression
24 "He shall give thee ___" (Prov. 29:17)
25 "For the ___ is red" (Matt. 16:2)
26 Constellation created by God
28 "Thou ___ come into the hand" (Prov. 6:3)
30 Group (abbr.)
31 Subject of parable worked here (Luke 15:15)
32 "Seest thou a ___ that is hasty" (Prov. 29:30)
35 "That they teach no other ___" (1 Tim. 1:3) (var.)
38 Paul: a ___ of the Law
40 Saul was ___ Paul
41 Drones
42 Rascal
43 David hid ___ caves
44 Fighter's first name
45 Florida west coast city
47 African country
48 Cat
49 "___ eateth, and wipeth her mouth" (Prov. 30:20)
50 Ca. university
52 Monkey
53 "Faithful witness will not ___" (Prov. 14:5)
54 Set up
57 Samson fought with a ___ bone (Judg. 15:16) (var.)
60 Speed
63 "When the wicked ___" (Prov. 11:10)
65 Range of hills
67 Naaman was ___ to obey Elisha (var.)
69 Capital of Norway
70 Awry
71 Double-reed instrument
72 "There was a swarm of ___" (Judg. 14:8)
73 "Better is a dinner of herbs ___ love is" (Prov. 15:17)
74 "The ___ is hated" (Prov. 14:20)
75 Superfast aircraft

DOWN

1 Rain ___ similar to contentious woman (Prov. 27:15)
2 Film maker
3 "It is his ___ to pass over a transgression" (Prov. 19:11)
4 "Day and night shall not ___" (Gen. 8:22) (pl.)
5 Bolus
6 Jesus died in ___ of me
7 Holding temporary position (abbr.)
8 Sidon to Ramah dir.
9 "Heaviness in the ___ of man" (Prov. 12:25)
10 Niche
11 "He that refraineth his ___ is wise" (Prov. 10:19)
12 "He caused an ___ wind to blow" (Ps. 78:26)
14 Deer relative
21 "Lest thou ___ be like unto him" (Prov. 26:4)
23 "They that ___ me love death" (Prov. 8:36)

29 "___ it, and make cakes" (Gen. 18:6)
30 Defunct football league
31 "I will requite thee in this ___" (2 Kings 9:26)
32 Airy (poet.)
33 Twisted
34 Saul turned ___ David (var.)
35 Fossil
36 Jacob and Esau were ___ rivals
38 Dimensions
39 Wing
43 Charges
45 Niches
46 "Yet they prepare their ___ in the summer" (Prov. 30:25)
49 "Let the ___ go, and take the young to thee" (Deut. 22:7)
51 Deborah was Rebekah's ___ (Gen. 35:8)
53 Eagle's nest
54 "As ___ beasts, in those things" (Jude 1:10)
55 "Thy want as an ___ man" (Prov. 6:11)
56 Tool mentioned in Bible (1 Sam. 13:21) (var.)
57 Like a wing
58 Peter was frightened by a (Matt 14:30)
60 Same
61 "He made him to ___ in the second chariot" (Gen. 41:43)
62 "Inhabitants of Canaan shall ___ away" (Ex. 15:15)
65 "But a foolish ___ spendeth it up" (Prov. 21:20)
67 Danish krone

35

Proverbs

by Sarah Lagerquist Simmons

ACROSS

1 Bum
5 "I will ___ off from the top" (Ezek. 17:22)
9 "Such as turn ___ unto their crooked ways" (Ps. 125:5)
14 Imitated
15 "Then said I, ___ am I" (Isa. 6:8)
16 "Come with us, let us lay wait for ___" (Prov. 1:11)
17 Smart person
18 "Thou shalt ___ up the tabernacle" (Ex. 26:30)
19 "They ___ fig leaves together (Gen. 3:7)
20 "Better is a ___ morsel" (Prov. 17:1)
21 Small scoop
23 "Knowledge is ___ unto him that understandeth" (Prov. 14:6)
24 Bow
26 Jump
28 Boxer Muhammad
29 Antelope
31 "The Lord that delivered me out of the ___" (1 Sam. 17:37)
34 Nationality of Biblical Egyptians
37 "If a ___ hearken to lies" (Prov. 29:12)
39 Excited
40 Umpire
41 Not one
42 "The ___ of the eyes rejoiceth the heart" (Prov. 15:30)
44 "I also will laugh at your ___" (Prov. 1:26)
47 "He will not regard ___ ransom" (Prov. 6:35)
48 Attention problem
50 "___ not thine heart be glad" (Prov. 24:17)
51 Sports group
52 Yellow melon
56 Prego's competition
59 Burrowing rodent
63 "Do they not ___ that devise evil?" (Prov. 14:22)
64 "When ye blow an ___" (Num. 10:5)
66 Capital of the Ukraine
67 Percussion instrument
68 Popular condiment
69 "An ___ soul shall suffer hunger" (Prov. 19:15)
70 "And the glede, and the ___" (Deut. 14:13)
71 Clean with bill
72 "Who also were in the ship mending their ___" (Mark 1:19)
73 "A bruised ___ shall he not break" (Isa. 42:3)

DOWN

1 "Spider taketh hold with her ___" (Prov. 30:28)
2 Musical production
3 "Hands are as gold rings set with the ___" (Song 5:14)
4 "Wherewith the ___ number of them is to be redeemed" (Num. 3:48)
5 Containing chromium
6 "They ___ to and fro" (Ps. 107:27)
7 Moses heard God's ___ voice
8 Brand of coffee alternative
9 Muscle group (abbr.)
10 "Yet a little ___, a little slumber" (Prov. 6:10)
11 Midwestern state
12 God made David's feet like ___ (2 Sam. 22:34) (var.)
13 Swirl
21 Painter of melting clocks
22 Doctoral degree
25 Express disgust
27 "We hanged ___ harps" (Ps. 137:2)

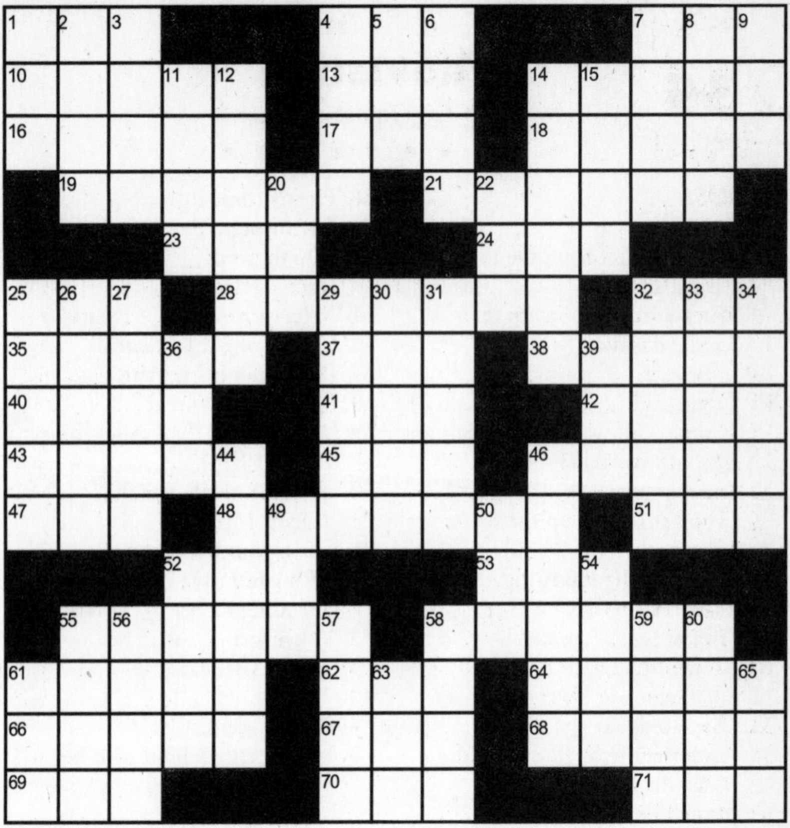

32 "___, O Lord" (Ps. 9:19)
33 "In the dry places like a ___" (Ps. 105:41)
34 "Create in me a ___ heart" (Ps. 51:10)
36 Discs
39 "How ___ did they provoke" (Ps. 78:40)
44 God created many ___ herbs
46 Amends (2 wds.)
49 ___ de Janeiro
50 Goddess
52 Modern-day Persia
54 "He brought ___ their heart" (Ps. 107:12)
55 "As a ___ that is told" (Ps. 90:9)
56 "Let thy hand be ___ the man" (Ps. 80:17)
57 Baby powder
58 Defender (abbr.)
59 "This is my ___ for ever" (Ps. 132:14)
60 "Righteous shall flourish like the palm ___" (Ps. 92:12)
61 "___ thy vows" (Ps. 50:14)
63 "___ condemn him when he is judged" (Ps. 37:33)
65 Education group

34

Psalms

by Sarah Lagerquist Simmons

ACROSS
1 Spiritedness
4 Bad (prefix)
7 Time
10 Toothbrush brand
13 Boxing great
14 Type of shorts
16 Deck
17 Ump
18 Opposite of Corinthian
19 Israel unleashed ___ against Jericho
21 Imprint
23 Shechem to Samaria dir.
24 Many Psalms ask for God's ___
25 Gorilla
28 "When thou with rebukes dost ___ man" (Ps. 39:11)
32 Shape of Noah's rainbow
35 "Lord will give ___ and glory" (Ps. 84:11)
37 "I shall be anointed with fresh ___" (Ps. 92:10)
38 Skunk-like African animal (var.)
40 "The ___ sitteth upon the flood" (Ps. 29:10)
41 Joseph's position (Gen. 42:6) (abbr.)
42 Quintet
43 King of Moab was ___ (Judg. 3:17)
45 Shoshonean
46 Jesus' boat was __ ___ (2 wds.)
47 Jacob ___ Leah
48 "Neither ___ his feet" (2 Sam. 19:24)
51 Gray sea eagle
52 Number of Noah's sons (Rom. num.)
53 "Lord's song in a ___ land" (Ps. 137:4) (var.)
55 Flatfish
58 Harmonize
61 Of the pope
62 "Go to the ___" (Prov. 6:6)
64 Idiot
66 "His name ___ is excellent" (Ps. 148:13)
67 "Upon the ___ of the righteous" (Ps. 125:3)
68 Beginning
69 Longing
70 "I ___ in the day time" (Ps. 22:2)
71 Drink

DOWN
1 Papa
2 Long time periods
3 "Thou wilt shew me the ___ of life" (Ps. 16:11)
4 Planet created by God
5 Lager
6 "They devised to take away my ___" (Ps. 31:13)
7 "His ___ to receive his ashes" (Ex. 27:3)
8 Skier's need
9 Facial twitch
11 "Thou shalt tread upon the ___ and adder" (Ps. 91:13)
12 Rebound
14 Give unwanted advice
15 Moses wore ___ or veil
20 "Do not ___ things unto me" (Job 13:20)
22 IBM competitor
25 Shining
26 Penetrate
27 "Which is neither ___ nor sown" (Deut. 21:4)
29 Absalom was a ___
30 "Pleasure to ___ in the day time" (2 Peter 2:13) (pl.)
31 Santa's helpers

28 Painter Richard
29 Side
30 Jabber
31 Stop
32 What a helicopter needs
33 Stage set
35 "Thy ___ is not waxen old" (Deut. 29:5)
37 "He shall be like a ___" (Ps. 1:3)
40 Abraham was a ___ (Gen. 20:13)
41 Lawyer (abbr.)
43 Guile
46 Imagine
47 "Grant me thy ___ graciously" (Ps. 119:29)
48 "Their words to the ___ of the world" (Ps. 19:4)
50 Store passageway
51 Direction
52 "But ___ has saved us" (Ps. 44:7)
53 "Let the sea ___" (Ps. 98:7)
54 "LORD, ___ me" (Ps. 6:2)
55 Active
56 Swarm
57 "They did ___ it with an omer" (Ex. 16:18)
60 "___, the LORD breaketh the cedars of Lebanon" (Ps. 29:5)
62 Expression of disgust

33 PSALMS

by Sarah Lagerquist Simmons

ACROSS
1 Mrs.
6 "King. . .is come out to seek a ___" (1 Sam. 26:20)
10 "Held my peace, even ___ good" (Ps. 39:2)
14 Lithe
15 "Blessed be the ___" (Ps. 68:19)
16 Jacob's son
17 He married Saul's daughter
18 American state
19 "I will make Jerusalem. . . ___ ___ of dragons" (Jer. 9:11) (2 wds.)
20 "But ___ the messenger came" (2 Kings 6:32)
21 Eye color
23 Slight
25 Wall support
26 Fen
27 "Then mayest thou for me ___ the counsel" (2 Sam. 15:34)
30 "Whose trust shall be a ___ web" (Job 8:14)
34 Tiny island
35 "He ___ on the ground" (John 9:6)
36 Month (abbr.)
38 Tabernacle tent post
39 "___ doth God know?" (Ps. 73:11)
40 "I ___ my couch with my tears" (Ps. 6:6)
42 "Even as a ___ gathereth" (Matt. 23:37)
43 "My ___ is also sore" (Ps. 6:3)
44 Jesus did ___ for our sins
45 Omelet cooker
48 Lamb was Last Supper's ___
49 "I do wait all the ___" (Ps. 25:5)
50 Comedian Griffith
51 Scattered, as the bones (Ps. 53:5)
54 "___ me under the shadow of thy wings" (Ps. 17:8)
55 Memory
58 Horse command
59 "Let thine ___ behold the things" (Ps. 17:2)
61 Indian currency
63 "There went over a ferry ___" (2 Sam. 19:18)
64 "Sealed them with his ___" (1 Kings 21:8)
65 Heron
66 "All his commandments are ___" (Ps. 111:7)
67 "Price of his ___ shall be" (Lev. 25:50)
68 Poetry in Psalms does not ___

DOWN
1 "Those that have ___ a covenant" (Ps. 50:5)
2 Seaweed substance
3 Plunge into water
4 Arab caliph
5 "I will ___ also of all thy work" (Ps. 77:12)
6 ___ did flow from Jesus' side
7 "And cast ___ upon my vesture" (Ps. 22:18)
8 Time
9 Affix
10 Rim
11 Remake
12 "That they may not pass ___" (Ps. 104:9)
13 "I was a reproach among all ___ enemies" (Ps. 31:11)
22 Furrow
24 "The fool hath said. . .There is no ___" (Ps. 14:1)
25 "___ out his wickedness" (Ps. 10:15)
27 "She brought forth butter in a lordly ___" (Judg. 5:25)

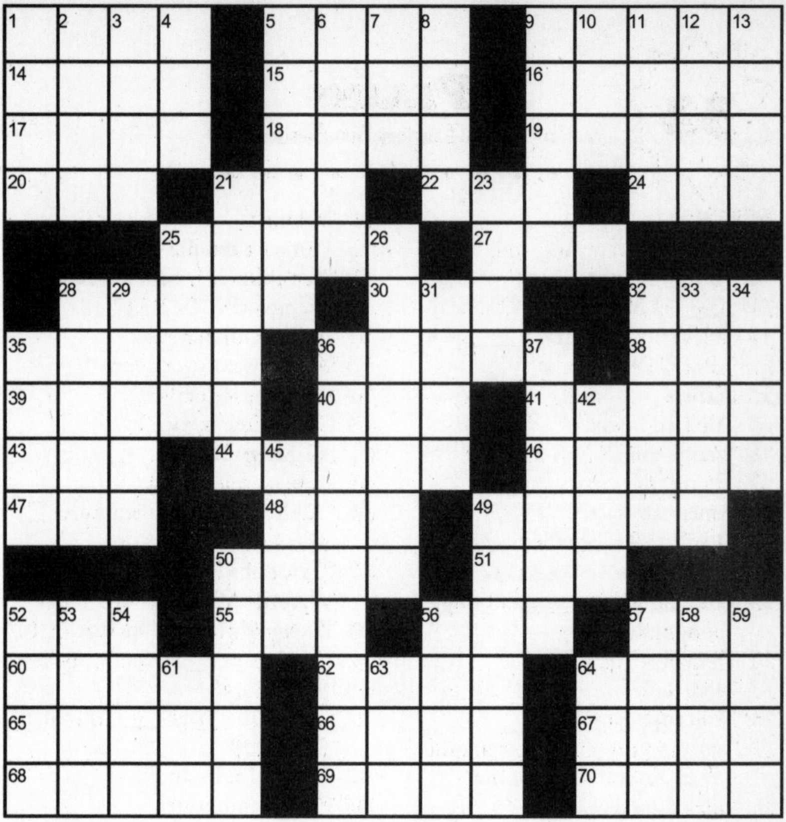

26 Streamlined
28 Fork prongs
29 David did ___ many Psalms
31 "There is a river. . .shall make glad the ___ of God" (Ps. 46:4)
32 "To keep them ___ in famine" (Ps. 33:19)
33 Solomon was a ___ son
34 "How much ___ man, that is a worm?" (Job 25:6)
35 Wind pointer
36 Moses was ____ water with gold (Ex. 32:20)
37 Moses was ___ than any man (Num. 12:3)
42 "Between blood and blood, between ___ and ___" (Deut. 17:8) (same wd. both blanks)
45 Next to Kauai
49 Skimps
50 Instructor
52 "The ___ and the lamb shall feed together" (Isa. 65:25)
53 Capital of Western Samoa
54 Convenience nonexistent in Bible times
56 Medicine amount
57 "Thou crownest the ___ with thy goodness" (Ps. 65:11)
58 Miriam's solo could be this (Ex. 15:21)
59 "Who is this ___ of glory?" (Ps. 24:10)
61 Rodent considered unclean (Lev. 11:29)
63 Head boss
64 Former USSR's secret police

32

Psalms

by Sarah Lagerquist Simmons

ACROSS

1 A sluggard does this well (Prov. 6:9)
5 Used on a horse (Prov. 26:3)
9 Dales
14 Sailor's "hey"
15 David's ___ : Build the Temple
16 Not Jesus' race
17 "Deliver me out of the ___" (Ps. 69:14)
18 Swerve
19 Vice ___
20 Soma
21 "He smote them ___ and thigh" (Judg. 15:8)
22 Weight per inch
24 Sixth sense
25 Father Christmas
27 "___ iniquity unto their iniquity" (Ps. 69:27)
28 Pluck
30 Stiff
32 "___ his commandments are sure" (Ps. 111:7)
35 Disease cause
36 Rainbow maker
38 "Proud have forged a ___ against me" (Ps. 119:69)
39 Senile
40 "How ___ did they provoke him" (Ps. 78:40)
41 Noah's story is of ___ proportions (pl.)
43 "He draweth him into his ___" (Ps. 10:9)
44 "Yet hath he respect unto the ___" (Ps. 138:6)
46 Rock and roll "King"
47 Joppa to Lydia dir.
48 "Why make ye this ___" (Mark 5:39)
49 Shoot clay pigeons
50 "Ye shall not eat of them that ___ the cud" (Deut. 14:7)
51 Oolong
52 Compact bundle
55 "Let us kneel before the Lord ___ maker" (Ps. 95:6)
56 Phone book (abbr.)
57 Wild ox
60 Musical production
62 Computer "button"
64 Lotion brand
65 Light purple flower
66 "The swallow a ___ for herself" (Ps. 84:3)
67 "So are the ways of every one that is greedy of ___" (Prov. 1:19)
68 "O ye of little ___" (Matt. 6:30)
69 The serpent ___ upon his belly (Gen. 3:14)
70 We are to ___ about God (Ps. 34:2)

DOWN

1 "Where is the ___ for a burnt offering?" (Gen. 22:7)
2 Buckeye State
3 "I have remembered thy name, O ___" (Ps. 119:55)
4 Caustic substance
5 "I may walk before God in the light of the ___" (Ps. 56:13)
6 David was an ___ shepherd
7 "We ___ not our signs" (Ps. 74:9)
8 "Yea, upon the ___ will I praise thee" (Ps. 43:4)
9 Saul's successor
10 "And ___ the lamp of God went out" (1 Sam. 3:3)
11 Psaltery (Ps. 71:22)
12 A ___ was sold for drink (Joel 3:3)
13 Metal fastener
21 Gretel's friend
23 God ___ He is only God (Isa. 45:18)
25 Was "insanely" jealous of David

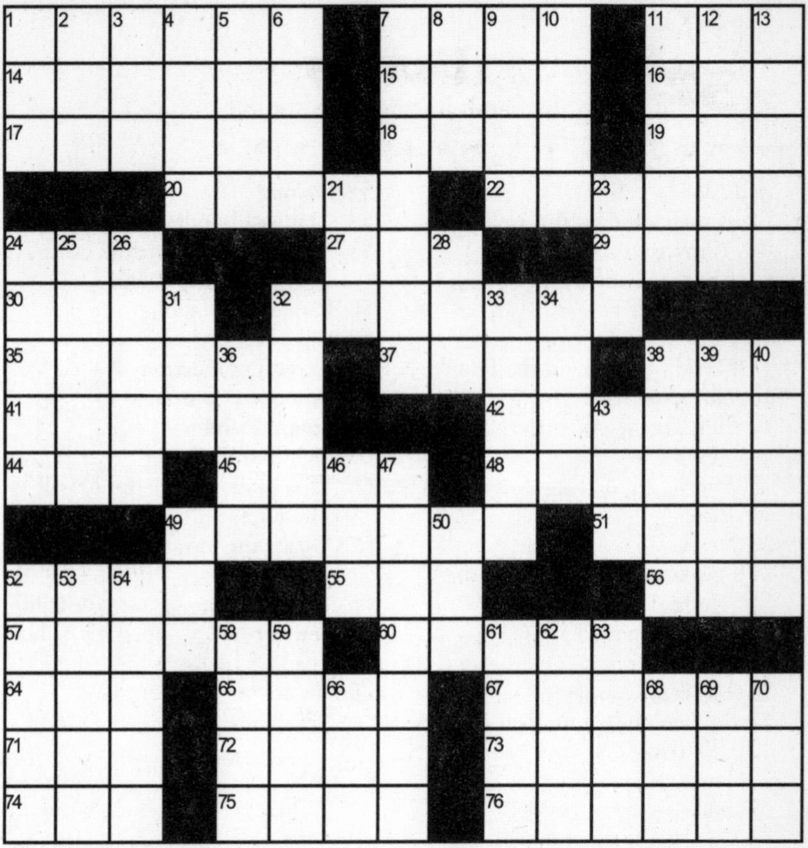

26 Cake confection
28 KJV rent
31 "I'm at a loss for words"
32 Describes Job's friends' advice
33 South African plain (var.)
34 Pitcher
36 Tidy
38 Feature of Daniel's lions
39 "Thou shalt not ___" (Ex. 20:15)
40 Describes Job (Job 1:8)
43 The Book's holder of power (Job 2:6)
46 Brainy test (abbr.)
47 Job's description of life, in a way (Job 3:23)
49 Much of it was at Job's eldest son's house (Job 1:18–19)
50 After he lost everything, what Job lived in, perhaps
52 Result of Job's sore boils, perhaps
53 Jesus, the Word (John 1:1) (Gr.)
54 Job's misery would ___ his patience (Job 3:1)
58 Skins of kids covered Jacob's (Gen. 27:16)
59 NT Book
61 "Canst thou ___ lightnings?" (Job 38:35)
62 Tub spread
63 Grass
66 "When it is ___, they are consumed" (Job 6:17)
68 School org.
69 Glutton's partner, slangily (Prov. 23:21)
70 Jerusalem to Amman dir.

31

Job

by Patricia Mitchell

• • • • • •

ACROSS

1 Book's question: Why do people ___?

7 Book's question: Does God ___?

11 Serpent's sound

14 Dye familiar to Lydia, perhaps (Acts 16:14)

15 Judas Iscariot took the wrong one (Matt. 26:14–15)

16 French friend

17 What the wicked do, but never repay (Ps. 37:21)

18 Choir section

19 Metal that can withstand fire (Num. 31:22–23)

20 The Book, in a way

22 Paul would ___ on a journey to Cyprus (Acts 13:4)

24 New York winter hour

27 Measurement (Ezek. 45:14)

29 Baruch's tools (Jer. 36:18)

30 "Be ___ with sandals" (Mark 6:9)

32 The Book's answer (Job 19:25) (2 wds.)

35 Albanian capital

37 What you sit on during worship (2 wds.)

38 Controversial food flavoring (abbr.)

41 Book before the Book

42 Musically smooth

44 Job's wife, e.g.

45 Paul was ___ during his trip to Cyprus (Acts 13:4)

48 Job's "comforters" did this a lot

49 Unbeliever, perhaps

51 Book's question: How does man ___ with grief?

52 Snow transport

55 London hour in January

56 Describes 11 Down

57 Sun circle

60 Cleaner choice

64 The Book takes place long ___

65 Job surely felt this when he said that "the Lord hath taken away" (Job 1:21)

67 Jesus said time would ___ before world's end (Matt. 24:6)

71 "Their houses are safe. . .neither is the ___ of God upon them" (Job 21:9)

72 Dept. of Commerce agencies

73 Physicist Isaac

74 Tyre to Amman dir.

75 French verbs

76 Job's friends would ___ their advice to Job (but not their home or money!)

DOWN

1 Each of Job's children had one, for short

2 One in Madrid

3 New Deal pres.

4 "The ___ of God is fallen from heaven" (Job 1:16)

5 The Book's lesson: They show when we presume to advise others

6 The Book's debates, almost

7 Name in color

8 It tells you when you've got mail

9 Eliphaz would ___ Job's innocence (Job 4:7–8)

10 Esau (Gen. 36:1)

11 Job's adversary (Job 1:10–11)

12 Look on the face of 9 Down, perhaps

13 Peter does this when he tries to walk on water (Matt. 14:30)

21 Job would ___ God's test (Job 42:10)

23 Repeat, in music

24 Colorado park

25 Summation of Job's reply to his wife, perhaps (Job 2:10)

37 Fashions
38 "The ___ out of the wood" (Ps. 80:13)
39 Coupe
40 "___ ye for me" (Est. 4:16)
41 "Planteth an ___, and the rain doth nourish it" (Isa. 44:14)
42 "Upon a pavement of ___, and blue" (Est. 1:6)
43 Nix
45 Behind
46 "Many of the ___. . .became Jews" (Est. 8:17)
48 Not moral nor immoral
49 Put behind bars
50 Dared
52 "Wherefore they called these days ___" (Est. 9:26)
56 "Whose heart is snares and ___" (Eccl. 7:26)
57 Ale
58 "To the king ___" (Est. 1:16)
59 Not mentioned in Esther
60 "___ it was chewed" (Num. 11:33)
61 Map direction
63 God's name is ___ (Ps. 111:9) (abbr.)
64 Cain's mother

30

Esther

by Sarah Lagerquist Simmons

• • • • • • • • • •

ACROSS

1 Arbiter
4 Keyboard key next to "!"
9 Elicit
14 Legume
15 Regions
16 Withered
17 David was Jonathan's ___
18 Jews were allowed to ___ (Est. 9:2)
19 "Duke Aholibamah, duke Elah, duke ___" (1 Chron. 1:52)
20 Acts out
22 Haman wanted to ___ Mordecai (Est. 6:4)
24 Costa ___
25 "They have taken gifts to ___ blood" (Ezek. 22:12)
27 Haman ended up with ___
31 "If thou wouldest ___ unto God betimes" (Job 8:5)
32 "There came a grievous ___ of flies" (Ex. 8:24)
33 Tweak
34 Notions
36 Sugar-free brand
38 East Indian tree
40 Esther's people ____ (Est. 4:16)
42 Cheek make up
43 Haman was a ___ man
44 "Neither ___ nor drink three days" (Est. 4:16)
45 Imitative
47 "They ___ the beams thereof" (Neh. 3:6)
51 "My doctrine shall ___ as the rain" (Deut. 32:2)
53 "Even darkness which may be ___" (Ex. 10:21)
54 Austen book
55 "As Mordecai had written ___ them" (Est. 9:23)
57 "I have given my maid into thy ___" (Gen. 16:5) (pl.)
59 Literary composition category
62 Clean
65 Furrow
66 God put planets into ___
67 Flat
68 "Their laws ___ diverse from all" (Est. 3:8)
69 Thinks
70 "Kept throughout ___ generation" (Est. 9:28)
71 "He ___ them with a cloud" (Ps. 78:14)

DOWN

1 Drug type
2 Unkind person
3 Esther lived in the ___
4 27th U.S. president
5 Eye part
6 "Make bare the ___" (Isa. 47:2)
7 Telegraphic signal
8 Bravery saved her people
9 Sports channel
10 Condescend, as to men of low estate (Rom. 12:16)
11 Vase
12 Executive director
13 European sea eagle
21 Encrusting
23 Naval rank (abbr.)
25 "The ___, and the pelican" (Lev. 11:18)
26 God ___ all knowledge
28 Wager
29 In the end, Haman ___
30 Mammal created on sixth day
32 "King Ahasuerus laud a tribute upon. . .the ___" (Est. 10:1)
35 Imbue
36 17th book of Bible (abbr.)

21 Utilizations
25 "The ___ of heaven, he will prosper" (Neh. 2:20)
26 Canal
28 "They set a ___" (Jer. 5:26)
29 "I will ___ me of mine adversaries" (Isa. 1:24)
30 Hurried
32 "Congregation. . .made booths, and ___" (Neh. 8:17)
34 "Overlaid it with the ___ gold" (1 Kings 10:18)
37 Essence
39 Christmas ___
40 "Now the man Moses was very ___" (Num. 12:3)
41 Middle Eastern country
42 Female horse
43 Clean animals (Lev. 11)
45 Ill-bred man
48 "Mourn ___, nor weep" (Neh. 8:9)
53 "Levites that ___" (Neh. 12:44)
54 Roman Catholic devotion
56 Sporty car brand
57 Style of Greek column
59 Time period
60 "Grant him ___ in the sight" (Neh. 1:11)
62 Swarmy
64 Disciple, informally
66 "They straightway left their ___, and followed" (Matt. 4:20)
67 Baking measurement (abbr.)
68 Environmental agency
69 Zero
70 "They read in the book in the ___" (Neh. 8:8)

29

Nehemiah

by Sarah Lagerquist Simmons

ACROSS

1 "The ___ of violence is in their hands" (Isa. 59:6)
4 Power unit
8 ___ does not matter in church (James 2:2–4)
14 "___ to thee, Moab!" (Num. 21:29)
15 Opera solo
16 Holy Ghost made this sound (Acts 2:2)
17 Boulevard (abbr.)
18 "Remember the ___, which is great and terrible" (Neh. 4:14)
19 Vent
20 Leprosy would ___ anyone
22 Dynamite
23 "They were much cast down in their own ___" (Neh. 6:16)
24 "Smite the city with the ___ of the sword" (2 Sam. 15:14)
27 "Let not the ___ of Jerusalem be opened" (Neh. 7:3)
31 "The ___, and all that is therein" (Neh. 9:6)
33 Earth created in this shape
35 Strike sharply
36 Choke
38 "Thou shalt surely ___" (Gen. 2:17)
39 Court suit
40 Imitative
44 "Concerning the Jews that had ___" (Neh. 1:2)
46 Periods of time
47 Nehemiah was the ___ of Hachaliah (Neh. 1:1)
49 Placed on Moses' basket
50 "Let now thine ___ be attentive" (Neh. 1:11)
51 "For the cherubims spread forth their ___ wings" (1 Kings 8:7)
52 "Thou camest ___ also upon mount Sinai" (Neh. 9:13)
55 "Women ___ their dough" (Jer. 7:18)
58 "There shall come forth a rod out of the ___ of Jesse" (Isa. 11:1)
61 Country in SE Asia
63 Lawman
65 David was a very ___ man
67 What a professor has
70 Belief
71 Ball holder
72 "Thou gavest also thy good ___" (Neh. 9:20)
73 King kept ___ of Mordecai's bravery (abbr.)
74 "Will they make an ___ in a day?" (Neh. 4:2)
75 "I was in Shushan the ___" (Neh. 1:1)
76 God knows ___ to all questions
77 "I testified against them in the ___" (Neh. 13:15)

DOWN

1 "Thou wast not ___" (Jer. 50:24)
2 Birds
3 Collapsible shelter
4 "The ___ of Jerusalem also is broken down" (Neh. 1:3)
5 "I ___ in the night" (Neh. 2:12)
6 "She painted her face, and ___ her head" (2 Kings 9:30)
7 Little bit
8 Spank
9 "What is this ___ that ye do?" (Neh. 2:19)
10 Artery
11 "Strong shall be as ___" (Isa. 1:31)
12 North American nation
13 Mousy

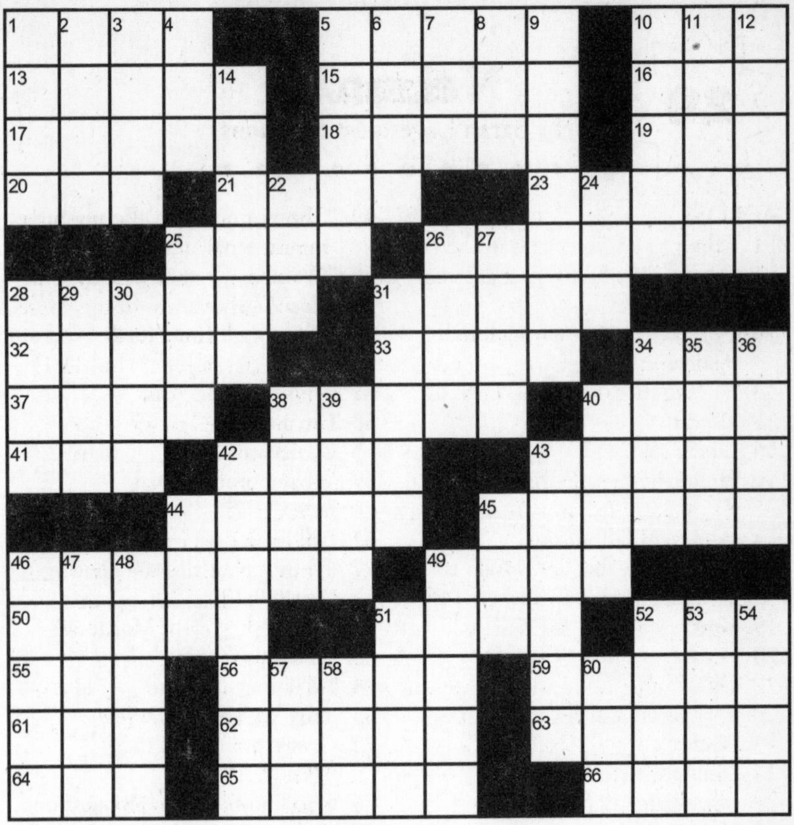

25 "Of the oaks of Bashan have they made thine ___" (Ezek. 27:6)
26 Experts
27 "God saw the light, ___ it was good" (Gen. 1:4)
28 France & Germany river
29 Jewish scribe
30 Golf shot
31 "There ___ you" (Ezra 1:3)
34 "Sin lieth at the ___" (Gen. 4:7)
35 "Be it known unto the ___" (Ezra 5:8)
36 When David brought the ark into Jerusalem, he was filled with ___
38 Smile
39 Haman tried to ___ Mordecai
40 The Israelites ___ through the dessert for 40 years
42 Similar Egyptian plague symptom
43 Cyrus was king of ___ (Ezra 1:2)
44 Contagious disease
45 "Needful for the house of thy ___" (Ezra 7:20)
46 Rascal
47 Shiny balloon material
48 Angry, as God was with Israel (2 Kings 17:18)
49 Achan took ___ (Josh. 7:1) (pl.)
51 "And weighed unto them the silver, and the ___" (Ezra 8:25)
52 ___ mater
53 College student
54 Carbonated drink
57 "Thou art my battle ___" (Jer. 51:20)
58 Israel was to ___ lepers
60 "The ___ shall take him by the heel" (Job 18:9)

28

Ezra

by Sarah Lagerquist Simmons

ACROSS

1 Compass point
5 "Wound the head of his enemies, and the hairy ___" (Ps. 68:21)
10 "The battle went sore against Saul, and the archers ___him" (1 Sam. 31:3)
13 Flower
15 Birch's cousin
16 "Hear O Israel, the LORD our God is ___ LORD" (Deut. 6:4)
17 "God said unto Jacob, "___, go up to Bethel" (Gen. 35:1)
18 Wind instrument
19 North American nation
20 Hit
21 "Who is the LORD, that I should ___ his voice" (Ex. 5:2)
23 Sits for a picture
25 Sonata
26 One who runs a race (1 Cor. 9:24)
28 Floral leaves
31 Moses' arms ___ during battle (Ex. 17:12)
32 Blue, as in tabernacle's curtain (Ex. 16:1)
33 "I have given every green herb for ___" (Gen. 1:30)
34 10 grams (abbr.)
37 "Many of them also which used curious ___" (Acts 19:19)
38 Holy ___
40 "God. . .hath made me forget all my ___" (Gen. 41:51)
41 Lab animal
42 Grain like wheat mentioned in Luke 3:17
43 Jacob was ___ to deceitfulness
44 David did ___ a stone at Goliath
45 Mr. Lucas
46 Grinning
49 "The ___ our God, to leave us a remnant" (Ezra 9:8)
50 Persian king during Ezra's time
51 "Cyrus. . .put them in the house of his ___" (Ezra 1:7)
52 Cancer charity
55 Wing
56 Touching the ark was ___ (1 Chron. 15:2)
59 Ice house
61 Tangle
62 "Magnify the LORD with me, and let us ___ his name" (Ps. 34:3)
63 David ___ his slingshot at Goliath
64 Before (prefix)
65 Tears
66 During his trial, Job had ___

DOWN

1 What Ehud did to Eglon (Judg. 3:21)
2 European monetary unit
3 Radar echo
4 Dinah was Joseph's
5 "I will for their ___ remember" (Lev. 26:45)
6 "He brought me. . .out of the miry ___" (Ps. 40:2)
7 Cutting tool (var.)
8 Sign of the zodiac
9 Ezra was one
10 "Bestow it out of the king's treasure ___" (Ezra 7:20)
11 The ephod was ___ with onyx stones (Ex. 25:7)
12 Gibe
14 "I viewed the ___, and the priests" (Ezra 8:15)
22 Large vehicle
24 "We will go with our young and with our ___" (Ex. 10:9)

27 Fashionable
29 "A people ___ with iniquity" (Isa. 1:4)
30 "Go forth. . .and fetch ___ branches" (Neh. 8:15)
31 __graph machine
32 Rational
33 "If ye. . .go and serve ___ gods" (2 Chron. 7:19)
34 Wrapped around Jonah's head (Jonah 2:5)
36 Pastrami on ___
39 Food energy (abbr.)
44 Thin band
46 Counterfeit
49 Talk
50 Card game
52 Azubah was Jehoshaphat's mother's ___ (2 Chron. 20:31)
54 What a dog returns to (Prov. 26:11), colloquially
55 Fun
56 Rant
57 "There was no more war unto the five and thirtieth ___" (2 Chron. 15:19)
58 Hold
59 "They ___ the house of the Lord" (2 Chron. 24:18)
60 Jesus' boat was ___ as he slept
61 Language
63 Resort hotel
65 __ Lanka

27 2 Chronicles

by Sarah Lagerquist Simmons

ACROSS

1 "Child shall play on the hole of the ___" (Isa. 11:8)
4 Before (prefix)
7 "I took the little book out of the angel's hand, and ___ it up" (Rev. 10:10)
10 Queen of __ visited Solomon (2 Chron. 9:1)
13 "Art not thou ___ God" (2 Chron. 20:7)
14 Jesus is preparing mine
16 People curse those who ___ (Prov. 11:26)
17 Womens' docs
18 "Moreover the brasen ___" (2 Chron. 1:5)
19 Old Testament prophet
21 Muddy
23 Cup
24 Family returning to Jerusalem (Neh. 7:47)
25 Number of commandments
28 "Then ___ spake unto all Israel" (2 Chron. 1:2)
32 "Had much cattle, both in the ___ country" (2 Chron. 26:10)
35 "Hezekiah humbled himself for the pride of his ___" (2 Chron. 32:26)
37 Boxer Muhammad
38 Angle less than 90 degrees
40 Pretentious
41 "Isaac was old, and his eyes were ___" (Gen. 27:1)
42 Suffer
43 Gunpowder need
45 Seth's mother
46 Traveled over regularly
47 "The ___ of the house of David" (Isa. 22:22)
48 Fiery
51 Luke was one of these (abbr.) (pl.)
52 Athletic association
53 Beak
55 Tending to snatch hastily
58 W. Cameroon seaport
61 "Remember the __"
62 Samaria to Shechem dir.
64 "Thou shalt plant vineyards, and ___ them" (Deut. 28:39)
66 "Solomon kept the feast ___ days" (2 Chron. 7:8)
67 Mammal created on sixth day
68 "Hezekiah commanded to ___ the burnt offering" (2 Chron. 29:27)
69 Downwind
70 Isaac's substitute sacrifice
71 Thai (var.)

DOWN

1 "He planteth an ___" (Isa. 44:14)
2 "So he drew off his ___" (Ruth 4:8)
3 Ring
4 Winnie the __
5 Abrade
6 Formerly (arch.)
7 Against (prefix)
8 Frog
9 "Ye therefore do greatly ___" (Mark 12:27)
11 "The ___ of a cup" (2 Chron. 4:5)
12 Adapt
14 Boat dock
15 Actress Jessica
20 "Hast thou not heard long ___" (2 Kings 19:25)
22 Military aid group
25 "Sacrificed thereon peace offerings and ___ offerings" (2 Chron. 33:16)
26 Disciples thought Jesus was ___ (Matt. 14:26)

26 Education beyond high school scrutinized (Brit.)
27 "The noise was heard ___ off" (Ezra 3:13)
28 "For we ___ not make ourselves of the number" (2 Cor. 10:12)
29 Stork-like bird
30 Church should work in ___ (Eph. 4:3)
31 Chicken
34 Japanese cedar
35 Elkanah was ___ the king (2 Chron. 28:7) (dial.)
36 "That they may fear ___, to walk in thy ways" (2 Chron. 6:31)
38 Joseph's many-colored garment
39 Female name
40 Threw (var.)
42 Straps
43 "They pluck the fatherless from the ___" (Job 24:9)
44 Prodigal son worked here
45 Group of modern-day Matthews
46 States of unconsciousness
47 Queen was taken ___ by Solomon's wisdom
48 Gutsy
49 Samson had more than one
51 Consumer
52 Pop
53 High school party
54 ___ of Green Gables
57 Grain
58 North American country
60 "Thy servants ___ skill to cut timber" (2 Chron. 2:8)

26

2 Chronicles

by Sarah Lagerquist Simmons

ACROSS
1 Brand of dog food
5 French painter Edgar
10 "My ___ did enter into his ears" (2 Sam. 22:7)
13 Monaco city Monte ___
15 ___ acid
16 Purple was ___ used in tabernacle
17 Chirp
18 Plastic
19 Southern U.S. state (abbr.)
20 Nation's goods' total value
21 Isaac was Abraham's ___
23 "Hezekiah commanded to ___ the burnt offering" (2 Chron. 29:27)
25 Jesus did ___ Jew and Gentile
26 The blacksmith "fashioneth it with ___" (Isa. 44:12)
28 Deprive of weapons
31 Becloud
32 Bottomless pit
33 Present day Babylonian neighbor
34 "worshiped God that ___ on the throne" (Rev. 19:4)
37 Skating ___
38 Product of Lebanon (2 Chron. 2:8)
40 Male name
41 Joseph could not ___ slavery (abbr.)
42 "The ___ spake to Manasseh" (2 Chron. 33:10)
43 Stroke over par (var.)
44 Sodom was a ___ city
45 California city
46 Choral composition
49 "He sacrificed. . .under every green ___" (2 Chron. 28:4)
50 God wants person who ___ Him
51 Constellation
52 Accountant
55 "They ___ my path" (Job 30:13)
56 "Then all the people went to the ___ of Baal" (2 Chron. 23:17)
59 "They laughed them to ___" (2 Chron. 30:10)
61 What it's worth
62 Jesus ___ our burdens (Matt 11:30)
63 Claw
64 "Hast thou with him spread out the ___" (Job 37:18)
65 "The ___ in their courses fought against Sisera" (Judg. 5:20)
66 Athaliah was Ahaziah's mother's ___ (2 Chron. 22:2)

DOWN
1 David ___ insane (1 Sam 21:13) (abbr.)
2 Yard
3 Mary went to ___ Jesus' body
4 Bravo! (Sp.)
5 "As ___ thy father walked" (2 Chron. 7:17)
6 Turkish official
7 "For a ___ and for a snare" (Isa. 8:14)
8 "Neither chose I ___ man to be a ruler over my people Israel" (2 Chron. 6:5)
9 ___ requested wisdom from God (2 Chron. 1:11)
10 Abrade
11 "There shall not fail thee a man to be ___ in Israel" (2 Chron. 7:18)
12 Joash became king at seven ___ (2 Chron. 24:1)
14 "Lest thou give thine honour unto ___" (Prov. 5:9)
22 Tree
24 Overseas money group
25 Moses used a kind of ___ (2 Cor. 3:13)

30 Breakfast starch
33 "Their words seemed to them as idle ___" (Luke 24:11)
35 "Every ___ shall bow" (Isa. 45:23)
40 Irritably
41 Engage in make-believe
42 Small boat
43 Duplicate
45 "___ the heavens be glad" (1 Chron. 16:31)
47 "___ thou through the wall in their sight" (Ezek. 12:5)
49 Excellent
50 Growth
51 "Let not his ___ head go down to the grave" (1 Kings 2:6)
52 Central American toad species
53 Coffee
54 "An ___ is nothing in the world" (1 Cor. 8:4)
55 Evil Roman emperor
56 Stare
59 Cry for help (abbr.)

25

1 Chronicles

by Sarah Lagerquist Simmons

ACROSS

1 Golf term
5 "So they ___ it up" (Micah 7:3)
9 Shellfish
13 "To stand every morning to. . . praise the Lord, and likewise at ___" (1 Chron. 23:30)
14 Buzz
15 Samson found one in a lion's carcass
16 The first home of the Ark of God
17 Card game
18 Acted like a monkey
19 Hoax
21 John wrote with ___ and ink (2 John 1:12) (pl.)
23 Beverage vessel
24 New Testament book (abbr.)
25 Zadok fulfilled this office (1 Chron. 24:6)
28 Person settling argument old-fashioned way
31 "Hezekiah was sick. . .and prayed unto the ___" (2 Chron. 32:24)
32 God did ___ the world spinning
34 Elijah hid in a cave's ___
36 *Arabian Nights*' Baba
37 Hail
38 "I will ___ them with a ___" (Jer. 15:7) (same wd. both blanks)
39 "As an eagle stirreth up her ___" (Deut. 32:11)
41 Worked
43 Jesus did ___ again
44 Bombed
46 Form an idea
48 "Which stilleth the noise of the ___" (Ps. 65:7)
49 Delilah did ___ Samson's hair
50 Talkative
53 Circus activity
57 Jellystone bear
58 A singer (1 Chron. 15:19)
60 It was Abram's ___ to lie
61 Kish's son (1 Chron. 8:33)
62 Small flock of birds
63 Military rank (abbr.)
64 Used to carry
65 Russian ruler
66 Plant in the lily family

DOWN

1 Cheese
2 "Phinehas. . .was the ruler___ them" (1 Chron. 9:20)
3 "David took. . .his clothes, and ___ them" (2 Sam. 1:11)
4 Lured, as Delilah did to Samson (Judg. 16:5) (past tense)
5 Hit
6 Grain
7 David prepared a place for it in his city (1 Chron. 15:29)
8 A foreteller, as Nathan (1 Chron. 17:1)
9 Funnyman Charlie ___
10 "Thou shalt not delay to offer the first of thy ___ fruits" (Ex. 22:29)
11 Assert
12 "Let them sing aloud upon their ___" (Ps. 149:5)
14 Arm joints
20 Alcohol-related illness (abbr.)
22 Leprosy did ___ Naaman
24 Blend
25 Princes hatched ___ against Daniel (Dan. 6:4)
26 Parts
27 European ethnic group
28 Jehoiada was buried in the city of ___ (2 Chron. 24:15–16)
29 Girl's name

29 The kind of man Cornelius was (Acts 10:22)
30 Like ash wood
31 Chirping sound
35 Toilet
36 Eber's son (1 Chron. 1:19)
38 European monetary unit
39 Joktan's father (1 Chron. 1:19)
40 District of ancient Attica
42 "David went out to ___ them" (1 Chron.12:17)
46 Rebekah ___ Abraham's servant's camels
47 "Yet this was a small thing in thine ___" (1 Chron. 17:17)
50 "Eat not of it ___" (Ex. 12:9)
52 Enclose
53 "There were precious ___ in it" (1 Chron. 20:2)
54 Italian city
55 Do very well
56 "They were ___ with bows" (1 Chron. 12:2)
57 Asher had four (1 Chron. 7:30)
59 State
61 "I went out. . .to the dung ___" (Neh. 2:13)
62 "The host of Sisera fell upon the ___ of the sword" (Judg. 4:16)
63 A prophet, as Samuel (1 Chron. 9:22)
65 Ohio's time zone (abbr.)
67 For

24

1 Chronicles

by Sarah Lagerquist Simmons

• • • • • • • • • •

ACROSS

1 Jesus' baby gifts had great ___
6 "Many women were there beholding ___ off" (Matt. 27:55)
10 Sonata
14 Incentive
15 "The man did as Joseph ___" (Gen. 43:17)
16 Valley
17 "They made ___ of pure gold" (Ex. 39:25)
18 Priest had to examine (Lev. 13:6)
19 Input
20 Refuge
22 Flightless birds
24 "The ___ of Sodom and Gomorrah is great" (Gen. 18:20)
25 Accumulate
27 Divided nation
29 Noah's son
32 "___ for eye" (Ex. 21:24)
33 "Pray for them which despitefully ___ you" (Matt. 5:44)
34 "After that miracles, then gifts of healings, ___" (1 Cor. 12:28)
37 "Have I ___ of mad men" (1 Sam. 21:15)
41 Japheth's brother
43 Moses put blood on Aaron's ___ (Lev. 8:23)
44 Hose
45 Kind
46 "Waters were on the face of the ___ earth" (Gen. 8:9)
48 Happens during sleep (abbr.)
49 Epoch
51 Babel in God's eyes
54 Access (2 wds.)
56 Representative
57 Gender
58 River dam
60 Scientific instruments
64 "Let us go up at ___" (Num. 13:30)
66 Gambol
68 Positive electrode
69 Opposite of yeses
70 Pitcher
71 Twilled cloth
72 Lot's wife became this
73 Pedestal part
74 Organic compound

DOWN

1 "___, Father"(Mark 14:36)
2 "Swift as the ___ upon the mountains" (1 Chron. 12:8)
3 "Noah ___ remained alive" (Gen. 7:23)
4 Muslim official
5 Take upon oneself
6 Stomach muscles (abbr.)
7 "Elders. . .fell upon their ___" (1 Chron. 21:16)
8 First man
9 "When thou with ___ dost correct man" (Ps. 39:11)
10 "Wherewith the ___ number of them is to be redeemed" (Num. 3:48)
11 "___ be unto thee" (1 Chron. 12:18)
12 Radical
13 "Every one that findeth me shall ___ me" (Gen. 4:14)
21 Noah's best subject in school
23 Chinese sauce
26 "Adam, ___, Enosh" (1 Chron. 1:1)
28 Tore, as Reuben did to his clothes (Gen. 37:29)

22 Central time zone (abbr.)
25 Earth's satellite (2 Kings 23:5)
26 Web-like
27 Sobbed (2 Kings 22:19)
28 How long Daniel was troubled (Dan. 4:19)
29 Cloth Jesus used to wash disciples' feet (John 13:5)
30 Damascus river (2 Kings 5:12)
31 Widow sold oil to pay ___ (2 Kings 4:7)
33 North American Indian
35 Jehoiachin's allotment (2 Kings 25:30)
36 Mesha, king of ___ (2 Kings 3:4)
37 "The ___ of the world" (Ps. 22:27)
39 Ranch guy
40 Dislodge
42 Mixture
45 Compass point (abbr.)
46 Garment father put on son (Luke 15:22)
47 Fraxinus Americana
48 Siblings (abbr.)
49 Writes out
51 Fawn
53 Billions of years
54 Hairless, like Elisha (2 Kings 2:23)
56 "There shall come a ___ out of Jacob" (Num. 24:17)
57 Sports channel
59 Weeding tool
61 "A reward of their shame that say, ___" (Ps. 70:3)
62 Remnant

23

2 Kings

by Kathy Hake

• • • • •

ACROSS

1 Rainbow
4 "Feet ___ with the. . .gospel" (Eph. 6:15)
8 Menahem exacted from ___ man fifty shekels of silver (2 Kings 15:20)
12 Scarf
13 Musical conclusion
14 Siamese
16 Taken temporarily, like axe (2 Kings 6:5)
18 Jehoash broke down wall of Jerusalem to ___ gate (2 Kings 14:13)
20 Brand of pain reliever
21 Sore
23 Elijah crossed Jordan on ___ ground (2 Kings 2:8)
24 "Was full from one ___ to another" (2 Kings 10:21)
25 Section of court where Isaiah heard God's word (2 Kings 20:4)
26 "All the days of his ___" (2 Kings 25:29)
27 Progressive politician of past
29 Crisp flat tortilla
32 Longest division of geological time
33 Owl sound
34 "Hoshea ___ his servant, and gave him presents" (2 Kings 17:3)
38 "He ___ ___ the idolatrous priests" (2 Kings 23:5) (2 wds.)
40 Berodachbaladan, king of ___ (2 Kings 20:12)
41 Company of performers
42 Father's brother's wife (Lev. 18:14)
43 Young boy who became sick (2 Kings 4:19)
44 Quandary
46 Loots, as Philistines did threshing floors (1 Sam. 23:1)
47 Hezekiah "shall not be ___ to deliver" (2 Kings 18:29)
50 What Jesus' disciples took while He prayed in garden
51 "LORD, ___ down thine ear, and hear" (2 Kings 19:16)
52 ___ Lanka
53 Cain's brother
55 Opposite of exalt (Luke 14:11)
58 Israel's king (2 Kings 18:10)
60 Naaman offered Gehazi two changes of ___ (2 Kings 5:23)
63 Seat placed in Elisha's room (2 Kings 4:10)
64 Jehoram's father (2 Kings 3:1)
65 Cover
66 Deliver, as Naaman did letter to king (2 Kings 5:5)
67 Christ's gift bringer
68 White-tailed sea eagle

DOWN

1 New Testament name for God
2 Crucifix
3 Incise (2 wds.)
4 Chide
5 "Remember now ___ I have walked" (2 Kings 20:3)
6 Praise poem
7 Dadaism follower
8 Engrave, as God did Ten Commandments
9 Type of greeting
10 Automobile
11 Sanskrit
15 Vassal
17 Jewelry father put on son's hand (Luke 15:22)
19 Cereal

26 Desert animals (2 Kings 8:9)
28 He asked for double portion of Elijah's spirit (2 Kings 2:9)
30 The LORD "shall pluck my feet out of the ___" (Ps. 25:15)
31 Make lace
32 Cunning
34 Title of respect (John 4:11)
36 Smear
37 Wood chopper that fell into water (2 Kings 6:5)
38 Contend
39 Person to whom money is owed (2 Kings 4:1)
40 Idol Israelites burned incense to (2 Kings 23:5)
42 Jehoiakim "did that which was ___" (2 Kings 23:37)
43 Discuss
45 Urge forward
47 Ice houses
48 Greeting Gehazi was not to use (2 Kings 4:29)
50 Animals Naaman gave to Gehazi (2 Kings 5:26)
52 Biblical outcast (2 Kings 5:27)
53 "Went unto their tents joyful and ___" (1 Kings 8:66)
54 Restaurant dinner listing
55 Labels
57 Stab with tusk (Ex. 21:28)
58 Writer Bombeck
60 Animal doctor (abbr.)
62 Jewel

22

2 Kings

by Kathy Hake

• • • • •

ACROSS

1 "Take my ___ in thine hand" (2 Kings 4:29)
6 Pouch
9 Doorway in Samaria where measure of fine flour was sold for shekel (2 Kings 7:1)
13 Height of chapter: ___ cubits (2 Kings 25:17)
14 Sheet
15 Moab's king (2 Kings 3:4)
16 "___ men went before the priests" (Josh. 6:9)
17 "___ him come now to me" (2 Kings 5:8)
18 Anesthetic
19 " ___ is the word of the LORD" (2 Kings 20:19)
20 Traded check for money
22 Avowal (Rom. 3:29)
23 African antelope
24 Smote by archers (1 Chron. 10:3)
25 Long narrative poem
27 Say hello (1 Sam. 25:5)
29 Renounces
33 Elisha did this over a dead child (2 Kings 4:34)
34 "Thine eyes shall not ___ all the evil" (2 Kings 22:20)
35 Grain Elisha cast in pot (2 Kings 4:41)
36 Josiah "walked in all the way of ___ his father" (2 Kings 22:2)
39 Government security agency (abbr.)
40 Miss Boop
41 Center of rotation
42 Make a mistake (Prov. 14:22)
43 Bad (prefix)
44 Apiary
46 Fertile desert area
49 Among
50 Roman deity
51 Girl
53 Time zone (abbr.)
56 Dilemma
58 Women's magazine
59 Depart, as Elisha refused to do from Elijah (2 Kings 2:2)
61 Digit priest put oil on (Lev. 14:28)
62 Company of men, such as Jesus' disciples
63 Holy messenger (2 Kings 19:35)
64 Lode yield
65 Express emotions
66 Fine dirt made by threshing (2 Kings 13:7)
67 Agent (abbr.)
68 Microwave laser

DOWN

1 Canned chili brand
2 Crowd together (Mark 3:9)
3 Equipment used in battle (2 Kings 20:13)
4 Give meal, as ravens did (1 Kings 17:4)
5 Supplied bread and water (1 Kings 18:13)
6 What a dropped melon does
7 Beers
8 Greek island of Aphrodite
9 "___ into the city" (2 Kings 7:12)
10 Pallid
11 Biblical you (2 Kings 1:13)
12 "He read in their ___" (2 Kings 23:2)
15 Doctor
20 Habitation broken in war (2 Kings 25:4)
21 Type of sword
24 "Hath shaken her ___ at thee" (2 Kings 19:21)

13 Stitched
21 Persia
22 Foreign Agricultural Service (abbr.)
25 Mennonite
27 "They that ___ in tears shall reap in joy" (Ps. 126:5)
29 Committee
30 Adoniram's father (1 Kings 4:6)
31 Brews
32 Mud (1 Kings 7:46)
33 Sixth sense (abbr.)
34 Omri's son (1 Kings 16:28)
35 Computer memory unit
36 __ vu
38 Bird's "thumb"
39 Compass point (abbr.)
43 South by west (abbr.)
45 Designated
46 Due
49 Wing
51 Tree Solomon used to make two cherubims (1 Kings 6:23)
53 Push roughly
54 Shin
55 The LORD spoke in ___ small voice (1 Kings 19:12)
56 Meat and potatoes dish
57 Fencing sword
58 Goofs
60 Drift
61 "Who is ___ to judge this thy so great a people?" (1 Kings 3:9)
62 Mentally alert
65 Enemies "___ them away captive" (1 Kings 8:48)
67 Precious stone

21

1 Kings

by Kathy Hake

• • • • •

ACROSS

1 Blemish
5 First New Testament book (abbr.)
9 Stinging insects
14 Hawaiian dancing
15 Captain of host (1 Kings 16:16)
16 Beach, where Solomon's navy was (1 Kings 9:26)
17 Metal (1 Kings 6:7)
18 Christmas song
19 Zeruah (1 Kings 11:26)
20 Hole (Gen. 37:24)
21 "The undersetters were of the very base ___" (1 Kings 7:34)
23 Organization (abbr.)
24 Large desert
26 Fire residue king had on face (1 Kings 20:41)
28 Hiram's "father was a ___ of Tyre" (1 Kings 7:14)
29 El __ (Texas city)
31 Expert
34 His son married Solomon's daughter (1 Kings 4:11)
37 Ceiling supports, built of cedar (1 Kings 6:15)
39 Reasons
40 "Came to pass at the ___ of three years" (1 Kings 2:39)
41 Jump, as priests did upon altar (1 Kings 18:26)
42 One laver contained forty of these (1 Kings 7:38)
44 Judah provoked LORD to ___ with sins (1 Kings 14:22)
47 North by east (abbr.)
48 False bible god (1 Kings 16:31)
50 Punching tool
51 Night bird of desert (Ps. 102:6)
52 Creatures (1 Kings 4:33)
56 "It shall bruise thy head, and thou shalt bruise his ___" (Gen. 3:15)
59 Elijah wondered if their god "sleepeth, and must be ___" (1 Kings 18:27)
63 Strike, as archers did Saul (1 Sam. 31:3)
64 Fourth month
66 He sacrificed meat to God (Gen. 4:4)
67 Mongolian desert
68 "Go and ___ other gods, and worship them" (1 Kings 9:6)
69 Run, as Rehoboam did to Jerusalem (1 Kings 12:18)
70 "Solomon did ___ in the sight of the LORD" (1 Kings 11:6)
71 His son lived in Aruboth (1 Kings 4:10)
72 "The thoughts of the diligent ___ only to plenteousness" (Prov. 21:5)
73 Solomon used threescore measures of this each day (1 Kings 4:22)

DOWN

1 Big boats Jehoshaphat made to carry gold (1 Kings 22:48)
2 Pope's governing organization
3 Where Baanah lived (1 Kings 4:16)
4 Bolted, as two of Shimei's servants did (1 Kings 2:39)
5 Billings' location
6 Minor prophet from Bethel
7 Very tall plant people dwelt under (1 Kings 4:25)
8 "Take away the remnant of the house of Jeroboam. . .___ it be all gone" (1 Kings 14:10)
9 Vane direction (abbr.)
10 Shisha's son (1 Kings 4:3)
11 Turfs
12 Experts

30 "The ___ of the covenant of the LORD" (1 Kings 3:15)
31 Tests, as God does our hearts (1 Chron. 29:17)
32 Solomon wanted to "discern between good and ___" (1 Kings 3:9)
35 "No God like thee, in heaven above, or on ___ beneath" (1 Kings 8:23)
37 Clip
38 Note of debt
39 Vow (1 Kings 2:43)
40 Cedar or hyssop (1 Kings 4:33)
41 Society (abbr.)
42 "The earth ___ with the sound" (1 Kings 1:40)
44 BB player ___ Abdul-Jabbar
45 ___ duck
47 Drills
48 "___ me, and know my thoughts" (Ps. 139:23)
49 "Queen of ___ heard of the fame" (1 Kings 10:1)
50 Recorded
54 Compared to Sinai (Gal. 4:25)
55 Island nation
56 Captains were told to fight only with ___ (1 Kings 22:31)
58 "Handful of ___ in a barrel" (1 Kings 17:12)
61 "Hiram came out from Tyre to ___ the cities" (1 Kings 9:12)
63 "___ they not written in the book?" (1 Kings 11:41)
64 Church leader (abbr.)
65 Negative answer (1 Kings 2:20)

20

1 Kings

by Kathy Hake

• • • • •

ACROSS

1 "Priests. . .which were not of the sons of ___" (1 Kings 12:31)
5 "The ___ thereof shall be as the wine of Lebanon" (Hos. 14:7)
10 Eighth month (1 Kings 6:38)
13 Glided
14 Jewish scripture
15 Pop
16 "Woman's child ___ in the night" (1 Kings 3:19)
17 "___ my heart to fear thy name" (Ps. 86:11)
18 "Good works for necessary ___" (Titus 3:14)
19 "King David was ___ and stricken in years" (1 Kings 1:1)
21 Tackle
23 Before (abbr.)
26 Liquid Zadok used to anoint Solomon (1 Kings 1:39)
28 Gives, as sinner does to sinner (Luke 6:34)
29 Relax, as Abner did around Saul (1 Sam. 26:7) (2 wds.)
32 Brasen rods which protected great cities (1 Kings 4:13)
33 Solomon was made ruler ___ Israel and Judah (1 Kings 1:35)
34 Squeak
36 Office furniture
37 Water nymph
38 Small particle
42 Bleacher
43 Paddles made from oaks of Bashan (Ezek. 27:6)
44 "___ the charge of the LORD" (1 Kings 2:3)
46 "Walking in the ___ of David" (1 Kings 3:3)
49 "To ___ the pride of all glory" (Isa. 23:9)
51 Son of ___, Solomon's officer (1 Kings 4:8)
52 Biddy
53 Cracker
57 Workout place
59 Dueling sword
60 Appearance
62 Take in
66 Where Jotham fled (Judg. 9:21)
67 One captain of Israel's hosts (1 Kings 2:5)
68 Location
69 Fleet's supreme commander (abbr.)
70 Angers
71 "Solomon raised a ___" (1 Kings 5:13)

DOWN

1 Least significant digit (abbr.)
2 Shiloh's priest (1 Kings 2:27)
3 Rival
4 Ahinadab's father (1 Kings 4:14)
5 Artist's workplace
6 Swindle
7 Little Mermaid's love
8 Treaty organization (abbr.)
9 "___ sat Solomon upon the throne" (1 Kings 2:12)
10 Brass vessels Hiram made (1 Kings 7:45)
11 Turn over
12 Keeps
15 "Art of ___ eyes" (Hab. 1:13)
20 Throw
22 Harsh criticism
23 Slog
24 Jabber
25 "Thine ___ may be open" (1 Kings 8:29)
27 Fellow laborer (Philem. 1:24)

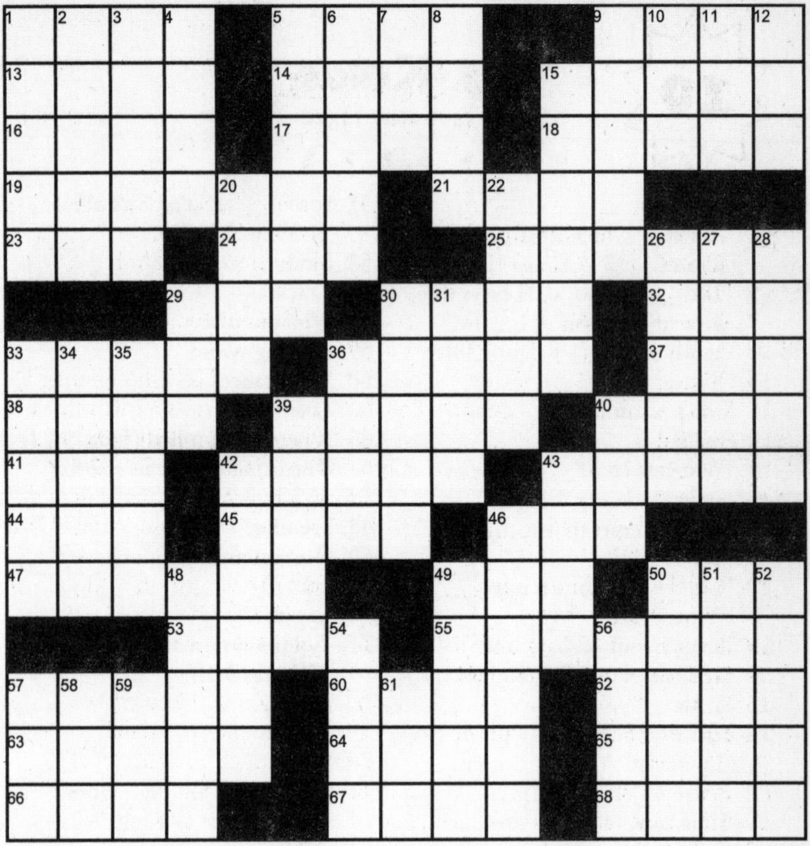

20 Religious song (Matt. 26:30)
22 Painter Richard
26 Banana oil e.g.
27 Cut the lawn
28 "If he be ___, there is tidings in his mouth" (2 Sam. 18:25)
29 "Lest he ___ him fenced cities" (2 Sam. 20:6)
30 Shiny metal (2 Sam. 8:10)
31 Am not
33 City in Nebraska
34 Roman marketplace (Acts 28:15)
35 Emblem
36 Duck
39 Southern girl
40 Archer's weapon Israelites were taught to use (2 Sam. 1:18)
42 Large grassy areas where soldiers camped (2 Sam. 11:11)
43 Absalom's great head covering (2 Sam. 14:26)
46 Delayed
48 Frosting
49 Oak seed
50 Seven closures (Rev. 5:1)
51 Throat infection
52 Writing
54 City David's enemies were coming from (2 Sam. 15:18)
56 Uh-uh
57 "Chasten him with the ___" (2 Sam. 7:14)
58 Spring month (abbr.)
59 Pod vegetable
61 Travel term

19

2 Samuel

by Kathy Hake

• • • • •

ACROSS

1 "Abner ___ himself strong" (2 Sam. 3:6)
5 Load
9 "Reward the doer of ___" (2 Sam. 3:39)
13 Winged
14 God's words are ___ (2 Sam. 7:28)
15 Food group
16 Singer
17 "Neither let there be ___" (2 Sam. 1:21)
18 "Let the young men now ___" (2 Sam. 2:14)
19 Zeruiah's son (2 Sam. 2:18)
21 God's dwelling (2 Sam. 7:6)
23 Center
24 Half of Chinese principle of harmony
25 Plan
29 Time zone (abbr.)
30 Reduce
32 Sun's name
33 "How ___ would I have gathered" (Matt. 23:37)
36 "The word of the LORD is ___" (2 Sam. 22:31)
37 Number of days David was in Ziklag (2 Sam. 1:1)
38 Deliberate
39 Legumes brought to David (2 Sam. 17:28)
40 "As though he had not ___ anointed" (2 Sam. 1:21)
41 "___ thou Asahel?" (2 Sam. 2:20)
42 Meal David made for Abner (2 Sam. 3:20)
43 Legion
44 Color
45 Evils
46 Michal "___ king David leaping" (2 Sam. 6:16)
47 Machir's father (2 Sam. 9:4)
49 Boxer Muhammad
50 Vane direction (abbr.)
53 Fly
55 Musical instruments (2 Sam. 6:5)
57 Quick
60 "If the sacrifice of his offering be ___" (Lev. 7:16) (2 wds.)
62 Boat movers not allowed on God's rivers (Isa. 33:21)
63 Swings wide, as Samuel does the doors of the house of the LORD (1 Sam. 3:15)
64 "Bind the ___ of thine head" (Ezek. 24:17)
65 Type of matter to be judged (Deut. 17:8)
66 Fishing tool (Hab. 1:15)
67 "Out of the ___ of the Philistines" (2 Sam. 19:9)
68 See

DOWN

1 Lady
2 Defense
3 Israel's second king (2 Sam. 2:4)
4 Long time periods
5 "I am in a great ___" (2 Sam. 24:14)
6 Queen of Sheba "came to Jerusalem with a very great ___" (1 Kings 10:2)
7 French "yes"
8 "Watchman ___ up to the roof" (2 Sam. 18:24)
9 What Hushai had on his head (2 Sam. 15:32)
10 Number of years David reigned in Hebron (2 Sam. 5:5) (Rom. num.)
11 Government agency (abbr.)
12 Used to make soap
15 "David ___ before the LORD" (2 Sam. 6:14)

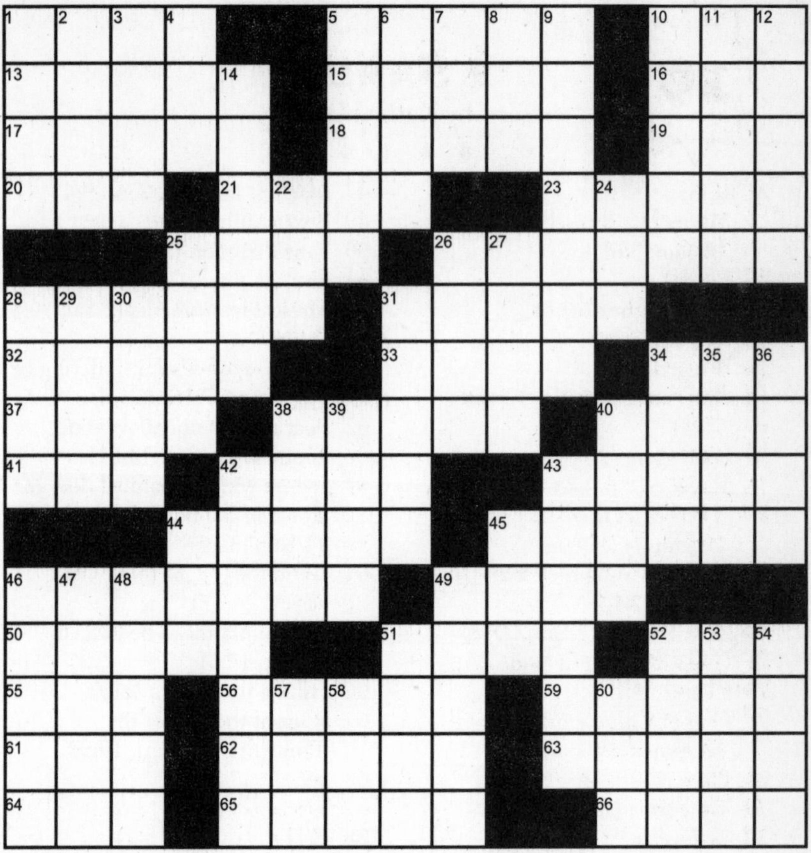

28 "Mercy shall not depart ___ from him" (2 Sam. 7:15)
29 Used to bind breastplate to rings of ephod (Ex. 39:21)
30 Iron tools (2 Sam. 12:31)
31 Herb
34 Zeruiah's son (2 Sam. 14:1)
35 "My cry did enter ___ his ears" (2 Sam. 22:7)
36 Tableland
38 People of this place became David's servants (2 Sam. 8:14)
39 Where Joab spoke with Abner (2 Sam. 3:27)
40 "Watchman cried, and ___ the king" (2 Sam. 18:25)
42 Comic
43 Land where Israel and Absalom pitched (2 Sam. 17:26)
44 Extremely swift jet (abbr.)
45 State leader (abbr.)
46 Stage
47 Cords Israelites brought to city (2 Sam. 17:13)
48 Sugar-free brand
49 Children playing in streets (Zech. 8:5)
51 Dues
52 Realm
53 Swing
54 Antes
57 Abner's father (2 Sam. 3:37)
58 Years Absalom lived in Jerusalem (2 Sam. 14:28)
60 Poor man's sole possession (2 Sam. 12:3)

18

2 Samuel

by Kathy Hake

• • • • •

ACROSS

1 Musical repeat
5 Stadium
10 Friend
13 Musical production
15 Imitation chocolate
16 Wide sash
17 Two lines of Moabites were sentenced to this (2 Sam. 8:2)
18 India language
19 Jonathan was Saul's
20 "He had made an ___ of speaking" (2 Sam. 13:36)
21 Cast metal of harrows and axes (2 Sam. 12:31)
23 "The meek will he ___ in judgment" (Ps. 25:9)
25 Tub spread
26 "I will ___ him with the rod" (2 Sam. 7:14)
28 Noisy situation (arch.)
31 Thailand citizens
32 "Saul ___ weaker" (2 Sam. 3:1)
33 Knoll, of Ammah (2 Sam. 2:24)
34 Mountain man Bridger
37 Pros
38 African country God brought Israel out of (2 Sam. 7:6)
40 Firm up muscles
41 "___ verily, their sound went into all the earth" (Rom. 10:18)
42 Eve's husband
43 Sheep-like animals (1 Sam. 25:2)
44 Killed, as David did Philistines (2 Sam. 8:1)
45 David cursed the mountains of this place (2 Sam. 1:21)
46 Presuppose, as prophet did (Deut. 18:20)
49 Type of ornaments (2 Sam. 1:24)
50 "LORD God of ___ was with him" (2 Sam. 5:10)
51 Mephibosheth's age when he fled (2 Sam. 4:4)
52 Loose gown worn at mass
55 26,000 men were ___ to war and battle (1 Chron. 7:40)
56 Entomb
59 Lofty habitation
61 "Now therefore let me ___ the king's face" (2 Sam. 14:32)
62 Stairway post
63 Lived, as Mephibosheth did in Jerusalem (2 Sam. 9:13)
64 Vane direction
65 Condition of people's heart (Acts 28:27)
66 Dines

DOWN

1 Regulation
2 They camped in ___ fields (2 Sam. 11:11)
3 Deceased, as David wanted Uriah to be (2 Sam. 11:21)
4 "Thou ___ great, O LORD" (2 Sam. 7:22)
5 Sneeze
6 "Neither let there be ___" (2 Sam. 1:21)
7 Gray sea eagle
8 City east of Eden (Gen. 4:16)
9 Nabal's wife (2 Sam. 2:2)
10 Suggest
11 Dwelt, as David did two days in Ziklag (2 Sam. 1:1)
12 Ephod's fabric (2 Sam. 6:14)
14 Jehoshaphat's father (2 Sam. 8:16)
22 Deep, dreaming sleep (abbr.)
24 Ship initials
25 Minerals
26 Snack food
27 Type of person awaiting healing (John 5:3)

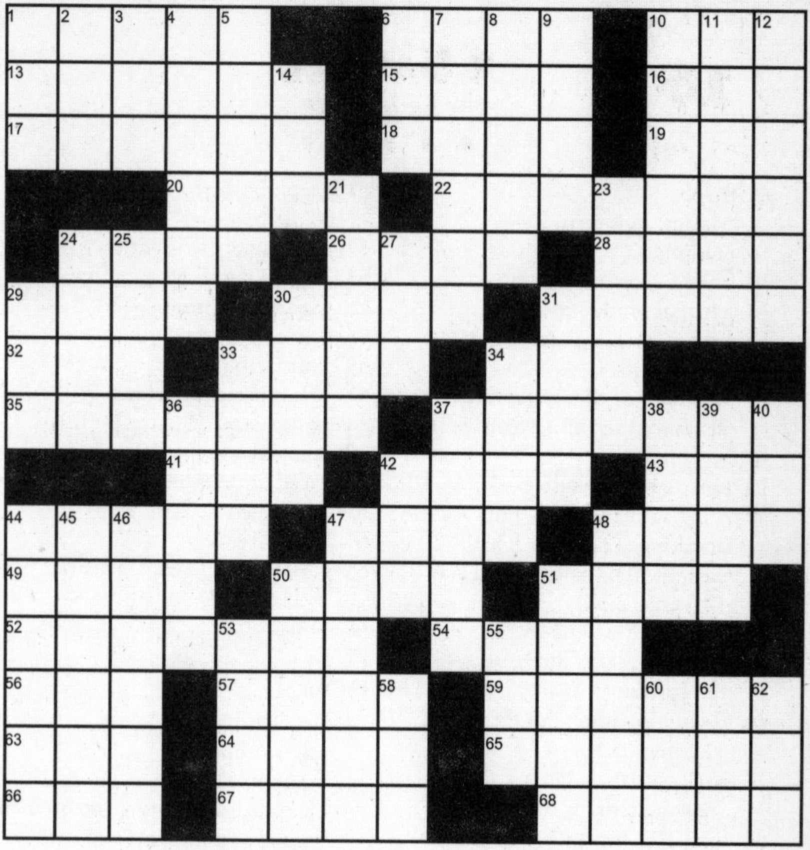

31 Move through water, as the iron (2 Kings 6:6)
33 Had four brasen wheels (1 Kings 7:30)
34 "___ no more so exceeding proudly" (1 Sam. 2:3)
36 Natural rooms where people hid (1 Sam. 13:6)
37 Public disorders
38 Heroic
39 Hannah "called his ___ Samuel" (1 Sam. 1:20)
40 Cooking measurement (abbr.)
42 "___ this child I prayed" (1 Sam. 1:27)
44 "Have ___ by one Spirit unto the Father" (Eph. 2:18)
45 David took ten of these to his brothers (1 Sam. 17:17)
46 Earwig
47 Flask David took to brothers (1 Sam. 16:20)
48 Cookie nut
50 "LORD came, and ___, and called" (1 Sam. 3:10)
51 Combustibles
53 ___ mater
55 Commercials
58 Bird that "gathereth her chickens under her wings" (Matt. 23:37)
60 Fasten, as kine (1 Sam. 6:7)
61 Winter hazard cast forth like morsels (Ps. 147:17)
62 Saul's uncle (1 Sam. 14:50)

17

1 Samuel

by Kathy Hake

• • • • •

ACROSS

1 Fancy boat
6 Hook
10 Second month (abbr.)
13 Beehive
15 Band instrument
16 Road (abbr.)
17 Unkind person
18 Raced
19 By way of
20 Space administration
22 Doings weighed by God (1 Sam. 2:3)
24 Part Dagon lost (1 Sam. 5:4)
26 Consumes offerings (1 Sam. 2:28)
28 Canal
29 Place where ark was carried (1 Sam. 5:8)
30 What Rahab did with scarlet thread (Josh. 2:18)
31 Fathers
32 Yang's partner
33 "Fear not; for thou hast ___ a son" (1 Sam. 4:20)
34 Number of Elkanah's wives (1 Sam. 1:2)
35 Pacify
37 Clothing Saul used to change appearance (1 Sam. 28:8)
41 Fire remains Tamar put on her head (2 Sam. 13:19)
42 Movie
43 Old-fashioned fathers
44 "The LORD killeth, and maketh ___" (1 Sam. 2:6)
47 Record where Samuel wrote (1 Sam. 10:25)
48 Weakling
49 Pointed cylinder
50 "The poorest ___ of the people" (2 Kings 24:14)
51 What Dagon fell on (1 Sam. 5:4)
52 Mary ___ (artist)
54 Israel's first king
56 First woman
57 Grudging (var.)
59 Under tooth's enamel
63 Part of a minute (abbr.)
64 Type of unclean animal (Lev. 11:30)
65 Channel for water (Isa. 19:10)
66 Fast plane (abbr.)
67 City in Yemen
68 Bovine

DOWN

1 Sweet potato
2 Animal brought by Tarshish navy (1 Kings 10:22)
3 Government security agency (abbr.)
4 Samuel's mother
5 Trinity
6 "They ___ not the land. . .by their own sword" (Ps. 44:3)
7 "We went ___, and set forth" (Acts 21:2)
8 Coerce, as priests threatened (1 Sam. 2:16)
9 "He will keep the ___ of his saints" (1 Sam. 2:9)
10 "Samuel. . .was in ___" (1 Sam. 2:26)
11 Show
12 Goliath threatened to feed David to these (1 Sam. 17:44)
14 Affirmative
21 Alight
23 Expression
24 One plague in Egypt (Ex. 9:25)
25 Volcano
27 Hotel with no room (Luke 2:7)
29 Swindle
30 Dagon lost ___ of his hands (1 Sam. 5:4)

30 Induct (2 wds.)
31 "The ___ is a doctrine of vanities" (Jer. 10:8)
32 Bush where Hagar set her son (Gen. 21:15)
33 Sibling's daughter
34 Harvest (Ruth 2:15)
35 "Bring to pass his ___" (Isa. 28:21)
37 Executive director (abbr.)
39 Tricky
41 "Shall ___ as lions' whelps" (Jer. 51:38)
43 Growling
46 Israel lost thirty thousand in battle (1 Sam. 4:10)
48 Test, as God did for Gideon (Judg. 7:4)
51 Communications Workers of America (abbr.)
53 Dinosaur
56 Chances of winning
57 "What aileth the people that they ___?" (1 Sam. 11:5)
58 Columbus's ship
60 "To hearken than the fat of ___" (1 Sam. 15:22)
61 "Eli sat upon a ___" (1 Sam. 4:13)
62 Opera solo
64 "They ___ up in the morning early" (1 Sam. 1:19)
65 Region
66 Hannah brought Samuel a coat every ___ (1 Sam. 2:19)
68 Compass point (abbr.)
70 Brain wave detector (abbr.)

16

1 Samuel

by Kathy Hake

• • • • •

ACROSS

1 Chinese seasoning
4 Dry stream beds
9 "___ them upon the table of thine heart" (Prov. 3:3)
14 Terminal abbr.
15 Home
16 Rough valley is neither ___ nor sown (Deut. 21:4)
17 Rested, as Eli did upon seat by post of temple (1 Sam. 1:9)
18 One spoil of war (1 Sam. 14:32)
19 Making a knot
20 Stone where Israelites "set down the ark" (1 Sam. 6:18)
22 Spoke
24 Pigpen
25 Proud ___ from God's commandments (Ps. 119:21)
27 Help, as men of Shechem did for Abimelech (Judg. 9:24)
29 Godly leaders (1 Sam. 15:30)
32 Hannah did not take ___ drink (1 Sam. 1:15)
35 Lager
36 "Let us ___ the ark" (1 Sam. 4:3)
38 Lily neither ___ nor spins (Luke 12:27)
40 God "smote the men of the ___" (1 Sam. 5:9)
42 "But be ye ___ of the word" (James 1:22)
44 "Earth shall ___" (Isa. 24:20)
45 "Ashamed when he is found" (Jer. 2:26)
47 "___ not. . .a daughter of Belial" (1 Sam. 1:16)
49 Coral reef
50 Use a key
52 Fruitless, like Hannah
54 Lord "bringeth ___, and lifteth up" (1 Sam. 2:7)
55 Seed bread
56 "A man after his ___ heart" (1 Sam. 13:14)
59 Relating to the ankle bone
63 Doctor's picture
67 Rationalism
69 Eagle's nest
71 Unrefined metal
72 Compact
73 Pine Tree State
74 "Sand which is on the ___ shore" (1 Sam. 13:5)
75 Produce eggs
76 Canned chili brand
77 A king "will set them to ___ his ground" (1 Sam. 8:12)

DOWN

1 Plateau
2 Prod
3 Fence opening where Saul met Samuel (1 Sam. 9:18)
4 Hannah "___ in bitterness of soul" (1 Sam. 1:10)
5 Hated (1 Sam. 2:17)
6 "LORD shall reward the ___ of evil" (2 Sam. 3:39)
7 Belief
8 Fall month (abbr.)
9 Mud (2 wds.)
10 Shaft of light
11 Part of eye
12 Where Israelites fled (1 Sam. 4:10)
13 Jittery
21 "Thou hast ___ captivity captive" (Ps. 68:18)
23 Hannah wept and did not ___ (1 Sam. 1:7)
26 Game official (abbr.)
28 Entryway where women assembled (1 Sam. 2:22)
29 Tohu's son (1 Sam. 1:1)

26 That (possessive)
28 Musical notation
29 Repairs (2 Chron. 24:12)
30 Ancient Indian
31 Naomi "___ with her daughters in law" (Ruth 1:6)
32 Lived, as Ruth did with her mother-in-law (Ruth 2:23)
33 Praises to the Lord (Rom. 15:11)
34 Partly frozen rain
35 Luau dish
37 Also known as (abbr.)
39 Special attention (abbr.)
41 Hawaiian island
43 "Seeing I am a ___?" (Ruth 2:10)
46 SE African country
48 "I will. . .___ with him" (Rev. 3:20)
51 "Lest I ___ mine own inheritance" (Ruth 4:6)
53 And so forth (abbr.)
56 Type of cedars to be cut down (Isa. 37:24)
57 Margarine substitute
58 Small ground plot (2 Kings 9:26)
60 Post-traumatic stress disorder (abbr.)
61 Short laugh
62 Afresh
64 "We cry, ___, Father" (Rom. 8:15)
65 Country where Naomi's family sojourned (Ruth 1:1)
66 "LORD shall judge the ___ of the earth" (1 Sam. 2:10)
68 Fall month (abbr.)
70 "The five men that went to ___" (Judg. 18:17)

15

Ruth

by Kathy Hake

• • • • •

ACROSS

1 "Fashioned it long ___" (Isa. 22:11)

4 "It grieveth me much for your ___" (Ruth 1:13)

9 Ruth was better to Naomi than ___ sons (Ruth 4:15)

14 "God was with the ___" (Gen. 21:20)

15 Sheep sound (Judg. 5:16)

16 Violence (Ezek. 7:23)

17 Number of Naomi's daughters-in-law (Ruth 1:8)

18 Opposite of full (Ruth 1:21)

19 Desert pond

20 Gumbo ingredient

22 "That his heart may discover ___" (Prov. 18:2)

24 "Thou ___ a virtuous woman" (Ruth 3:11)

25 Colossal

27 College football conference (abbr.)

29 She was "cumbered about much serving" (Luke 10:40)

32 Inhabits, as Naomi does in Moab (Ruth 1:4)

35 Brand of dispensable candy

36 Plant material lion will eat like the ox (Isa. 11:7)

38 "Almighty hath ___ very bitterly" (Ruth 1:20)

40 Upon

42 Wood and iron harnesses (Jer. 28:13)

44 "Cast into the fire for ___" (Ezek. 15:4)

45 Perfect

47 Enhances the flavor

49 Winter month (abbr.)

50 Plot

52 Most correct

54 America (abbr.)

55 "___ to teach" (2 Tim. 2:24)

56 Upper part of ladder to heaven (Gen. 28:12)

59 Parentless child (Lam. 5:3)

63 "They ___ to Bethlehem" (Ruth 1:22)

67 Mete out

69 Fire tool of gold (1 Kings 7:49)

71 Cape ___, peninsula of NE Tunisia

72 Trickle into

73 What a king will take a tenth of (1 Sam. 8:17)

74 Not good; part cast away (Matt. 13:48)

75 Gambling game

76 "Endued me with a good ___" (Gen. 30:20)

77 Gut muscles (abbr.)

DOWN

1 Singing voice

2 Look

3 Smell

4 South by east (abbr.)

5 "The ___ hath afflicted me" (Ruth 1:21)

6 "She ___ fast by the maidens of Boaz" (Ruth 2:23)

7 Feeds, as Boaz (Ruth 3:7)

8 Eye infection (var.)

9 Jibed

10 Epoch

11 Permission to enter a foreign country

12 Native ruler

13 "As an eagle stirreth up her ___" (Deut. 32:11)

21 Abridged (abbr.)

23 Ruth was Naomi's daughter-in-___

24 Mythical Greek deity
25 Ground (Judg. 2:1)
26 Pairs
27 "This is nothing ___ save the sword of Gideon" (Judg. 7:14)
28 See secretly (Josh. 14:7)
29 What men asked Gideon to do (Judg. 8:22)
30 What unrighteous do in the day time (2 Peter 2:13)
31 Main impact
34 Arched, as a bow (Ps. 7:12)
35 Elliptical
36 Samson's mother could not eat anything from this plant (Judg. 13:14)
38 Sharpen
39 Mined metals
40 Very reluctant (var.)
42 Army leader, as Sisera (Judg. 4:2)
43 Beaches (Judg. 11:22)
44 Eglon was a fat one (Judg. 3:17)
45 Hobo
46 Organic compound
47 Samson could not ___ his head (Judg. 16:19)
48 Healed (Luke 7:21)
49 Crush of people around Jesus (Luke 19:3)
51 A wolfhound
52 Vegetable
53 Honey makers Samson found in lion carcass (Judg. 14:8)
54 Organization that promotes cause (abbr.)
57 Cow sound
58 Energy unit (abbr.)
60 U.S. Navy rank

14

Judges

by Kathy Hake

ACROSS

1 Negative (prefix)
5 Speak without preparation
10 Furthest back
13 Baseball player Yogi
15 City manager
16 "Go and ___ in wait in the vineyards" (Judg. 21:20)
17 Shiny metal Philistines bound Samson with (Judg. 16:21)
18 Athletic field
19 2,000 pounds
20 High naval rank (abbr.)
21 "All the men of Israel were gathered against the city, ___ together as one man" (Judg. 20:11)
23 "Ye thought evil against me; but God ___it unto good" (Gen. 50:20)
25 Big cat (Judg. 14:8)
26 Prophetess (Judg. 4:4)
28 Secret mission (Judg. 3:19)
31 Jacob took Esau ten of these (Gen. 32:15)
32 Taking to court
33 "There ___ up fire out of the rock, and consumed the flesh and the unleavened cakes" (Judg. 6:21)
34 King in Celtic mythology
37 Walk slowly
38 Gideon was least in his father's ___ (Judg. 6:15)
40 Israel's priests came from this tribe (Deut. 31:9)
41 "___ the hand of the house of Joseph prevailed" (Judg. 1:35)
42 Cob vegetable Samson burned (Judg. 15:5)
43 Mr. O'Brien
44 Impressionist painter
45 Container Jael gave Sisera (Judg. 4:19)
46 Survives (Judg. 3:26)
49 Tola's father (Judg. 10:1)
50 Divert
51 Samson's strong limbs (Judg. 15:14)
52 Kimono sash
55 Dark, oily material
56 Ramble
59 Samson "had ___ the honey out of the carcase of the lion" (Judg. 14:9)
61 Adam's wife
62 Tiny amounts
63 "Dogs came and licked his ___" (Luke 16:21)
64 Sea Israelites walked to (Judg. 11:16)
65 Parts of speech
66 "If they bind me ___ with new ropes that never were occupied, then shall I be weak" (Judg. 16:11)

DOWN

1 Father (Rom. 8:15)
2 Goody two shoes
3 Trolley car
4 Tax agency (abbr.)
5 Vigorously
6 Weapon (Job 41:26)
7 Caustic substance
8 Cation
9 Thorny bush trees asked to reign over them (Judg. 9:14)
10 Holy table (Judg. 21:4)
11 Female singer ___ Apple
12 Day people came up out of Jordan and encamped in Gilgal (Josh. 4:19)
14 Posing questions (Luke 2:46)
22 Land where Cain dwelt (Gen. 4:16)

28 Scent
29 Not his
30 "___ no man any thing, but to love" (Rom. 13:8)
32 Fled, as Jotham did (Judg. 9:21)
35 "___ of his finger" (Luke 16:24)
36 "Why make ye this ___?" (Mark 5:39)
37 Moved rhythmically (Judg. 21:23)
38 Footgear Joshua removed (Josh. 5:15)
39 Greek goddess of youth
40 See ya!
41 Frequency (abbr.)
42 Type of memory (abbr.)
43 "LORD ___ every man's sword" (Judg. 7:22)
45 Disappointed, as Ahab (1 Kings 21:5)
46 Hurry
48 "___ not yourselves" (Rom. 12:19)
49 Purple
50 Second brightest star in constellation Taurus
52 Mount where Barak went (Judg. 4:12)
56 Other places Israelites hid from Midianites (Judg. 6:2)
57 Where Abimelech stood to fight against the city (Judg. 9:44)
58 Graven image
59 Fuel
60 Rodent
61 Important span of time
63 Tyrannosaurus ___
64 Business title ending (abbr.)

13

Judges

by Kathy Hake

ACROSS

1 "We will go up by ___ against it" (Judg. 20:9)
4 Greek word meaning love
9 Small, freshwater fish
14 "They said ___ to another" (Judg. 6:29)
15 Pepper plant
16 Throng
17 "Sand by the ___ side for multitude" (Judg. 7:12)
18 What Gideon requested for his men (Judg. 8:5)
19 People fled to a strong ___ in Thebez (Judg. 9:51)
20 Jabin's army captain (Judg. 4:7)
22 "Children of the ___ lay along" (Judg. 7:12)
24 Adam's garden
25 Philosopher Karl
27 Santa call (2 wds.)
31 Abimelech "beat down the city, and sowed it with ___" (Judg. 9:45)
32 Wash off
33 Morning moisture Gideon requested (Judg. 6:37)
34 European nation
36 Love intensely
38 Shrivel up
40 Trees of Lebanon (Judg. 9:15)
42 Wooly animals destroyed by Israel's enemy (Judg. 6:4)
43 He fought against Israel (Judg. 11:20)
44 Jephthah's home (Judg. 11:3)
45 Bundle of grain used as offering (Lev. 23:15)
47 One place Israelites hid from Midianites (Judg. 6:2)
51 "His daughter came out to ___ him" (Judg. 11:34)
53 Cab
54 "Israel did ___ in the sight of the LORD" (Judg. 6:1)
55 Totals
57 He "threshed wheat by the winepress" (Judg. 6:11)
59 Loon-like seabird
62 Trio
65 Licensing organization for UK newspapers (abbr.)
66 Went to Egypt with Moses
67 Musical "slow"
68 "___ thee down" (Judg. 7:9)
69 Heavenly lights Deborah and Barak sang about (Judg. 5:20)
70 "That ye may ___" (1 Cor. 14:12)
71 ICAO code for Ethiopian Airlines (abbr.)

DOWN

1 Defeats
2 New York Indian
3 Prickly herb
4 Reduce (abbr.)
5 Ehud's father (Judg. 3:15)
6 "I. . .___ it up" (Rev. 10:10)
7 Pod vegetable
8 "Jephthah went with the ___" (Judg. 11:11)
9 Fifth book in the New Testament
10 A food Gideon gave an angel (Judg. 6:19)
11 "Thou hast brought me very ___" (Judg. 11:35)
12 Ram's mate, used for sacrifice (Lev. 14:10)
13 Computerized database of U.S. drivers (abbr.)
21 Wanting nothing (James 1:4)
23 Abimelech's cutting tool (Judg. 9:48)
25 Sisera's drink (Judg. 4:19)
26 Some

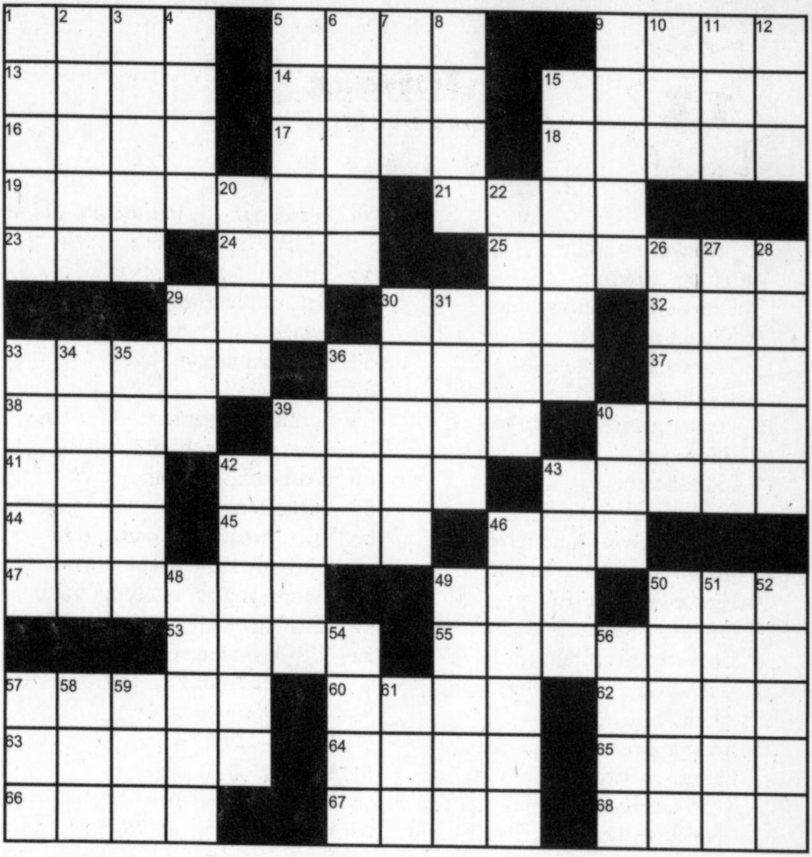

12 Cooking tool Tamar used (2 Sam. 13:9)
15 "___ her in whatsoever business" (Rom. 16:2)
20 Sailor's "hey"
22 Resource
26 Deluxe
27 "O ___ and see" (Ps. 34:8)
28 Under a beard (2 wds.)
29 "Give ___, O ye" (Deut. 32:1)
30 Steam bath
31 Great man among Anakims (Josh. 14:15)
33 Belt
34 Ocean jewel of great price (Matt. 13:46)
35 Sri ___
36 Pros opposites
39 Challenges
40 Assist
42 Silently
43 Israelites' inheritance (Josh. 1:6)
46 Large people occupying land Israelites wanted (Josh. 12:4)
48 Foreign nations were snares and ___ for Israel (Josh. 23:13)
49 Another spoil of war (Josh. 22:8)
50 Raccoon-like animal
51 Cycle
52 Saying
54 Towering, as the Anakims (Deut. 2:21)
56 Organization (abbr.)
57 "___ had brought them up to the roof" (Josh. 2:6)
58 Sticky black substance
59 Government agency (abbr.)
61 Meaningless refrain

12

Joshua

by Kathy Hake

ACROSS

1 David did weep and ___ for his child (2 Sam. 12:21)

5 Footwear

9 "Pluck away his ___" (Lev. 1:16)

13 Reverberate

14 Joshua commanded Israelites to keep this spoil (along with 49 Down) (Josh. 22:8)

15 Playing field

16 "The place whereon ___ standest is holy" (Josh. 5:15)

17 Part of sword used to kill (Josh. 10:28)

18 Number of days Israelites marched around Jericho

19 "Be strong and of a good ______" (Josh. 1:9)

21 Bezer and Golan were cities of refuge to the ___ (Josh 20:8)

23 "This our bread we took ___ for our provision" (Josh 9:12)

24 Rahab and ___ family were spared

25 Afternoon nap

29 Aurora

30 Talk back

32 Football conference (abbr.)

33 Spread out

36 Insertion mark

37 Tree (Isa. 44:14)

38 "Lest he ___ my soul like a lion" (Ps. 7:2)

39 "O thou of little faith, wherefore didst thou ___?" (Matt. 14:31)

40 Opposed

41 "Joshua sent messengers, and they ___ unto the tent" (Josh. 7:22)

42 This ceased after Israelites found food in Canaan (Josh. 5:12)

43 "To whom then will ye ___ God?" (Isa. 40:18)

44 Accompanied Israelites around wall of Jericho (Josh. 6:8)

45 __ Major (Big Dipper)

46 One of the armed tribes (Josh. 4:12)

47 North American river

49 Container

50 Accountant (abbr.)

53 "Your God hath given you ___" (Josh. 1:13)

55 Signaled by audio

57 What thief came to do (John 10:10)

60 Actor Alda

62 Nothing

63 "___ is that people, whose God is the LORD" (Ps. 144:15)

64 "Save that which was ___" (Matt. 18:11)

65 Buck

66 Epochs

67 "Shall suffer ___" (2 Cor. 3:15)

68 Floor covering

DOWN

1 "Elders of Gilead went to ___ Jephthah" (Judg. 11:5)

2 Sound of a sneeze

3 Joshua's command to people on last day circling Jericho's walls (Josh. 6:16)

4 Travel around

5 Attacks

6 Flax was "laid in ___ upon the roof" (Josh. 2:6)

7 Tooth

8 "Every ___ shall bow" (Isa. 45:23)

9 Greek island (Acts 27:7)

10 Pastor (abbr.)

11 "Not ___ thing hath failed thereof" (Josh. 23:14)

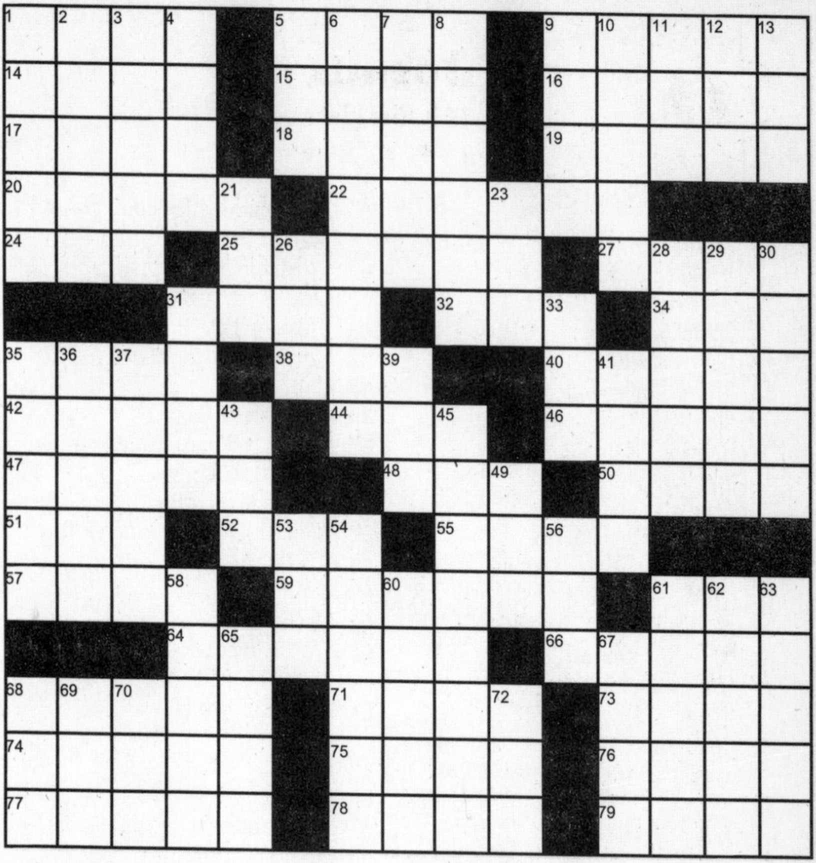

23 Airport abbr.
26 What Israelites were commanded to obey
28 "God in heaven above, and in ___ beneath" (Josh. 2:11)
29 Agricultural student
30 Small amount
31 Hurried from enemies (Judg. 5:30)
33 Football assoc.
35 Cramp
36 Banned
37 Musical based on life of Eva Perón
39 "Meditate therein ___ and night" (Josh. 1:8)
41 Grain
43 Eastern state (abbr.)
45 Royal palace
49 Killed in action (abbr.)
53 "Pharisees fast ___" (Matt. 9:14)
54 Long scolding
56 Non-nuclear energy (abbr.)
58 Zippor's son (Josh. 24:9)
60 Man who bought Shechem for 100 pieces of silver (Josh. 24:32)
61 Jephunneh's son (Josh. 14:13)
62 What Joshua wrote a copy of the law on (Josh. 8:32)
63 "Get you unto your ___" (Josh. 22:4)
65 Manasseh's children who inherited land of Gilead (Josh. 17:6)
67 "A ___ of blue" (Ex. 39:21)
68 Center
69 Time period
70 ICAO code for Albanian Airlines
72 Dekaliter (abbr.)

11

Joshua

by Kathy Hake

ACROSS

1 Wild beast (Ps. 80:13)
5 Judah's border "went up to ___" (Josh. 15:3)
9 Cowboy rope
14 "___, Father" (Mark 14:36)
15 Burnt offering (1 Sam. 6:14)
16 Painting prop
17 Northeast by north (abbr.)
18 Continent where Paul ministered
19 "Your foot shall ___ upon" (Josh. 1:3)
20 Japanese city
22 "Talk no ___ ___ exceeding proudly" (1 Sam. 2:3) (2 wds.)
24 Concord e.g.
25 Heavenly body idolatrous priests burned incense to (2 Kings 23:5)
27 Orderly
31 "___ ye not, but pursue after your enemies" (Josh. 10:19)
32 Tribe with seventh lot (Josh. 19:40)
34 At 110, Joshua said, "I am. . . stricken in ___" (Josh. 23:2)
35 God counts each ___ we take (Job 31:4)
38 After couple ___, Jesus turned water into wine
40 David said the proud ___ lies against him (Ps. 119:69)
42 "A ___ work of a sapphire stone" (Ex. 24:10)
44 Pat lightly
46 One language on Jesus' cross (Luke 23:38)
47 "Judah shall ___ in their coast" (Josh. 18:5)
48 Chatter
50 "And ___ took up the ark" (Josh. 3:6)
51 Drunkard
52 "The sixth ___" (Josh. 19:32)
55 Forsaking the Lord and serving strange gods (Josh. 24:19–20)
57 Balak, king of ___ (Josh. 24:9)
59 Fiji denizen
61 GMT-0600
64 Stellar
66 Excite
68 Form of greeting
71 Vinegary
73 Hebrew name meaning oak
74 Metropolitan
75 Wharf
76 Penny
77 What Israel turned before their enemies (Josh. 7:8)
78 Mount where Joshua built altar (Josh. 8:30)
79 Village in eastern Hungary

DOWN

1 Jordan's river edges that overflow (Josh. 3:15)
2 Heeds Lord's commands
3 Monastery superior
4 Scold
5 Precedes an alias (abbr.)
6 "Neither be thou ___" (Josh. 1:9)
7 Negatively charged particle
8 "The tabernacle was ___ up" (Ex. 40:17)
9 Allows
10 Eleazar's father (Josh. 24:33)
11 Compass point
12 Israelites passed through Red ___ on dry land (Josh. 4:23)
13 "Destroyed. . .young and ___" (Josh. 6:21)
21 Choose

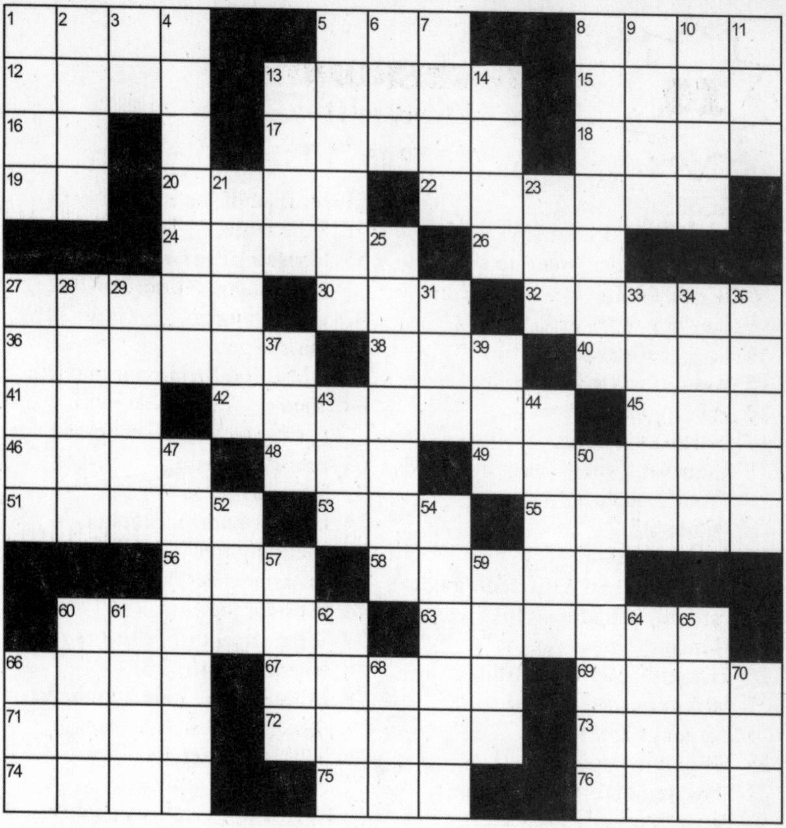

28 Promised land flowed with milk and this (Lev. 20:24)
29 Of the king
31 Accountant (abbr.)
33 "The poor shall never ___" (Deut. 15:11)
34 Camels' offspring (Gen. 32:15)
35 "The LORD said unto me, '___' " (Deut. 10:11)
37 Rainy month (abbr.)
39 Facial twitch
43 "The oath which he ___ sworn" (Deut. 7:8)
44 Bovine
47 The people were to do this before God (Deut. 12:18)
50 Father of Hebrew nation
52 Electromagnetic unit
54 Phantom
57 God will bless the fruit of this (Deut. 7:13)
59 Uncertain
60 Philippines' national sport
61 Men found horses and asses ___ (2 Kings 7:10)
62 Cranny
64 Hawkeye State
65 God's word was written on its posts (Deut. 11:20)
66 Binding oath
68 God sent Moses to the ___ of Pisgah (Deut. 3:27)
70 "Fowl that may ___ above the earth" (Gen. 1:20)

10

DEUTERONOMY

by Mary A. Hake

• • • • • •

ACROSS

1 Smallest group under captains (Deut. 1:15)
5 Some offerings were cooked in one (Lev. 6:21)
8 Medicine amount
12 Woof's partner in weaving
13 "Ye ___ the deeds of your fathers" (Luke 11:48)
15 Thought
16 "I have caused thee to see ___" (Deut. 34:4)
17 Wild meat dish
18 City near Dead Sea (Deut. 34:3)
19 Its cap. is Halifax
20 They "___ thy covenant" (Deut. 33:9)
22 Tables of sacrifice (Deut. 7:5)
24 Painter's stand
26 Telegraphic signal
27 Show indifference
30 Part of a minute (abbr.)
32 Bangladesh capital
36 Hype
38 "___ to teach" (1 Tim. 3:2)
40 Balaam's father (Deut. 23:4)
41 "If ___ man take a wife" (Deut. 22:13)
42 Son of Joseph (Deut. 33:17)
45 Boxing great
46 "___ the Lord thy God" (Deut. 6:2)
48 "When he saw them, he ____ to meet them" (Gen. 18:2)
49 Olive trees would grow here (Deut. 28:40)
51 10th U.S. president
53 This brought manna (Ex. 16:13–15)
55 Very fat
56 A Hebrew
58 Less wet
60 Horizontal above-ground stem
63 Moses told the people not to be this (Deut. 1:17)
66 Number of bullocks offered on 6th day (Num. 29:29) (Rom. num.)
67 Design
69 "The swine, because it divideth the ____" (Deut. 14:8)
71 Middle Eastern oil conglomerate (abbr.)
72 Plunder in war
73 Truant (abbr.)
74 Walk in water
75 Kilometers per hour (abbr.)
76 Jesus' mother

DOWN

1 Jacob to Esau (Gen. 25:24)
2 Consumes food (Deut. 32:13)
3 Naval Reserve (abbr.)
4 Talked aloud (2 wds.)
5 Broad ones covered altar (Num. 16:39)
6 "God delivered ___ unto us" (Deut. 2:36)
7 Severe inflammation of mouth
8 An area near Red Sea (Deut. 1:1)
9 Scent
10 These waters had abundance (Deut. 33:19)
11 This could be plucked by hand (Deut. 23:25)
13 Wine is like their venom (Deut. 32:33)
14 "The fallow deer, and the ____ goat" (Deut. 14:5)
21 Unclean bird (Deut. 14:12)
23 Little bit
25 God gave Isaiah the tongue of what? (Isa. 50:4)
27 "The candlestick was of beaten gold, unto the ____" (Num. 8:4)

22 This crop withstood plague (Ex. 9:32)
25 Lookout who goes ahead of army
26 Desert plants
27 It was made of shittim wood (Deut. 10:3)
29 They dwelt in Hazerim (Deut. 2:23)
30 Those committing 61 Across were to do this (Deut. 22:22)
32 Delight in
33 God says He kills and makes ___ (Deut. 32:39)
34 Irritate
35 Senior Airmen (abbr.)
36 "The LORD alone ___ lead him" (Deut. 32:12)
38 American tax agency (abbr.)
42 U.S. espionage bureau (abbr.)
43 Snake-like fish
47 Faithful
49 A Hebrew celebration (Deut. 16)
50 "___ the judgment is God's" (Deut. 1:17)
52 Place they abode (Deut. 1:46)
55 Dry grass bedding (Isa. 11:7)
57 Seek prey (Gen. 27:5)
58 Hebrews could eat the fallow one (Deut. 14:5)
59 Old Norse poetry collection
60 "___ as of a woman in travail" (Jer. 22:23)
61 Bird classification
62 Part of foot anointed (Lev. 14:14)
63 "The LORD he is God; there is none ___" (Deut. 4:35)
64 "___ an altar unto the LORD" (2 Sam. 24:18)
65 Pronoun used 3 times in Deut. 1:12
68 Papua New Guinean language

9

DEUTERONOMY

by Mary A. Hake

• • • • • •

ACROSS

1 It precedes Ephesians (abbr.)
4 City overthrown by God (Deut. 29:23)
9 Made brooks blackish (Job 6:16)
12 Popular chocolate cookie
14 What Moses did to stone tables (Deut. 9:17)
15 "The cattle we took for a ___" (Deut. 2:35)
16 India's champion of the poor (Phoolan)
17 "Get thee down quickly from ___" (Deut. 9:12)
18 "He ___ upon a cherub" (Ps. 18:10)
19 Ship used by disciples
21 Worker bees
23 God saved by His stretched-out ___ (Deut. 4:34)
24 Number of workdays in week (Deut. 5:13)
25 Large amount
28 Unhappy (1 Sam. 1:18)
31 Nest of young birds
35 Fearful
37 Days Passover lasted (Deut. 16:3) (Rom. num.)
39 Samuel's mentor (1 Sam. 3:6)
40 Honey and oil came from one (Deut. 32:13)
41 More frozen
43 This is to be put away (Deut. 24:7)
44 Austria (abbr.)
45 Moses' eyes never became this (Deut. 34:7)
46 Arm covering
48 Rebellious one's neck (Deut. 31:27)
51 "___ now of the days that are past" (Deut. 4:32)
53 Women's fashion magazine
54 Mythical Greek goddess
56 Repeated exclamation in Psalms (Ps. 35:21)
58 "Thou didst ___ out of the land of Egypt" (Deut. 9:7)
61 Forbidden by 7th commandment (Deut. 5:18)
66 Enhanced Data Acquisition System (abbr.)
67 Unclean bird (Deut. 14:14)
69 Margarine
70 Revise
71 Spear support
72 Jacob's brother (Deut. 2:4)
73 How Esau approached Jacob (Gen. 33:4)
74 "I ___ above all things" (3 John 1:2)
75 Disobey (James 1:16)

DOWN

1 "Thou shalt have none other ___ before me" (Deut. 5:7)
2 Space
3 Priestly tribe (Deut. 31:9)
4 Israel was to ___ idols (Deut. 7:26)
5 Visions (Deut. 13:1)
6 N-Methylanthraniloyl (abbr.)
7 Official dog registry (abbr.)
8 A heart that does this will not be deceived (Deut. 11:16)
9 King Og's bedstead (Deut. 3:11)
10 Assign property to another
11 "The ____ of the LORD thy God are always upon it" (Deut. 11:12)
13 Used to anoint (Deut. 28:40)
15 Substitute
20 "The man did as Joseph ___" (Gen. 43:17)

22 Joshua's father (Num. 11:28)
25 Prophetic
27 Aaron's name was written on Levi's (Num. 17:3)
29 Royal
30 They wouldn't let Israel pass (Num. 20:21)
31 A clean woman "shall be ___" (Num. 5:28)
32 Moses said, "If thou ___ thus with me, kill me" (Num. 11:15)
33 Offenders were to ___ 1/5 more in restitution (Num. 5:7)
34 Drink rapidly
35 "The LORD appointed ___ ___ time" (Ex. 9:5) (2 wds.)
36 Why do the heathen do this? (Ps. 2:1)
38 Entrances or passages (arch.)
39 "The Canaanites dwell by the ____" (Num. 13:29)
43 Considerate attention (abbr.)
45 Fruit of 27 Down (Num. 17:8)
46 Balaam compared Israel to this (Num. 24:9)
49 Type of tree (Isa. 44:14)
51 "The cloud ___ upon the tabernacle" (Num. 9:18)
53 Emanations
54 Things
55 Type of wood priest used (Num. 19:6)
56 Tree juices (Ps. 104:16) (pl.)
57 "The cock shall not ____" (John 13:38)
58 Last Stuart monarch
60 Swiss-like cheese
61 Raised platform (arch.)
62 God gives this in season
65 Moses told his father-in-law, "Leave us ___" (Num. 10:31)
67 Common illness

8

NUMBERS

by Mary A. Hake

• • • • • •

ACROSS

1 What drowsiness clothes a man with (Prov. 23:21)

5 Caleb said, "Let us go up at ___" (Num. 13:30)

9 Follower of Jamaican subculture

14 Small ornamental lady's bag

15 Measure of electric current strength

16 Nocturnal, odd-toed mammal

17 Nazarites let this grow (Num. 6:5)

18 Time of day Passover was celebrated (Num. 9:11)

19 Descendant of Gad (Num. 26:17)

20 Aaron was 123 years ___ when he died (Num. 33:39)

21 Heavy work shoe

23 "One ___ five hundred pence" (Luke 7:41)

24 Threescore and twelve thousand were offered to God (Num. 31:33)

26 Container for the ashes of dead

28 Daniel "___ no pleasant bread" (Dan. 10:3)

29 Nevada city

31 Regulates food and health items (abbr.)

34 People did this with the quails (Num. 11:32)

37 Paul ___ not speak of some things (Rom. 15:18) (past tense)

39 Father of Gaddi (Num. 13:11)

40 "Hast thou not heard long ___" (2 Kings 19:25)

41 "Let her not be as one ____ (Num. 12:12)

42 Israel was this to God (Isa. 45:4)

44 Son of Pedahzur (Num. 1:10)

47 The Lord's servant is to be ___ to teach (2 Tim. 2:24)

48 Eliasaph was his son (Num. 3:24)

50 Levites did this to lamps

51 American College of Surgeons (abbr.)

52 Tile design

56 If one spreads, the person's unclean (Lev. 13:8)

59 Son of Kohath (Num. 3:19)

63 A Native American tribe

64 Border of Moab (Num. 21:13)

66 College head

67 Wilma Flintstone's husband

68 South African ethnic group

69 Among

70 "Eloi, ___ sabachthani?" (Mark 15:34)

71 This savor pleases the Lord (Num. 15)

72 "Every ___ inheritance" (Num. 33:54)

73 Former Soviet Union (abbr.)

DOWN

1 The spies searched Zin unto here (Num. 13:21)

2 "Our years as _ ___ that is told" (Ps. 90:9) (2 wds.)

3 "I will ____ thee with mine eye" (Ps. 32:8)

4 Joseph's brothers addressed him this way in Egypt (Gen. 43:20)

5 Priests were appointed to do this to the vessels (1 Chron. 9:29)

6 De __ (from the beginning)

7 Gadfly

8 Active volcano

9 Rapid Transit Authority (abbr.)

10 Moses' brother (Num. 2:1)

11 Eject forcefully

12 "Son of man, take thee a _____" (Ezek. 4:1)

13 Dry

21 Hebrew letter often added to many place names (John 1:28)

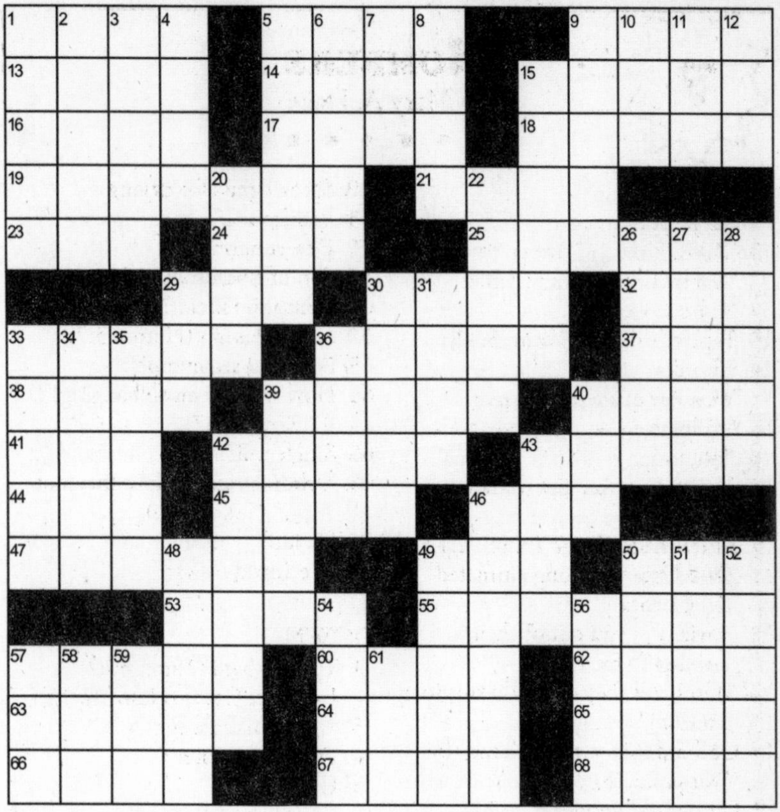

29 "It went ___ with Moses for their sakes" (Ps. 106:32)
30 Ropes on court hangings (Num. 4:26)
31 "If a man vow __ ____ unto the Lord" (Num. 30:2)(2 wds.)
33 Wilderness area (Num. 10:12)
34 Paul did not do this with his power (1 Cor. 9:18)
35 Vegetable people longed for (Num. 11:5)
36 Talk show host
39 Valley where Israel camped (Num. 21:12)
40 Descendant of Benjamin (Num. 26:40)
42 Son of Gideoni (Num. 1:11)
43 Drink offering (Num. 15:5)
46 Their western one was the great sea (Num. 34:6)
48 Son of Zebulun (Num. 26:26)
49 Type of offering (Num. 15:19)
50 Large striped cat
51 Algebraic morphism
52 Little wooded valleys
54 Small boat
56 Soft mineral
57 It spoke to Balaam (Num. 22:28)
58 "He smote them ___ and thigh" (Judg. 15:8)
59 Anger
61 "Deliver thyself as a ___ from the. . .hunter" (Prov. 6:5)

7

Numbers

by Mary A. Hake

ACROSS

1 Air pollution
5 "All that are ____ to go forth to war in Israel" (Num. 1:3)
9 Short remnant
13 Type of offering (Num. 6:20)
14 Chunk
15 West African republic
16 Study of supply and demand (abbr.)
17 Ancient plucked instrument
18 Hardship
19 Ammishaddai's son (Num. 1:12)
21 2004 Oscar-winning animated documentary
23 "I will ___ you out of their bondage" (Ex. 6:6)
24 Moses said they could do this for a month
25 God did this to the ass's mouth (Num. 22:28)
29 Computer brand
30 Heave offering (Num. 15:20)
32 Street (abbr.)
33 Ancestor of Eliab (Num. 26:8)
36 "I give thee my ___" (Song 7:12)
37 Liquid measure (Num. 15:4)
38 Cain's murdered brother
39 Nothings
40 Alphabet
41 Herb (Luke 11:42)
42 Root beer brand (3 words)
43 Priest was to do this with curses (Num. 5:23)
44 "Who shall ___ counsel" (Num. 27:21)
45 Founders of 12 tribes relationship (abbr.)
46 Moses was to ___ Hebrews to make fringes (Num. 15:38)
47 Scotland's loch monster
49 Japanese for *book*
50 Spread grass for drying
53 Whirlpool
55 Desert hermit
57 Son of Enan (Num. 1:15)
60 Canaanite king (Num. 33:40)
62 Son of Joseph (Num. 13:7)
63 Mythical sea nymph
64 How women made hangings (2 Kings 23:7)
65 Single unit
66 Deborah sang, "Have they not ___?" (Judg. 5:30)
67 Sly look
68 Greek god of war

DOWN

1 Take an oath (Num. 30:2)
2 Father of Geuel (Num. 13:15)
3 Shaped like an egg
4 DNA component
5 Glowing
6 Utter impulsively
7 Used to divide the land (Num. 26:56)
8 Balaam prophesied its affliction (Num. 24:24)
9 "The Lord make his face ___ upon thee" (Num. 6:25)
10 Children's running game
11 One (Sp.)
12 The instruments of ministry were to be put on this (Num. 4:12)
15 A Nazarite could not have this fruit (Num. 6:3)
20 African ox
22 Heifers chosen couldn't have worn these (Num. 19:2)
26 Vophsi's son (Num. 13:14)
27 Kick out
28 Having a high mass per unit volume

24 "I ___ the LORD your God" (Lev. 11:44)
25 To place in sight
26 Aaron did this to the sacrifice (Lev. 9:8)
27 Proofreader's insertion mark
28 Pointed corners of altar
29 Ring-tailed animal
30 Best musical, Tony award 1980
31 "Poor, and fallen in ___" (Lev. 25:35)
34 Ornamental feather
36 Mythological Irish princess
41 Taught one-on-one
42 May be woolen or linen (Lev. 13:47)
43 Fruit of the land (Lev. 26:4)
44 Chubbier
46 "Thou shalt not avenge, ___ bear any grudge" (Lev. 19:18)
48 Compass point, 22.50 degrees
50 "The land is ___" (Lev. 25:23)
51 "It went ___ with Moses" (Ps. 106:32)
52 Jael drove one into Sisera (Judg. 4:21)
53 Type of flour used with offering (Lev. 2:1)
54 Presentation
55 Unclean animal (Lev. 11:30)
56 Union (abbr.)
57 "A homer of barley ___ shall be valued" (Lev. 27:16)
60 Men weren't to do this to the corners of their beards (Lev. 19:27)

6

LEVITICUS

by Mary A. Hake

● ● ● ● ● ●

ACROSS

1 Drench
5 Foul up
9 "The priest ___ is anointed" (Lev. 4:5)
13 ___ Stanley Gardner
14 Accompanist's instrument
15 "Lest he ___ thee to the judge" (Luke 12:58)
16 For fear that (used 3 times in Lev. 10)
17 Wading bird, unclean to eat (Lev. 11:19)
18 Humor writer Bombeck
19 Right ear, hand, and this anointed (Lev. 14:14)
20 Type of man to be honored
21 Plays
23 This was to have a Sabbath rest (Lev. 25)
25 Plant fungus
26 Connive
29 Made happier
32 Part of the Thai language family
33 Twelve of gold listed in Num. 7
35 "Be unclean until the ___" (Lev. 15:27)
37 People did this in their hearts (Ps. 95:10)
38 Ten Commandments
39 God casts this like morsels (Ps. 147:17)
40 "There ___ out fire from the LORD" (Lev. 10:2)
42 Bowels
44 Parent-teacher groups
45 Wave caused by earthquake
47 Set-in wood strips
49 If beasts did this, the meat was unclean (Lev. 17:15)
50 Restaurant food list
51 "Do according to all that they ___ thee" (Deut. 17:10)
54 Problems
58 Animal den
59 To correct
61 Model
62 A scarlet one saved Rahab (Josh. 2:21)
63 God's ____ was not to be profaned (Lev. 18:21)
64 "I am the LORD, and there is none ___" (Isa. 45:5)
65 "God ___ the people" (Ex. 13:18)
66 Temporary Restraining Order (abbr.)
67 The high priest was not to do this to his clothes (Lev. 21:10)

DOWN

1 God swore by his own ___ (Ex. 32:13)
2 Chocolate sandwich cookie
3 "I ___ will do this" (Lev. 26:16)
4 "He struck it into the pan, or _____" (1 Sam. 2:14)
5 Mixed seed was not to be sown there (Lev. 19:19)
6 Pork fat
7 Card game
8 Hebrews were not to make brothers become any (Lev. 25:42)
9 Performance venue (Brit.)
10 Offenders were to make amends for this (Lev. 5:16)
11 _____ mater
12 Oolong and orange pekoe
14 Communication devices
22 "Ye tithe mint and ___" (Luke 11:42)

29 Ballet step
30 "Neither shall he go in to any ____ body" (Lev. 21:11)
32 Of the kidney
34 Those with more than four of these were unclean
35 Brother of 2nd degree (1 Chron. 15:18)
37 God would make the earth like this (Lev. 26:19)
38 Unclean animal (Lev. 11:19)
39 "Let the living bird loose into the ___ field" (Lev. 14:7)
40 "If thou ___ offer a burnt offering" (Judg. 13:16)
42 Its cap. is Dover
43 European Aerospace Co.
45 Choose
46 Coiffure
47 Fancy
48 Capital of Spain
49 Italian city
51 Men were not to mar its corners (Lev. 19:27)
52 False name
54 Israel smote with this part of sword (Num. 21:24)
56 "How ___ did they provoke him in the wilderness" (Ps. 78:40)
59 Tokyo's original name
61 Large African antelope
62 Moray
63 Locomotive tracks (abbr.)

5

LEVITICUS

by Mary A. Hake

• • • • • •

ACROSS

1 Unclean bird (Lev. 11:19)
6 Ship's spar (Isa. 33:23)
10 "Bring to pass his ___" (Isa. 28:21)
13 Antiseptic solution
15 Some dwell in a walled one (Lev. 25:29)
16 Golf ball holder
17 Old fellow
18 Strategic Research Investment Reserve (abbr.)
19 High explosive
20 Margarine
22 Sacrifice could not have one
24 Suspected leprosy was ___ up 7 days (Lev. 13:4)
26 Membrane (Lev. 3:4)
28 Metal
29 Corner crops were left for them (Lev. 23:22)
30 Beasts' homes (Job 37:8)
31 Support Equipment Requirements Review (abbr.)
33 Everyone (Lev. 24:14)
34 Accomplishment
35 "His offering __ a burnt sacrifice" (Lev. 1:3)
36 Legume
38 "Fall upon any sowing seed which is to __ ____" (Lev. 11:37) (2 wds.)
41 Color rams' skins were dyed (Ex. 35:7)
42 College administrative officer
44 East Indian herb
45 Piglet
48 Type of offering (Lev. 2)
49 "Come and ___ the priest" (Lev. 14:35)
50 Firstfruits' corn was green (Lev. 2:14)
51 Hairless (Lev. 13:40)
52 Father's brother's wife (Lev. 18:14)
53 Flax oil
55 "The ___ of thy foot have rest" (Deut. 28:65)
57 Epoch
58 Challenge (1 Cor. 6:1)
60 Priest dipped this into offering's blood (Lev. 4:6)
64 Cent. Daylight Time
65 Framework of bars
66 Simon's occupation (Acts 10)
67 Priest's digit anointed with blood (Lev. 14:14)
68 Root of the taro (arch.)
69 "Afflict your ___" (Lev. 16:31)

DOWN

1 Ill (Lev. 15:33)
2 "Is any thing ___ hard for the LORD?" (Gen. 18:14)
3 Number to be redeemed (Num. 3:48)
4 God's people were not to rule each other with this (Lev. 25:46)
5 Camels did this by a well (Gen. 24:11) (past tense)
6 Master of Ceremonies (pl.)
7 Commuter plane
8 "If it appear ___ in the garment" (Lev. 13:57)
9 King Hiram's city (1 Kings 5:1)
10 Clothes (Jer. 2:32)
11 It held burning coals (Lev. 16:12)
12 Ninth Hebrew letter
14 "How long will it be ___ they believe?" (Num. 14:11)
21 Large body of water
23 Leader of Israel
24 Fly alone
25 Place where priests ate (Lev. 7:6)
27 Industrious insect (Prov. 6:6)

33 "All men are ___" (Ps. 116:11)
34 A fool
35 Hur's son (Ex. 31:2)
37 Tau Epsilon Phi (abbr.)
39 Babies were "delivered ___ the midwives come" (Ex. 1:19)
41 Four were on brass grate (Ex. 38:5)
43 Ahead-of-Time (abbr.)
46 Moses' son (Ex. 2:22)
48 God "made the sea ___ land" (Ex. 14:21)
51 Tap
53 Ye
56 Passover sacrifice
57 70s guerilla movement in Oman
58 Dry metric tons (abbr.)
60 Rings from these were used for the gold calf (Ex. 32)
61 Esau's descendants (Ex. 15:15)
62 Greeting (It.)
63 Command (arch.)
65 Sea's noise (Ps. 98:7)
66 Pharaoh accused Hebrews of being ____ (Ex. 5:17)
67 Blend
69 Air Traffic Operations (abbr.)
71 Letter to the Editor (abbr.)

4

Exodus

by Mary A. Hake

• • • • • •

ACROSS

1 Jesus asked, "Why make ye this ___?" (Mark 5:39)
4 Tenth part (Num. 18:26)
9 Father (Sp.)
14 Multitude that left was a _____ (Ex. 12:38) (pres. tense)
15 Last son of Jacob listed, Ex. 1:1–4
16 Related to upper pelvic bone
17 "This is ___ of the Hebrews' children" (Ex. 2:6)
18 Moses wrote #90
19 Shorter forearm bone (pl.)
20 Pharaoh to Egypt (Ex. 6:11)
22 Fleet
24 Measure of light output (abbr.)
25 Curved line
27 Inland Northwest (abbr.)
29 Eastern deity
32 Son of Merari (Ex. 6:19)
35 Decorative vase
36 Manna's ____ was like honey (Ex. 16:31)
38 Moses turned ___ to see (Ex. 3:4)
40 "Gather a certain ___ every day" (Ex. 16:4)
42 Son of Zorobabel (Luke 3:27)
44 Goats' ____ was spun for tabernacle curtains (Ex. 26:7)
45 Cake glaze
47 Priest's garment set with gems (Ex. 25:7)
49 Young hart (Song 2:9)
50 Leaders of Israel (Ex. 3:16)
52 Lovers' meeting
54 Science Research Assoc.
55 Slang greeting
56 "The ___ cannot leave his father" (Gen. 44:22)
59 Moses said, "I am slow of ___" (Ex. 4:10)
64 Put in breastplate with Thummim (Ex. 28:30)
68 City in the plain of Siddim (Gen. 10:19)
70 Father of Maasiai (1 Chron. 9:12)
72 Lyric poem
73 Slogan
74 Cook with fire (Ex. 12:8)
75 Entire (Ex. 1:5)
76 "Put thine hand into thy ___" (Ex. 4:7)
77 The LORD ___ Egypt's firstborn (Ex. 12:29)
78 Sea that God parted (Ex. 14)

DOWN

1 One of chief priests (Neh. 12:7)
2 Islamic exams
3 Peace offering animals (Ex. 24:5)
4 Rap
5 Tribe of Israel (Ex. 1:3)
6 Western Indian desert
7 Turns a ship (James 3:4)
8 Bulgarian river
9 Deadly fish
10 Wing
11 Accomplished
12 "He wrote also letters to ___ on the LORD" (2 Chron. 32:17)
13 Oasis with 12 wells (Ex. 15:27)
21 Israelite tribe (Ex. 1:4)
23 Divides circle in half (abbr.)
26 Remote Digital Terminal (abbr.)
28 Laver held water to do this (Ex. 40:30)
29 Orthopedic support
30 Passover lasted from the 1st ___ 7th day (Ex. 12:15)
31 These brought boils (Ex. 9:8–9)
32 Net

26 Bear constellation
27 Siestas
28 Look over quickly
29 Persia
30 The children of Israel were ___ afraid (Ex. 14:10)
31 Jewel in fourth row of breastplate (Ex. 28:20)
34 Jaunty
35 Isaiah said to do this to the law (Isa. 8:16)
36 Pharaoh accused the workers of being this (Ex. 5:8)
38 Sound from Mount Sinai (Ex. 19:16)
39 Concept
40 Where the lice came from (Ex. 8:17)
42 "I will ___ them of children" (Jer. 15:7)
43 Firstborn of Israel (Ex. 6:14)
44 It turned into a serpent (Ex. 7:10)
45 Moses neither ate __ drank for 40 days (Ex. 34:28)
46 Cowboy's rope
47 Aaron's second son (Ex. 6:23)
48 "How much ___ punishment" (Heb. 10:29)
49 Every man and ___ suffered plagues
51 Eliezer was named for God's ___ (Ex. 18:4)
52 An unclean animal (Lev. 11:6)
53 Organization for a common interest (abbr.)
54 "I will ___ with thee" (Ex. 25:22)
57 Dirty animal
58 Negative answer (Gen. 42:10)
60 Furrow

3

EXODUS

by Mary A. Hake

• • • • • •

ACROSS

1 "Pharaoh commanded the ___ day" (Ex. 5:6)
5 Second gem in breastplate (Ex. 28:17)
10 Car speed (abbr.)
13 Pack animal of Andes
15 The pillar of cloud helped the Hebrews ___ the Egyptians
16 Time period
17 Narcotic
18 Aaron's first son (Ex. 6:23)
19 Aholiab's tribe (Ex. 31:6)
20 Husk
21 Truant (abbr.)
23 Paul said, commands would "perish with the ___" (Col. 2:22)
25 Winged
26 Use a key
28 Miriam to Moses
31 Hitler girlfriend Eva
32 Curve
33 Sports channel
34 Pressure unit (abbr.)
37 Retirees' organization (abbr.)
38 Italian money
40 "In very ___ for this cause" God raised up Pharaoh (Ex. 9:16)
41 Direction Israelites headed from Egypt
42 "As it were the ___ of heaven in his clearness" (Ex. 24:10)
43 Rustic
44 Priest of Midian (Ex. 2:18)
45 Nuzzle
46 Dodger Tommy ___
49 Fight, like Israel had with 14 Down
50 "The glory of the LORD ___ upon Mount Sinai" (Ex. 24:16)
51 "Hail smote every ___ of the field" (Ex. 9:25)
52 Canaanites descended from him
55 Title of respect used by Joseph's brothers (Gen. 43:20)
56 Sleep disorder
59 God used the Red Sea to do this to Pharaoh's men
61 Amram married Jochebed and ___ bore two sons (Ex. 6:20)
62 Saints' prayers are in golden ones (Rev. 5:8)
63 Miriam fetched her mother as one for Moses (Ex. 2:7)
64 Pronoun Moses used to refer to God
65 Nation Hebrew slaves fled
66 The tabernacle was one of these (Ex. 26)

DOWN

1 Mess
2 Brand of dog food
3 Pharaoh's daughter sent hers to get the basket-boat
4 Flightless Australian bird
5 God's covenant was "after the ___ of these words" (Ex. 34:27)
6 Egg-shaped
7 Cushion
8 Professional association for dentists (abbr.)
9 Tribe of Israel (Ex. 1:3)
10 Physician
11 Trick
12 The vail was to ___ on four pillars (Ex. 26:31–32)
14 They fought Israel in Rephidim (Ex. 17:8)
22 Joshua thought this caused the noise (Ex. 32:17)
24 Every Hebrew one was to be drowned (Ex. 1:22)
25 Upon

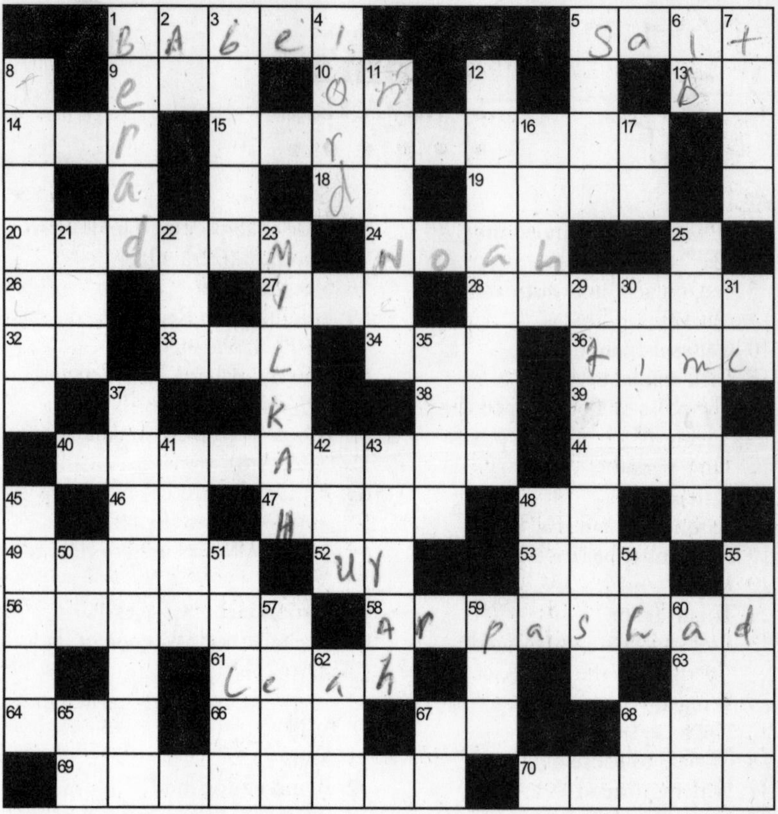

29 Jacob's fifth son (Gen. 30:18)
30 Joseph told his brothers to come ___ (Gen. 45:4)
31 A traveled way (abbr.)
35 A servant ___ him 10,000 talents (Matt. 18:24)
37 Isaac's well of "room" (Gen. 26:22)
41 Invigorates
42 Note of debt
43 Abram's father (Gen. 11:26)
45 Sarah's burial cave is near here (Gen. 23:19)
48 Expression of contempt
50 Note after la
51 King Melchizedek's city (Gen. 14:18)
54 Hatchet
55 Shinab's kingdom (Gen. 14:2)
57 Slight
59 Pastry
60 Sarah died at Kiriath ____ (Gen. 23:2 NIV)
62 Camera's auto-bracketing (abbr.)
65 Like
67 Train track (abbr.)
68 Host (abbr.)